SAFE HOUSES ARE DANGEROUS

SAFE HOUSES
ARE DANGEROUS

HELEN LONG

Foreword
by
'PAT O'LEARY'
General Sir Albert-Marie Guérisse
GC, KBE, DSO

WILLIAM KIMBER · LONDON

First published in 1985 by
WILLIAM KIMBER & CO. LIMITED
100 Jermyn Street, London, SW1Y 6EE

© Helen Long, 1985

ISBN 0-7183-0551-5

Typeset by Grove Graphics, Tring
and printed and bound in Great Britain by
The Garden City Press, Limited
Letchworth, Hertfordshire SG6 1JS

For I was an hungered, and ye gave me meat:
I was thirsty, and ye gave me drink:
I was a stranger, and ye took me in:

Naked, and ye clothed me:
I was sick, and ye visited me:
I was in prison, and ye came unto me.

Matthew, Chapter XXV, verses 35 and 36

Part of a lesson read at the service at the
Central Church of the Royal Air Force at St
Clement Danes in London, on the occasion of
the dedication of a bronze memorial to
'Helpers', on 21st June 1981.

Contents

List of Illustrations

ILLUSTRATIONS IN THE TEXT

Foreword
by 'Pat O'Leary'
General Sir Albert-Marie Guérisse
GC, KBE, DSO

First of all I would like to thank Helen Long, the author of this beautiful book, for having given me the opportunity to write this preface, to pay tribute to those men and women of the great 'escaping' family. I admired and loved them dearly, and never cease to think of them.

Helen Long's uncle and aunt, Dr and Madame Rodocanachi, are amongst those brave people whose quiet courage and modesty were equal to the dangers they faced. It was in their home in Marseille that I found refuge in August 1941.

Captain Ian Garrow had been living clandestinely with them for several months, and it was from their home that he ran the first escape line of its kind . . . a network which had been built up from scratch, and which led to his arrest scarcely three months later when I was called upon to continue his work.

The greater proportion of those who were to need safe housing along the routes out of Holland, Belgium and Luxembourg via the Rodocanachis and the Nouveaus were RAF crews. From these safe houses escapers were dispersed along the Mediterranean from Monaco to Perpignan whilst awaiting the crossing of the Pyrenees, or clandestine embarkation on Royal Navy Q-Ships out of Gibraltar.

But the price paid by the *passeurs*, the discreet people who ran safe houses, was a heavy one indeed, because of the Gestapo, the Vichy Police and traitors.

Dr Rodocanachi was to die in a concentration camp; Louis Nouveau would survive, and miraculously would return from one. Others, countless others would be executed by firing squads, beheaded, hanged . . . exterminated.

When I myself was arrested by the Nazis, I was amazed to find that the network had been baptised THE ACROPOLIS LINE by the Gestapo. No more fitting recognition could have been afforded the Greeks of France, for the part that they played in the adventure of escape and evasion.

I am always greatly moved when I think of the courage of the RAF crews, and the brave people who went to their rescue when they were shot down, the gallant keepers of those very dangerous places . . . 'safe' houses.

Brussels, February 1985

Preface

A letter that I received from someone who had just taken my book *Change Into Uniform* out of his public library, along with another book, provided a strange coincidence that gave me food for thought.

'You mention your uncle Dr Georges Rodocanachi of Marseille in your story', he wrote. 'Was this the same Dr Rodocanachi whose name is mentioned in several war books that I have read? By a strange coincidence, he was referred to in the other book I took from my library on the same day as yours. It was such an unusual and eye-catching name that it caught my imagination.

'If this was the same man', my correspondent continued, 'then has his story been told, and if so, then what is the name of the book?'

Odd, I thought, for I also had read references to my uncle and aunt, but even I knew of no book giving any real details of their wartime activities. What I knew was garnered from the family, which was a close one, but there were large portions that only others who had been involved with them, could fill for me.

It was in this fashion that I attempted to piece together the wartime experiences of my uncle Georges and his wife Fanny, my paternal aunt. My researches led me to surprising and intriguing events, and to meet those still alive, and read about those who shared a clandestine life with my aunt and uncle in Marseille from 1940 to 1944.

H.L.

Acknowledgements

First of all I want to express my gratitude to my husband Aidan for his unfailing enthusiasm and patience, as together over four years we paid a number of visits to Marseille, and shared the clandestine life that was lived there some forty years ago. He has in fact been my 'guide' and 'helper' all along.

I wish to thank my son Christopher Long, Mr John Venmore-Rowland, and Mrs Amy Myers for their invaluable help with the writing of this book; and many others who were generous and supportive with their personal stories and reminiscences. In particular, words alone cannot express my warm appreciation of all the help I have received from Pat O'Leary, on the two occasions when my husband and I visited him and his wife Sylvia at their home in Brussels.

I am also greatly indebted to Mrs Elizabeth Lucas Harrison, Secretary of the RAF Escaping Society, who has been most important in my research, putting me in touch with members of the Society, and 'helpers' at home and overseas. For her generosity, and for the use of her late husband Louis Nouveau's manuscript and illustrations, and permission to quote from his book *Des Capitaines par Milliers*, I am profoundly grateful to Madame Renée Nouveau MBE.

For permission to quote from Mr Airey Neave's books *Saturday at M19*, and *They Have Their Exits* I am indebted to the publishers Hodder & Stoughton, and to Lady Airey of Abingdon herself, for sharing with me her husband's recollections and reactions. I would also like to express my thanks to Mr. Vincent Brome, for permission to quote from his book *The Way Back*, in which he has already made this journey with Pat O'Leary as his guide.

I also take this opportunity to thank Mr Neil M. Caskie, brother of the late Rev Donald Caskie for his help, and the publishers Macdonald, for permission to quote from *The Tartan Pimpernel*. To Mrs James Langley MBE, my appreciation for all her trouble and kindness, and for

15

permission to quote from her late husband's book *Fight Another Day*...
'Jimmy' too was generosity personified when first I began to gather
material for this story. To 'Griff', Group Captain Frank Griffiths, my
thanks for so much help, and for his generous permission to quote from
his book *Winged Hours,* published by William Kimber. To William
Kimber & Co my thanks for permission to quote from *Secret Sunday*
by Donald Darling (1975), *Fighter Pilot: A Self-Portrait* by George
Barclay (1976), and *Safer than a Known Way* by Philip Newman
(1983). I am also much obliged to Mr Alan Cooper for the benefit of
his wisdom and experience.

Amongst the many who at my request were good enough to search
their memories, looking back over some forty years, sometimes not
without painful nostalgia, and who helped me with material and sug-
gestions, my gratitude – like this story – straddles the English Channel,
as my warm appreciation goes out to : Madame Netta Zarifi, Monsieur
Georges M. Zarifi, Madame Hélène Vlasto, Madame Françoise Rodo-
canachi, Monsieur Georges P. Rodocanachi, Lady Daphne Straight,
Mrs Elizabeth Furse, Monsieur Jean-Pierre Nouveau, Air Chief
Marshal Sir Lewis Hodges, Air Marshal Sir Denis Crowley-Milling,
Mr Derrick Nabarro, Mr 'Scotty' Brazill, Wing Commander 'Taffy'
F. W. Higginson, Mr Pat Hickton, Mademoiselle Marie-Thérèse
Palluel, Madame Tom Kenny.

Marseille

Summer 1940

The whole world knew that France had fallen.

But did the whole of France know? How could it when newspapers failed to appear, and six million French people were away from home, on the move, and unable to have regular access to the wireless?

'In any case,' everyone was saying, 'the radio is already totally unreliable, corrupted, and so biassed that it's just not worth listening to it.'

Thus, for want of official news, rumours and counter rumours were bandied about in an atmosphere of treachery and suspicion.

Incredibly, even people living only a few miles distant from Dunkirk had been unaware that Britain with her gallant band of small rescue ships had evacuated the beaches there under ferocious enemy bombardment. It had seemed quite impossible that in such a short time the Allies could have been so totally overrun and cornered at Dunkirk. The German forces had invaded Belgium on 10th May and by 22nd June they had forced the French government to sign an armistice in the forest of Compiègne.

There was much criticism of the British armada so hastily mounted, which had left behind many former allies. The British themselves had made a miraculous retreat, and remained safe for the time being on their small island.

Although evacuating some 336,000 troops, the British did abandon, and allow to fall into enemy hands several thousand French troops, British troops, and vast quantities of arms and equipment. There is no doubt that by this audacious operation Britain had saved the bulk of her Expeditionary Force. But what a way to treat an ally: simply to depart.

If you wanted to make out a case of this kind, then most assuredly you could. Especially if you felt disinclined to see this war drag on. It was annoying, to put it mildly, to see the British now safely out of it, and protected from immediate invasion in a way that France could never be, by a moat – the Channel. Incredibly, and unreasonably, Britain was apparently determined to continue the fight.

British troops had, not unnaturally, been given priority in embarkation at Dunkirk, a fact which travelled around France, helped by the Germans, who were only too happy to make use of this anti-British propaganda. Thus in the summer of 1940, the French viewed the defiant and naïve enthusiasm of the British for continuing the war, with distaste, and were not impressed. Very few rallied around Britain in her self-appointed role as sole protagonist aided by the small numbers of patriots from occupied countries who were beginning to reach England to continue the fight.

The remnants of the British servicemen gathered in groups in the north heard talk of possibilities of escape out of France by crossing the Pyrenees into neutral Spain, and on to Gibraltar, and a boat to take them home.

French railwaymen were inclined to allow a fair amount of hitch-hiking on their trains by British troops. Others travelled on weary feet, hidden away in the homes of courageous people, who were forbidden by the new government to offer food or lodging to Germany's enemies.

The men did not have documents, money for food, lodging, or travel, or way to exchange their uniforms for civilian clothes. Some were suffering from wounds that had long gone untreated : yet they dared not declare themselves and seek medical aid. All were exhausted, hungry, disillusioned, and confused, and very few spoke more than a word or two of schoolboy French.

A line of refugees from Paris poured south to mingle with the remnants of the British Expeditionary Force, and others whose goal was Bordeaux and Marseille. These included French, Belgian, Dutch, and Polish troops who had avoided capture during the short sharp campaign of 1940. There were even Frenchmen whose prisons had been destroyed by bombing, and whose prison officers had fled before the enemy, leaving them free to escape.

There were also those who feared being sent to Germany as forced labourers, who didn't want to work in mines, factories, or on farms, nor help support the German and Italian war economy.

Thousands of desperate Jews from various European countries had an overriding ambition to get out of the occupied zone, France having by this time been carved in two, and away from the shameful surveillance of Vichy France.

Many weary British troops arriving at the Gare St Charles, Marseille's main station, found rest and refreshment at a government sponsored canteen there. Under the supervision of a Greek resident of long-standing in the town, Madame Zarifi, Red Cross volunteers manned this canteen day and night.

On 18th June 1940 General de Gaulle had broadcast from London, appealing to all French men and women to join him and continue the fight. On 2nd July Marshal Pétain, following the armistice, set up the Vichy government, and this self-appointed chief of the new French state, replaced the Third Republic, and began to govern by decree.

The citizens of Marseille had always prospered from international trade, but British ships had ceased to call. French vessels, however, continued to sail to Algiers, Tunis, Casablanca, and Beirut. And since the USA was not yet at war, ships still came and went across the Atlantic.

The town had emerged unscathed from the fighting in May and June 1940. Initially there was little change in the city's life, except that the German-Italian Armistice Commission took up residence in the best hotel on the Canebière, the main street, the Hôtel Louvre et Paix.

Now there was a massive feeling abroad of conflicting loyalties, and suspicion, and more than a smell of corruption hung over the town. Disguised Gestapo men kept silent watch, gendarmes could no longer be trusted, and parents felt compelled now to keep their usually lively and uninhibited children under strict control, lest they speak out of turn within the hearing of dangerous ears.

The new Vichy government was busy concentrating police energies on the business of rounding up British servicemen on the run. Thus, whilst some residents in the town were determined to cause as little aggravation and conflict with the new régime as possible, others reacted against the powers now vested in the greatly feared Milice.* These, after all, were French: down in the south the locals had to admit that the new masters were more difficult to fault *(car ils sont si corrects)*.

* The Vichy, or French Milice were a paramilitary body of Fascist Frenchmen, estimated to number roughly 45,000 throughout the whole of France. Alongside these in Marseille were *les flics*, the gendarmes. These local policemen regulated traffic, and their function was to deal with petty offences and parochial matters. But they were always liable to be working with the Milice.

Safe Houses Are Dangerous

The division between Occupied and Unoccupied France

Those who arrived in Marseille had individual ideas of the promised land. For the Jews and Spaniards it was North or South America. For the men of the Allied forces it was England. And for others it was French North Africa or the Middle East.

The black market in food, restaurants, hotels and trade generally, flourished, and accommodation of any kind at any price soon became hard to find. Many, notably the French, believed that the British Secret Service would soon set up escape lines. British officers out on parole were driven to prevaricate by saying that if the opportunity did arise, they would surely see what they could do to help.

These officers were housed in a temporary prison, at the old Fort St Jean which the Vichy administration used to contain officers and men of all three British services, who would otherwise have been on the run. This fort had been the collecting depot for volunteers for the Foreign Legion. Provided that they attended the weekly Monday morning roll-calls when ration cards were issued to individual officers, by the French Commandant, they were free to come and go as they pleased. Food had become so scarce and expensive that there was never any difficulty in selling ration cards, which enabled the British officers to live quite comfortably in a modest hotel.

The simple construction of the latrines at the fort, with their chimney-like outlets straight down into the sea, and the metal bars set into the stone to serve as seats, were soon exploited by British prisoners to whom parole was denied. Ropes were attached to the bars, and escapers clutching shoes and clothes in waterproof bags, descended the rope and ducked under the outer wall of the fort.

As an escape route it was perfect, though the swim to shore or the jetty close by was none too pleasant, since sewage disposal was left to the tide, which in the Mediterranean is not renowned for its rise and fall.

Captain Ian Garrow, a Seaforth Highlander of the 51st Highland Division, soon became very *persona grata* in several Marseille homes. Having escaped capture at St Valéry on the north coast of France at the end of May 1940, he had made his way south, taking with him four Highlanders from Glasgow. Together they survived many hazards as they travelled the length of France, and showing considerable enterprise and resource, Ian Garrow turned up in Marseille in October, to find the town full of a disorientated crowd of British servicemen. Their plight struck him as desperate, and he felt it his duty to try to rescue them from inevitable arrest, and removal to prisoner of war camps and prisons.

To return them to active service at such a critical stage of the war, he would need a number of local people who could be trusted to hide and feed these men, and keep them off tthe streets until he could somehow make arrangements to get them back to Britain. But where did one start to look for such 'helpers'?

He was a tall man, conspicuously so in a country not renowned for the stature of its people. He had no money, no pre-war contacts or introductions to anyone in the town, and no strings that he might pull. But his quiet manner, straight look, and pleasant ways soon commended him to the few civilians he had come to know.

He well knew his limitations. But soon he learnt his way about Marseille. Desperate as he was to locate safe housing, he was not one to be hurried into friendship or commitment. So, testing each foothold until he knew it to be secure, he moved about the town keeping his eyes and ears open.

The need for secret accommodation was becoming more acute every day. Yet neighbours of 'helpers' would surely notice that something was going on. And not too many people seemed well disposed towards the British. It was a risky business even to begin to ask around. He soon carved out for himself a niche within a small, cultured, and fiercely pro-British circle, amongst whom were several Greek residents of long standing in the town.

Garrow realised that political affiliations established during the Spanish Civil War still coloured attitudes. Some French people had been pro-Fascist, others had favoured the Communist forces, whilst others still, detested both. Franco had been backed by Hitler and Mussolini: and the Communists had enjoyed the support of Russia – and Communists everywhere. A large number of those who had favoured the Fascists were now inclined to support Pétain. But to the Communists, both Germany and Pétain were anathema. Many Communist supporters, with a very small number of people who had not supported either side during the Spanish Civil War, were now disposed to support the British.

Non-Communists who were trying to help British nationals and service personnel to escape from France felt an instinctive reluctance to involve themselves with, or put their trust in known Communist sympathisers. Indeed it was to be several years before General de Gaulle himself would entertain the idea of accepting Communists into his entourage, or would consider offering help to their Resistance movements in France.

The Communists knew that they had nothing to gain from the Nazis: and early on, in the weeks and months following the débâcle at Dunkirk, they began to develop underground organisations, and to print anti-German tracts and literature.

There was news filtering down from the north of internment and oppressive measures being taken by the Germans and the local Milice, against such militants and dissidents, who were in fact the very earliest resisters in the field. Life was clearly beginning to become dangerous in the occupied zone, as it would surely also become in the south too, especially if the enemy ever decided to occupy the rest of France, as they eventually did on 11th November 1942.

It was going to be a risky business if local people became involved in sheltering and hiding British troops on the run, and details of punishments that would result for anyone caught doing so, were already well advertised on bill-boards and hoardings all over France, and were enough to freeze the blood.

Garrow began to receive clandestine messages from people who were willing and eager to help. But how easy it might be to make a false and irrevocable move at this delicate stage, by showing one's hand to the wrong person. He felt an increasing urgency as the men continued to arrive in the town, but dared not leave any offer of help to chance, seeing it as a port in a storm.

He must sift every contact, check and cross-check, and learn to be suspicious. Already he himself was making good use of just such hospitality, living and eating with his new friends, and spending his nights in various houses and flats, flitting like a shadowy moth between them.

His French, despite his strong Scottish accent, was actually improving. He was also getting to know a great deal about people's ways of living, their politics, skills, occupations, hobbies, contacts and so on. He needed to be aware of their financial circumstances, what accommodation was on offer, whether it was in secluded places, and what leisure time 'helpers' would be able and willing to devote to certain activities.

He was at great pains to be sure that they understood and appreciated that they would be running grave life-and-death risks, which once embarked upon, would be irreversible. All this information could be given and exchanged without any commitment having actually been entered into by either side. It was the least he could do for those civilians who were apparently prepared and eager to help in spite of possible torture and, or death if caught.

He also owed it to the many men who would in due course reach Marseille, trusting entirely in his selection and provision of a truly safe house whilst waiting in the town.

The stage is just about set now, and the time has come for the players in this story of the dangerous game of escape and evasion, to take their places.

CHAPTER ONE

The Rodocanachis Join the Line

Summer and autumn 1940

I last saw my uncle Dr Georges Rodocanachi at Frinton-on-Sea, on 3rd September 1939. His open-topped Panhard sports car with its French number plates disappeared down the drive of a house called Maryland, as my family waved him on his way home to Marseille.

We had all foregathered with anxious foreboding, to hear the announcement of the declaration of war from Mr Neville Chamberlain at 11.15 that morning. My uncle Georges had known at once that he must return home and be available at his hospital. We were all gathered together as we did every summer at my Greek grandmother's behest, at the large, well appointed house close to a good golf course, and tennis club, which she took for the pleasure of welcoming her three children and their families.

Both my father's sisters, though Greek, lived in Marseille, and they and their children were like the swallows to us, heralding with their arrival, the advent of the summer holidays. They came in foreign cars with strange-looking number-plates, wore elegant French clothes, smoked continental cigarettes, and filled the house with a mixture of French, Greek, and English voices. We were the 'English' cousins, and there existed between us all a strong bond of family affection.

Now that the die was cast and we were at war, in various languages urgent plans were made. It was obvious that the foreign-based members of the family must head for home immediately. Cross-Channel traffic was sure to be oversubscribed, and would soon cease altogether. Instantly at war, France and Britain were once again ranged against the same common enemy as had confronted them in World War I.

By telephone flights were confirmed, sleepers on continental trains reserved, cars booked on to ferries, and telegrams sent to families in France, Greece, Switzerland and Egypt. In a flurry of foreign cars, nannies, children and babies, with their grown-ups scattered 'for the duration'.

In this fashion did Fanny and Georges Rodocanachi and Fanny's sister Netta Zarifi return to Marseille. For, as the doctor had said at the time : 'I must go at once. I shall be needed back at the hospital.'

In France as in Britain, everyone was prepared to wage total war immediately. But for months on end the *drôle de guerre*, the phoney war continued : an anti-climax in both countries which was liable to generate a sort of wolf-wolf situation in which it would be easy for resolution and fervour to fade away. But in Marseille the continual stream of Jews fleeing ahead of the Nazis, and seeking a safe harbour overseas, was a constant reminder of one grim side of war.

Dr Rodocanachi had by now been appointed examining medical officer for Jewish immigrants desirous of being accepted as residents in the United States of America. He had been asked to undertake this onerous task by the American Consul, Mr Fullerton, with whom he had had a number of contacts in the past.

America was still at this time a neutral country, and hundreds of Jews had taken up residence in the town in the hopes of getting clearance to go to the USA whilst ships still sailed there.

My uncle was charged with passing as fit for immigration only such as would not be likely to be a liability or financial burden on the state. People with tuberculosis, congenital illnesses, or mental or physical handicaps of any kind were unacceptable. It was an arduous and time-consuming task for my uncle did all the laboratory tests in his own small surgery in his flat, and there were endless forms and questionnaires to be filled in. He was under ever-increasing pressure to hasten the rate of these examinations, since fresh arrivals added to the crowds reaching the town hourly. Those who would not be fit to leave the country were for him a great sorrow, and he shared with them the desperation of their situation, for nobody had any illusions about the fate that awaited those who remained behind. The Vichy government was not exactly averse to currying favour with its new masters by indulging in anti-semitic activity on its own account. A twelve-year-old boy, confined to a wheel-chair, aware that his family would never go without him, committed suicide rather than hold them back.

For my uncle it was an agony to have to fail to pass as fit some supplicant or other : for this was how many of them appeared. Over 60,000 Jews were deported eastward from France during the war years, of whom only 2,800 returned. With all his professional conscience and integrity, and the delicate sensitivity that were so much a part of his character, he tried to reconcile his honesty with the immense compassion he felt for these victims of Nazi hatred.

The race was on to get the Jewish refugees safely beyond the Nazis' reach : yet no offers of personal jewellery, or money hidden about their persons could sway the doctor to do the impossible. He did it in any case, if his conscience so dictated, though he found the situation exhausting and emotionally draining. It was physically a great strain on him as he drove himself to fit in this extra work, alongside his usual daily round of consultations, visits to patients, and hospitals.

Georges Rodocanachi, born a British subject in Liverpool on 27th February 1876, of Greek parents who like himself were British, had spent his schooldays at the Lycée of Marseille, and went on to study medicine at the Faculté in Paris.

He qualified as a doctor in 1903, and began practising as a family doctor in Marseille the same year. He specialised in the care of infants and young children, and over the years became renowned for his skill and dedication to his work.

When World War I was declared, he made strenuous unsuccessful efforts to be included among the doctors who were being sent to the front. A letter from the War Office in Whitehall, dated 6th April 1915, regretted that since his name did not appear in the British Register, he was ineligible for a temporary commission in the Royal Army Medical Corps. It was suggested that he try to obtain suitable employment in the French Red Cross, as his French medical qualifications did not allow him to be sent to the British front.

In France, however, being a British subject, he was refused permission to be sent to the French front. He was frustrated and infuriated at his crazy predicament.

He simply couldn't accept that he was destined to remain at the hospital in Marseille, spending the rest of the war earning a good salary while others went to the front line. Nor did the idea of working purely as a Red Cross doctor appeal to him. He knew that he would only be satisfied when he was able to function as a doctor with one of the fighting services. To that end he was forced to accept that the only way to do so would be to renounce his British citizenship, and become a naturalised French subject.

These negotiations took time, and whilst continuing at work at his hospital in Marseille, he awaited his elusive call-up papers with impatience.

At last his efforts were rewarded and he joined the 24th Bataillon of the Chasseurs Alpins, which were among the finest troops in France. He took part in the campaigns of Alsace, of the Somme and others, and distinguished himself by his courage, endurance, his spirit of initiative, and the splendid example he gave to his men. He won seven citations, amongst which were the l'Ordre de l'Armée, the Croix de Guerre avec Palmes, and the Légion d'Honneur, which was awarded to him up at the front by Pétain himself. He was wounded twice, and gassed once : the war over, he returned to Marseille to resume his work in the town.

His wife Fanny (née Vlasto), was also of Greek parentage, born on 28th November 1884 in Paris. She spent her girlhood in London where on 20th June 1907 they were married. She was by birth French. She was a fastidious, elegant and sophisticated woman, unselfconsciously artistic in a throw-away, unstudied fashion. She was dressed and groomed with a chic that was almost tangible, and her home reflected her femininity and good taste. She preferred ivory, amber and jade to pearls and diamonds, and when she discarded her jewellery, it lay in pools of warm glowing colour on chiffoniers and escritoires, amidst a pretty clutter of tasselled worry-beads, pot-pourri, and books.

Her impeccable dress-sense was the more pleasing because it appeared to be so effortlessly achieved, and her slim brown arms and wrists tinkled with gold and ivory bracelets. Her small trim feet in hand-made, low-heeled shoes were turned out at ten-to-two, as so many of her generation were taught elegantly to walk, and twinkled about her home across parqueted floors.

Both she and her husband spoke fluent English, and their links with Britain were close and reinforced every year when they crossed the Channel to spend those summer holidays amidst their many relations. Fanny Rodocanachi's mother delighted, as did all her guests, in the summer house parties that drew the family together. Their affection therefore for Britain and the British people was a dominant factor in the Rodocanachis' lives, and they felt united in war now as they had always been in peace-time.

The flat that the Rodocanachis lived in at number 21 Rue Roux de

Brignoles was large, and patients took the old wrought-iron birdcage of a lift to the second floor, or walked up the stone staircase. The bell at the front-door was answered by an elderly maid in uniform. Séraphine had been with them for many years, a loyal and devoted member of the household who was destined to remain in their service, sharing with them the dangers and dramatic events that would take place in that seemingly innocent doctor's residence.

From 7 a.m. until 11 p.m. my uncle worked at the business of packing in his Jewish patients, alongside his normal work-load. In the course of two years he examined over 2,000 Jewish would-be emigrants. But he himself was far from well and was already aware that he was suffering from heart disease, and had frequent painful attacks of angina pectoris.

Unwilling to be beholden to the hated Vichy government for anything, once they had taken power following the signing of the armistice, he would not claim for petrol for his car,* to which as a doctor he would have been entitled. He preferred to walk from one visit to another, or take a tram.

Occasionally he would call a gasogène taxi† in an emergency, but most of the time he was a familiar figure walking about the town. No call for help was ever ignored by him, and he would go to the bedside of an ailing child at any hour of the day or night. And as he travelled about his practice, he became ever more aware of the desperate plight of British troops loose about the town.

Haunted by the ignominious defeat of France, and stricken by what he saw as the odious betrayal by Vichy in signing the armistice, in a defiant gesture of disgust and rebellion Georges Rodoncanachi tore off the tiny ribbon he had always worn in the buttonhole of the lapel of his jacket. The miniature symbol of the Légion d'Honneur pinned to his tunic on the battlefield at Verdun by Pétain, himself the hero of Verdun, had now become an agony : the very negation of the pride he had for many long years taken in the wearing of it.

It was at this point that he and Fanny, distraught at the passive role they were now to play in a war they considered that Britain was right

---

* A Panhard, a quality car built by the French firm Panhard. The company was in existence from 1889–1967, but was absorbed into the Renault company in 1965.
† Fuelled by charcoal at that time, which was carried in bags at the back of the car. Some taxis had to recharge gas cylinders en route.

in her determination to go on fighting, together decided that they would do something to further Britain's war effort.

Already Georges was involved with the newly reopened Seamen's Mission in the Rue de Forbin, after its organiser, the Reverend Donald Caskie, had been put in touch with him via the American Embassy, and Georges was caring medically for the men hidden there.

Donald Caskie confided to him that most of the men were not civilians or seamen, but escapers and evaders awaiting the hoped-for return via Ian Garrow's escape route. My uncle issued an open invitation to all the men, that they would be welcome at his home at any time.

As a result of his frequent medical calls at the Fort St Jean, the same invitation was extended to the British officers there, who were allowed out into the town on parole.

Sadly this privilege did not include other ranks, but a number of the officers soon began calling at 21 Rue Roux de Brignoles, and enjoying the civilised atmosphere, the relief of being able to talk freely in English with local people, and the pleasure of borrowing books in English. There was invariably a great deal of coming and going of patients, and it proved easy enough to slip in and out amongst them without attracting attention. The concierge in the hall was always watching, but there was no way that she could tell who was a patient, and who was not.

Men on the run, sporting their often ill-fitting French civilian clothes felt embarrassed, conspicuous, and vulnerable as they slipped past her. Avoiding using the dangerous lift within which they might find themselves closeted with unsuitable fellow-passengers, they headed for the doctor's flat via the stone stairs with studied nonchalance.

Those who chanced to arrive for the first time during surgery hours were instantly admitted. They couldn't be endangered by having to hang about in the street, and were shown into the waiting-room to sit amongst the patients, shoulders hunched, heads bowed, simulating illness and a disinclination to talk, they awaited the call from the door: *au suivant s'il vous plaît:* next one please. Once within the sound-proofed consulting-room they declared themselves, and after a brief purposeful interview and vetting, were given any necessary first-aid treatment, and passed through a communicating door which led into Fanny's own room.

Had the concierge ever thought to count those who went up, and checked the score against those who left the building, she would at times have noticed an interesting discrepancy.

It was in this fashion that as an anxious mother, Mrs Elizabeth Haden-Guest brought her two-year-old son Anthony to see Dr Rodocanachi in 1940. She and the boy had escape from Oflag 124 at Besançon and after hiding up with a friend in Paris, had succeeded in crossing the demarcation line by crawling along on hands and knees. Arrived in Marseille the little boy was clearly far from well, and Elizabeth had been advised by Mr Fullerton of the US Consulate to take the child to see Dr Rodocanachi. There followed a number of visits to her at the Hôtel de Noailles in the Canebière, and the diagnosis that the child was suffering from rickets, the result of prison food and living conditions.

During one of these visits Elizabeth, herself already involved in the dangerous business of helping British troops on the run, told the doctor that they were desperate for someone like himself to join them. A doctor who knew the town like the back of his hand, spoke perfect English, and had a network of grateful patients would be of inestimable value. His irreproachable reputation and personal contacts with hospitals, the police and other authorities in the town would be an enormous asset.

Trusting instinctively that she could safely confide in him, she told him of two other active workers in the new enterprise: Captain Ian Garrow, and a young Canadian civilian called Tom Kenny. She pleaded with him to join them, and to suggest another entirely reliable helper with local knowledge and potentially valuable contacts in the area.

The line was to attempt with the help of a handful only of hand-picked people to whip British officers and men off the streets from under the very noses of the French and German authorities, whisk them out of sight, and see them safely, they hoped, led by Spanish guides across the Pyrenees, into neutral Spain and back to the UK.

It would be necessary to reclothe them in civilian dress, keep them hidden away, fed, provided with forged papers, photographs, and supplied with enough French money to enable them to pass unnoticed until they could be handed over into the care of paid guides.

It was an imaginative and ambitious scheme, for people who had never before been involved in clandestine business, and who were themselves at the time escaping. A touching story of three young amateurs, relying on their commonsense and commitment alone, learning as they went along, and sustained by an overwhelming hatred of the enemy.

In this jungle of enemy watchfulness they would surely make terrifying mistakes: and in circumstances where to err might indeed be human, but would assuredly lead one or all of them to almost certain torture and death. It would not be a game for the squeamish, or those with too vivid an imagination.

The risks being asked of civilian helpers, as these courageous people came to be called, were potentially horrendous. Only those with a passionate sense of patriotism, loyalty to the cause and to fellow helpers, and a shared hatred of the enemy, were willing to take such risks.

There was no shortage of people around the town it seemed, who were glad that the armistice had been signed, and it was all over. There would be no more air raids, no more soldiers killed, and 'perhaps it won't be so bad', they said. 'Those German bastards don't seem too dreadful!'

Many believed that the British would in time be beaten, and didn't foresee the draconian conditions that would be imposed on France. Reasoning with short-term interest in mind, they displayed their photographs of Pétain, began to learn how to play the black market, and since they could not envisage an early end to the occupation of their country, saw collaboration with Germany as a paying and acceptable proposition.

'Helpers', on the contrary, yearned to support their erstwhile allies, though it would be an extremely dangerous and lonely way of life, attracting no praise, no sympathy if things went wrong, no promotion, no uniform to be worn with pride, no medals and no financial reward. How were such people to be located up and down an alien country without giving oneself away and showing one's hand?

Ian Garrow had met the Rodocanachis on a number of occasions, and had visited them at their flat. But for some time he had kept away, and they had wondered why. Now that Elizabeth Haden-Guest had told him what Garrow was planning, the Rodocanachis understood, and appreciated the young man's thoughtful concern for his new friends' safety. His considerate behaviour commended him to the older man who was by this time himself anxious to become involved in the proposed rescue operation, but well appreciated that it was as perilous

(Right) Doctor Georges
Rodocanachi. Just qualified.

(Below) On the right Madame
Fanny Rodocanachi with her
son Kostia. Centre Madame
Netta Zarifi holding her eldest
child, Fanny. Dated 1912.

(Right) Madame Rodocanachi.

(Below) Doctor Georges Rodocanachi, taken at the beginning of World War II. He is seen sitting at his desk in his consulting-room at 21 Rue Roux de Brignoles, Marseille. He still at that time wore his tiny Légion d'Honneur ribbon in his button-hole.

to become entangled with the wrong colleague upon such compromising business, as to have a traitor in one's midst.

Having by this time seen his own men safely on their way home to England, Garrow was determined to remain in France. The desperate plight of hundreds of British troops around him led him to believe that it would be more valuable for the war effort if he used his now considerable experience in France to get men out. It was at this point that my uncle and aunt decided to offer their home as a Safe House. This was a momentous decision, from which, once embarked upon, there was no going back.

In old Séraphine they knew that they had a staunch and faithful ally, and they took her into their confidence. But no warnings that they gave her of the risks she would be running if she remained in their employment at the flat, could make her change her mind. Together the three elderly people began to make their arrangements for hiding men.

The penalties for harbouring, feeding, or rendering first aid to the enemies of Germany were well publicised. But worse even than these enormities, was the returning to the UK of men to resume the battle. The penalty for such disobedience was deportation to Germany, and after torturing to extract information, almost certain death in a concentration camp. Posters threatening *l'échafaud*, the scaffold, were on hoardings, and nailed to trees all over France.

The Rodocanachis were aware that they had an incomparable cover in that a surgery took place at their flat twice every day. People came, with or without an appointment, and strangers were always liable to call without arousing suspicion amongst the neighbours.

Maids and concierges could be wonderful allies, or, just as easily, deadly enemies. But at the doctor's home the concierge was accustomed to the strange and erratic hours of his night calls. And the town was full of strangers and potential new patients. Nevertheless it was her business to notice who came and went past her little curtained window in the hall : and she was known to be rabidly pro-Pétain, as were most of her kind at that time. She was also well aware that the Rodocanachis were immensely pro-British, visited Britain every summer, and had always had visitors staying with them from England.

Fanny decided that when the men arrived, she would recommend that they came purposefully straight up the stairs as though they were expected and knew their way.

Number 21, Rue Roux de Brignoles, Marseille

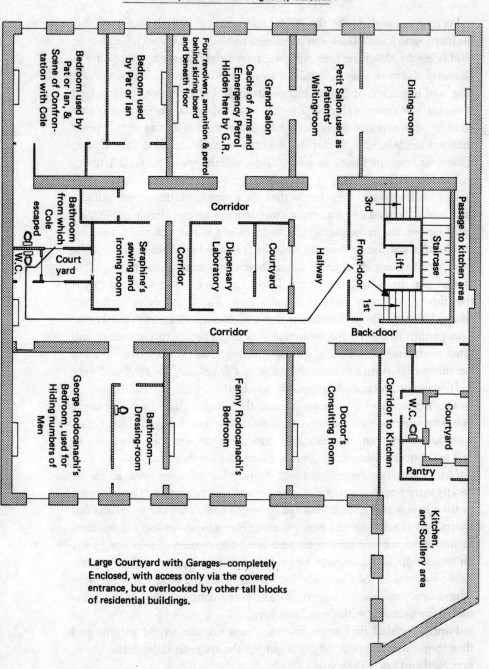

Impressive Gateway, and Entrance to Covered Passage to Large Courtyard and Garages at rear.

Bedroom used by Pat or Ian, & Scene of Confrontation with Cole

Bedroom used by Pat or Ian

Bedroom used by Pat or Ian

Four revolvers, ammunition & petrol behind skirting board and beneath floor.

Cache of Arms and Emergency Petrol Hidden here by G.R.

Grand Salon

Petit Salon used as Patients' Waiting-room

Dining-room

Corridor

3rd

Passage to kitchen area

Bathroom from which Cole escaped

Cole escaped

W.C.

Court yard

Seraphine's sewing and ironing room

Corridor

Corridor

Dispensary Laboratory

Courtyard

Hallway

Front-door

Lift

Staircase

1st

Corridor

Back-door

George Rodocanachi's Bedroom, used for Hiding numbers of Men

Bathroom— Dressing-room

Fanny Rodocanachi's Bedroom

Doctor's Consulting Room

Corridor to Kitchen

W.C.

Courtyard

Pantry

Kitchen, and Scullery area

Large Courtyard with Garages—completely Enclosed, with access only via the covered entrance, but overlooked by other tall blocks of residential buildings.

Weighing up the pros and cons, the Rodocanachis recognised that they enjoyed a number of advantages in their own particular set-up, which would make their Safe House safer than some might have been. It was unfortunate that they had no outside fire-escape staircase. But they had no dog to bark at strangers : only the silent family cat Mistigri. Nor did they any longer have small children living with them. These were to become essential requirements of Safe House keepers as recommended by MI9, the British department set up in London to deal with escape and evasion.

The Rodocanachis' only child, a son, Kostia, lived in Egypt, and would not be compromised. They therefore felt themselves free to make such plans, and take such risks as they both felt were justified, and to use their own money should this be necessary.

The flat was close to the Vieux Port at the heart of the town : the place where most escapers and evaders had been advised to head for. It was also no distance from Donald Caskie's Seamen's Mission, and the oldest and most densely populated part of the town, wherein it would be easiest to escape and get oneself lost in an emergency. It was a large flat, capable of housing a number of people. There were two spacious bedrooms well away from the front-door, and the part of the flat into which the patients penetrated.

It was also good to be upstairs on the second floor, where nobody could peer in through windows, or break in from the street. The flat below belonged to Fanny's loyal and discreet niece, Helen Vlasto, who would keep her own counsel.

The front-door and tradesmen's entrance both faced the lift and gave on to the main staircase, should an alternative emergency means of escape be required.

Like many old French buildings, there were three *cours:* tube-like shafts down through the flats, with the windows of bathrooms and lavatories of all the flats opening into shafts, which were open to the air at the top. This arrangement made it impossible for anyone outside to see how much use was being made of any of these small rooms. So long as the windows remained closed, and no lights were switched on unusually frequently, the other residents in the building would not notice anything unusual. But the men must be warned never to open any of those small windows giving on to the *cours*, or they might come face to face with other residents in the building, since there was only a short distance at a right-angle between one small room and another on the next wall.

Séraphine was soon to become adept at sensing a 'visitor'. A questioning _'le docteur?'_ and she would usher a silent man into the waiting-room to the right of the front-door. No more words would be required until she beckoned the man who sat, head in hands, feigning sleep or pain.

The flat could be noisy at times, loud with the piping of young children's voices, complaining at having to wait. The wailing of punctured babies, and the general business of a doctor's place of work made it restless, and impregnated with the heady smell of medicaments.

Fanny Rodocanachi has recorded that : *

His waiting-room being constantly full, and hall and corridors of the flat invaded by immigrants, the constant coming and going of patients made such a to-do and stir in the house that the concierges and neighbours were unable to realise that the flat was nearly always full of escaping men.

Dr Rodocanachi came and went, his friends of the Organisation were in and out all day long . . . this perpetual tumult prevented that anyone could find out what was actually happening in the flat.

Dr Rodocanachi had by this time been appointed to the medical board of the Military Hospital Michel-Levy. He undertook to examine British men, and to decide if they were or were not fit for further military service. Those who were unfit were to be repatriated. The rest, as prisoners of war, would remain in camps or prisons until hostilities ceased.

He accepted this new appointment since it would bring him into close and regular contact with British troops, and he envisaged that he might from time to time have an opportunity to do something useful outside his professional work, to help those unfortunate men. Like Garrow, he was desperate to help rescue men from the fate of God only knew what frustrations and privations in camps and prisons, and get them back into the fray as soon as possible.

The Medical Repatriation Board was run by the Vichy Armistice Commission, and included German and French doctors, alongside whom he functioned as 'American Representative'. This he saw as at

* She left typed notes of their activities with her son Kostia after her death.

least an opportunity to try to find as many as possible unfit for further military service. It was the duty of all servicemen to make every effort to return to base, and they had all been trained and briefed in how this might be done. My uncle did his best to help them. Prompted and coached by him if he felt that this was necessary to help improve their chances, he used his energies and his resourcefulness to rescue as many men as possible. Fanny records his work at this time, thus:

It is impossible to relate here the tale of the acrobatic medical feats accomplished by him between 1940 and the last meeting of the Medical Board in August 1942. The number of false certificates, the cautious advice given beforehand when he could get in touch with them, the tricks and expediencies which he cleverly contrived to simulate disease and physical disabilities.

All the old fraudulent and ingenious systems* that he had noticed during the war 1914–1918, when swindlers tried to avoid medical duties – all that was contrary and in such absolute contrast to his whole medical career, so loyal and so splendidly honest, he exploited during those sittings at the Medical Board.

He who was so proud and conscientious abased himself to beg complaisant certificates and attestations from his fellow doctors, so as to help to confirm the cases so fraudulently presented as unfit.

The radiographs which he interpreted at his will to denote so-called lung trouble, counsels for simulated heart disease, faulty sight, assumed deafness, as in the case of Whitney Straight for example – never found a better field for his energies.

The daily contacts with British troops were to ·prove invaluable to Garrow: and it wasn't just medicaments and sympathy that my uncle left with patients he visited in prison.

At the Seamen's Mission he was a regular visitor, and for Donald, a welcome support and adviser. He also undertook the care of the many British civilians still remaining in a country that was no longer the ally she had been. Living on meagre grants sent out by the British Government, many anxious and lonely people survived in shabby bed-sits and small hotels, short of funds and proper feeding. Nannies, not only from Marseille, but gathered together now from all over France, nursery-

* See Appendices.

maids, governesses, the earliest of au-pair girls, butlers, servants, monks, nuns, office workers, clairvoyants, prostitutes, hotel kitchen staff, members of Embassy and Consulate staffs, chauffeurs, dancers from the *Folies Bergère*, croupiers, jockeys and trainers ... all these British nationals awaiting repatriation lingered on in France, where many of them had spent the greater part of their lives.

For them the English-speaking doctor was a godlike figure, and they kept him busy and in close touch with British problems and possibilities, which information was useful to Ian.

There was a new intensity about him now, for his early attempts at organising and paying guides to take men across the mountains had worked well. His decision to seek help from the Rodocanachis had been a wise one : for at their flat his needs of both money for the line, and eventually a Safe House for himself to live in were met. To him, by word of mouth only, came all the business of the organisation.

He quickly established that Spanish guides were essential, but that they also cost much money. Civilian helpers too had to be reimbursed as quickly as possible, for expenses they incurred in hiding, feeding, and clothing 'parcels'* they sent on to Marseille. Many of these helpers were humble people, farmers and the like, and couldn't be expected to wait for payment. If this escape work was to continue, to become safer, and be expanded as surely it must, then he would need regular and reliable funding.

At this early stage in 1940 he was still having to depend on local support, though he was hoping that if he could only hang on long enough to prove that his system worked, London where an escape and evasion department was now becoming active would come up with regular finance to keep him going.

In the meantime he was safely off the streets where he was aware that he was beginning to attract unwelcome attention. His exceptional height and his broad Scottish accent made it difficult for him to pass unnoticed.

As a result of Elizabeth's urgent appeal to Dr Rodocanachi, after much soul-searching and careful thought, he had made contact with her and said that he would 'give you the son of a Greek family. A brave boy whose parents should probably not get involved.' And he had given

* One of a number of words used by helpers to refer to escapers and evaders passing along the Line.

the line, in addition to his own help, his beloved nephew Georges Zarifi, who was immediately to become a valued and most practical courier and supporter of the organisation.

CHAPTER TWO

Donald Caskie and the Seamen's Mission

Summer and Autumn 1940

The Reverend Donald Caskie's Seamen's Mission was at 46 Rue de Forbin, across the horseshoe-shaped inlet of water, on the opposite side of the Vieux Port from the Rodocanachis, and close to the docks. He had not long been in Marseille himself, when he established his Safe House. Formerly Presbyterian Minister of the Scottish Church in the Rue Bayard in Paris, he had fled in front of the enemy on 11th June 1940. The exodus from the capital was unstoppable that day. The *grande peur* was that one might be caught like a rat in occupied Paris. Few cared how or why they left, in their desperation to be elsewhere, and Caskie travelled south with his congregation, exposed to shelling and dive-bombing along roads that led to the Mediterranean.

He had never made any secret of his attitude to the Nazi régime, proclaiming it from his Parisian pulpit Sunday after Sunday. Having paid a last visit to older members of his congregation who would not be able to take flight, he deposited ten years' accumulation of sermons in manuscript in the cellar at the manse. He was never to see them again, for his concierge was to tell him later that the Germans had shown little interest in the church silver, but considerable interest in the matter of his preaching.

A simple pastor with an enthusiastic and unquenchable faith in his God, and through Him, in his own ability to make something of the seemingly hopeless plight in which he and his flock now found themselves, he heeded what he understood as his Master's plan for him, and headed for Marseille. Here chaos greeted him.

And in the midst of all this – and standing out clearly and in sharp contrast to everyone else, were the great numbers of British troops dangerously talking English, and self-consciously decked out in second-hand civilian clothes. With nobody to feed or organise them they risked being apprehended by the authorities, and scooped off the streets and into prisoner of war camps or prisons.

Prepared for an atmosphere of suspicion, and well aware that the British were no longer seen as friends and allies, he approached the police with due courtesy and diffidence. With him went Mr Dean, erstwhile British Consul from Nice. Messrs Dean and Dodds had been well known over the years as the smartest Consuls in Europe, and had dealt with the Duke of Windsor* at a critical time in his life in France.

The police were polite and very sympathetic. But already they were in the hands of the new authority, which made its own rules and regulations clear. They sent him to the Special Branch where, with total confidence in the urgency and rightness of his request, he demanded accommodation for stranded British nationals, at this time still permitted to leave occupied France.

However, they were powerless. Within the hierarchy of the new web of functionaries, they were themselves caught up in the invisible threads of the newly set-up Vichy Police state system. Bewildered, ill-at-ease and not yet comfortable in their new role, and unable suddenly to adapt to a method of policing that was contrary to the French mentality, they did their best to help him.

A senior man said that he knew the padre was the only British priest still at liberty in France. They could arrange for him to go home if he wished. Typically, he refused their offer of repatriation.

With that, and a few gentle admonitions as to what he could, and most assuredly could not do, they suggested that he might care to reopen the deserted Seamen's Mission building at number 46 Rue de Forbin. They warned him that he would be watched; to beware of sudden raids; let no soldier be found hiding there; trust no one. Those warnings were given in all sincerity, and he knew that they had done all that they reasonably could.

It is not unheard of that a building such as this should arise out of nothing to serve its purpose, and should then, after a brief flowering disappear into oblivion. Sadly that corner site has now been redeveloped, and no sign or plaque has been set up there to mark the spot where local people still remember that there were 'goings-on' at the British Reverend's centre there during the war.

Humble and unplanned as this building was, it played an invaluable

* The Windsors had fled Paris at dawn on 30th May heading south, and leaving their house in boulevard Suchet, to a German caretaker. It was eventually handed back to them in perfect order in 1944, having been sealed by the Swiss Legation.

part in the resistance in the south of France. Unpretentious, like the man who created this refuge, its very modesty was a distraction in itself and belied the links it came to have with MI9 in London.

Though it was to be under close surveillance by the local police until its closure early in 1942, it was not taken too seriously by those who failed to appreciate the importance of this innocent-looking staging-post in the network of escape routes out of Europe. In the same way that Garrow with his almost music-hall Scottish appearance was thought to be a simple unsophisticated spy, so was Caskie the gentle, unworldly priest underestimated.

Mercifully he was to be permitted to remain long enough at large to handle the last of the stragglers from the British Expeditionary Force, and later such aircrews as reached him from wherever they had crashed or been shot down in France.

Most of these, after living rough for weeks amongst strangers who didn't understand or speak English, reached the Mission exhausted and ravenous. For them the family-style meals taken around the long table in the Common Room, which looked not unlike a hospital ward, were a blessed relief, and an opportunity at last safely to speak English – even, amazingly with the local doctor.

With the £200 that Caskie had on his person, he hired beds and blankets, and with no previous experience of conducting clandestine activities, or leading a double life, he managed to survive, along with his protégés, in a hostile environment, and in very dangerous times. He simply opened his doors, and with uncharacteristic caution, and a furtive glance up and down the street, welcomed and hustled his compromising visitors inside. Those who were fit, he set to work cleaning the place up, though most of his lads were in a pretty bad way, and began to reach him from all over France, as soon as he was in business. There were even three sailors waiting for him outside the building when he arrived to take possession of it.

Clearly word had got around within the underground network of the town. No doubt the police or the American consulate had spread the news. The sailors helped him to put up a notice above his door : NOW OPEN TO BRITISH CIVILIANS AND SEAMEN ONLY, it read, and the Mission was already in operation by mid-July 1940. But Donald was busily making plans for sheltering other servicemen who might come to his door.

His was a quite different sort of Safe House from the one that the Rodocanachis were to run. It was a purpose-built club-house, with tough floors, stout fittings, entirely suitable for housing numbers of men, and with all the usual washing and lavatory arrangements.

It was a free-standing building with nobody living above or below, so he never had to bother to provide slippers, or forbid too frequent pulling of lavatory or bath plugs, or the making of too much refuse for collection. His ash-trays could overflow, and the dustmen wouldn't query full dustbins.

There were ping-pong and billiard tables, darts boards, and he soon collected reading material in English and packs of cards. There was a piano, and a gramophone, and he had a right to be seen taking men in. But these had to be dressed in civilian clothes, or as seamen, in or out of uniform, and be able to produce the requisite papers should the police ask to see them.

The American Consul, acting under international law, was an invaluable ally. Responsible for handling British affairs, he was only too delighted to replace 'lost' papers, and dished them out from a seemingly inexhaustible store. The generous largesse, and the pleasure that it seemed to afford him to supply them, splendidly adorned with an imposing red, heavily embossed and ornate American seal, encouraged Donald to feel free to request them as and when he needed them. They greatly impressed the authorities, who were entirely happy with these bogus symbols of practical Anglo-American friendship.

It was also of course, expected that English would be spoken in the British Seamen's building, and a splendid cross-section of the accents of the British Isles soon filled the Mission at all hours of the day, and far into the night.

Donald's urgent need was for food, and civilian clothes. Since no man must be found in uniform, other than a seaman's, upon the premises, he was forced to hide the men in prepared bolt-holes as soon as they arrived. And there they remained, until he could dress them in civilian clothes. Floorboards were prised up, and adequate hiding-places created in which a man could lie low in an emergency.

Soon there were man-sized spaces all over the place : between the joists, behind cupboards, and beneath the roof. Various doors and entrances were cleverly disguised, and panels constructed so that they could be slipped quickly and smoothly into place in a crisis. And these came with monotonous regularity. They were raided every morning at six, which became such a routine that they were ready for it. In time, however, Donald managed to amass enough clothing in advance, that new arrivals were soon kitted out and able to move freely about the building. These bundles of extra clothes they hid in the cellar, wrapped in blankets, behind heaps of coal.

Getting rid of incriminating discarded uniforms was quite a business. It involved going out at night, and heaving the weighted parcels into the sea in the dock area, where the big ships came and went, creating more movement. There was no other safe way of disposing of such tell-tale stuff, and with virtually no tide, it had to be weighted and lowered silently into deep water.

Food was a continual problem, since none of the men had a ration card. Not that these guaranteed food, but those with ration cards were at least permitted to stand in food queues. Every morning at about four o'clock, Donald would sally forth in search of food. In time he built up an excellent relationship with the Greek and Cypriot merchants of the Vieux Port, in whom he confided the truth.

He told me that without their generous help, he would have been in great difficulty. There were so many hungry young mouths to feed, and bodies to build up ready for the marathon trek across the mountains.

Once the organisation was in full swing, Donald, like the Rodocanachis, was kept informed about the movement of parcels along the line. A professional visit from the doctor would have him preparing the next batch of men for departure, as well as relieved to be advised about the care of individual men, some still nursing wounds from Dunkirk, or injured in air crashes.

Dr Rodocanachi was a popular and familiar figure at the Mission, where he lingered after surgery was done, to join in the simple daily service. He also joined the congregation there on Sundays, taking the opportunity to have a quick word with Donald, to check on arrangements made, agree or confirm details, or gather information for Ian to take back to the headquarters at his flat.

Caskie said to me he had absolutely no idea that the 'good doctor' too was running a Safe House at his home. That was how things had to be done. It was always best not to know what others were doing. The fewer names one knew, the better. Sooner or later one might be arrested, and questions would be asked.

In the meantime, with his cherubic, innocent face, and his kindly commonsense, he followed where his conscience led him, whilst Ian handled the business of arranging the arrivals and departures of the men.

Together these two Scots were seen as a couple of front men by the Vichy pro-German police, who kept a close watch on the Mission in the hopes of catching Caskie out, and being able to pull in the *real* secret agent.

Though the escape network appreciated the benefits of Caskie's Safe House, there were some who never felt quite at ease in the cosy, chatty atmosphere that prevailed there. The place tended to be over-full of worthy, domesticated women, nannies, governesses, ladies' maids and the like who had volunteered to help the young bachelor priest. As good Christians, according to their individual skills they sewed, mended, did the housework, cooked, and cared for the sick and convalescent.

Donald was delighted to have such practical support, and secretarial help from members of the British Embassy and Consulate staff.

The only nannies that Elizabeth Haden-Guest, now a courier for what had rapidly become an organised escape line, reckoned were really safe, and unlikely to gossip and threaten their activities, were those still working and living in families, who didn't feel the need to go to the Mission.

The others, from all over France, shared an anxious insecure world, for most of them were simple souls, far from home and family, and from the supportive employers with whom many of them had spent the greater part of their lives. They foregathered in the kindly atmosphere of the British Minister's home, seeing him as their hero. They altered and adapted to fit individual men the strange assortment of second-hand clothes Donald had managed to buy from Arab traders who weren't interested in politics, and weren't fussy about their destination, just so long as the money was good, and Donald never left any of his British uniforms behind. And the money *was* good by then, with donations and loans being drummed up by Ian and his new agent, Louis Nouveau, in Marseille, and along the Riviera.

The Mission was becoming an exceptional Safe House, which with just a little luck might survive the interest it aroused in the authorities. Just so long as nobody tripped up even once, and allowed a chink to show in the armour of righteousness that Donald wore.

He was now not only supplying shelter, food, medical care, and a starting point for escapers about to be linked with the guides, but also making a home-from-home for all those lonely British ladies of France who had time to kill, and were accustomed to being kept busy and feel needed. The police watched them as they came and went and moved around the town, thinking them harmless and of no account. But not all nannies were so innocent, and there were many British nannies among upper-class families in France. The French tended to have Irish nannies for religious reasons, whilst the Greeks preferred to employ English women whose Protestantism was not in conflict with the Orthodox church.

From their prestigious pivots of power they dominated their households, reigning supreme in their upstairs nursery floors and wings: remote, sound-proofed, a subtle fifth column. And wherever there was a nanny, a man might be hidden. A network of nannies regularly hid men, though often enough their employers were unaware of what went on in their own nurseries.

At the château de Montredon, the home of the Comte and Comtesse de Pastré, Nanny, with the connivance of Nadia, the daughter of the house, but unbeknown to her parents, formed part of the nanny-network, and could be counted upon for a night-nursery bed at any time.

To evader Jimmy Langley, later of MI9, and Elizabeth Haden-Guest, security conscious and trained to be reticent and discreet, the Mission was a nightmare. They felt exposed and endangered just by being there. Jimmy, nursing the painful and suppurating remains of the arm he had lost at Dunkirk, was pointed towards the Mission by the American Consul as soon as he reached Marseille. He wrote in his book *Fight Another Day*,*

But an hour spent in the club was enough to make me aware of the dangers of discussing any schemes for escape with the inmates. Moreover, I was able to guess, accurately as it was to be proved, that the French police must be fully aware of the plots hatched within its precincts. In fact it was only allowed to remain open because it was such an excellent source of information about clandestine British activities.

* Published by Collins in 1974.

At this time I doubt if the French had any paid informer who was a permanent habitué, but later they certainly did.

The result was that as British escape activities increased in Marseille, to the irritation of the Germans, the French were always able to answer the latter's complaints by saying that they had the Seamen's Mission well covered .

Donald kept his flock within the fold, allowing them out in ones and twos to walk about close to the Mission. He felt they would have gone mad with frustration had they never been allowed out. Apart from his early morning forays for food, and nightly burials at sea of discarded uniforms, he himself scarcely left the building.

In any case he never felt at ease away from home, preferring to be the one to open the door to callers. He never knew when someone might come with orders about arrivals and departures, giving the familiar three sharp raps, and asking for 'Donald Duck'. Hovering about outside the building, looking lost and anxious and dangerously still in uniform, such a person would be hustled inside.

'I needed to hear immediately of any break-out from the various prisons and camps that held our lads in case they were heading my way,' Donald told me. He was aware that he was being watched from a window across the street. The curtains didn't quite hide a silhouette which kept silent vigil day and night, and he was anxious that none of his men should have to answer the door in his absence.

In time most people concerned with the line came knocking on his door. Bruce Dowding, alias *Mason*, was one such caller at the Mission at the instigation of Donald Caskie. He had been living in the area for some years and was consequently bilingual, although he was immediately stamped as an Australian by his accent. Like many Australians he was a big man, with the fair looks common to many of them.

He was working closely with Garrow, and in and out of the Rodocanachis' flat. Men were escorted in ever larger parties, via Perpignan, across the Pyrenees, to Barcelona in neutral Spain, and back to the UK. But there was always a desperate need for more totally dedicated and reliable bilingual helpers, without the domestic ties that would involve explanation to family or friends.

Suitable candidates were rare, and ever more in demand as the *réseau* (network) was extended, and became more ambitious. Helpers prepared to hide and feed escapers and evaders had to be visited. They needed to be paid, and to be given instructions that could only be passed to them by word of mouth.

Their enthusiasm and commitment to the dangerous work they had undertaken had to be confirmed and under-pinned. Some needed encouragement, and appreciation, others had to be closed down because their cover had been blown. If a Safe House was no longer safe, then such a place was more dangerous than anywhere else in France for men to be heading for. A blown Safe House had to be closed down immediately, all outstanding expenses repaid, and everyone in the organisation advised of the new situation.

Safe houses were not all like the Rodocanachis' flat. Far from it. Agents and parcels alike had to get used to some highly unconventional lodging houses. *Maisons de rendezvous* were quite frequently used. A cross between a hotel and a brothel, a *maison de rendezvous* provided rooms that whether by night or day could be paid for by the hour by gentlemen bringing their female companionship with them. Discretion was paramount, and the police exercised an equal discretion since it was by no means certain whom they might discover if they were to raid them. They were ideal temporary overnight lodging places for agents arriving in Marseille with evaders or escapers in tow.

Maisons de rendezvous were bad enough, but brothels too became part of the organisation. These were splendid cover, and offered the cheapest and best coffee in Marseille at that time. They tended to be run by Italians who had fled because they were anti-Fascist. As such, they were equally anti-Nazi.

Elizabeth Haden-Guest recalls that every night they used to go to the local brothel, being the cheapest and safest place for hiding a man or men at short notice for a night or two. Even her small son Anthony lived with her in one of those unsavoury places. When she had to go out during the day, she left him with the chambermaids.

They were usually kind, motherly souls who asked no questions, and were trained to be discreet which suited her well. They loved having the little boy with them, and took him from one gaudy room to another as they remade beds all day long.

Brothels were Elizabeth's own particular forte, her coup you might say, because the others didn't know and appreciate the possibilities and virtues of brothels as she did. Ian with his strict Scottish upbringing in

The Vieux Port at Marseille. The Pont Transbordeur was blown up by the Germans in 1943 along with much of the old quarter.

The Fort St Jean photographed from the Pont Transbordeur. The Nouveaus' flat overlooked this fort and the Pont.

(Left) Donald Caskie in the uniform of officiating Chaplain to the Forces, a post he filled from 1944-5 after the liberation of Paris and his own release from prison.

(Below) The mission building as it was during those months of its great importance to the line. Entrance was on the extreme left.

C/o Room 166,
The War Office,
London.S.W.1.

M.I.9(b)/E/13/33/ 7th November,1941.
1331/P

Dear *Dr. Garrow*

    Enclosed is a photograph taken
in August, in which you will recognize
Capt. Garrow.   Our latest advices are
that he is in the best of health and
spirits.

    You will appreciate that we
cannot give you fuller details about the
photograph, such as to how or ~~whom~~ *where*
the group was taken and so on.
Please do not show the photograph to
others.

    We hope, but can not promise, to
be able later to get a letter
through from your Son to you.

      Yours *Sincerely*

          H.B. de Bruyne
          Capt. GS.

Dr. A. G. Garrow,
15 Woodside Place,
GLASGOW.

*Ian Garrow was in touch with M19 in London during 1940 through Donald
Darling in Lisbon. Their concern for him and the secrecy with which his
operations were cloaked are reflected in this letter from M19 to Captain
Garrow's father in 1941.*

a doctor's house could not. Nor could Donald, the Presbyterian Minister from the Manse. And as for dear Dr Rodocanachi . . .

Elizabeth was not new to the game of espionage and counter-espionage, and knew from experience the merits of the splendid anonymity that the seedier joints in a place like Marseille could afford. Born in Esthonia of a Russian father and Germano-Esthonian mother, she considers herself to be of Russian-Baltic birth. By religion partly Orthodox and partly Jewish, she was a young Communist in the 1930's.

She had been working with Red Aid and in 1934 had been sentenced to death by the Nazis for helping political prisoners to escape. Her brother-in-law David Haden-Guest, a militant Communist, was killed in Spain.

At the beginning of the war Elizabeth's husband was in America. They had American papers, and she possessed Clipper tickets for herself and her baby son. But she decided to stay on, preferring to remain in France helping to fight it out, and enrolled as an ambulance driver in the north.

Because of her privileged social and financial position, and because she had always worked for and aligned herself with the 'people', she felt that she could not at that critical time simply run away to safety.

After giving the slip to four German guards who were taking her from prison at Besançon to Paris, she hid for a time with a girl-friend in Paris. A grim journey south and across the perilous demarcation line with her small son, saw her join the crowds gathering in Marseille.

There with the child in tow, she presented herself at the American Consulate, to be confronted by Major Dodds of Dean and Dodds. She explained that she had recently escaped from Oflag 142 at the Citadelle at Besançon. His response was to say routinely : 'No room at all – anywhere in Marseille. And no money whatsoever. You'll have to take the child outside and await your turn in the queue for repatriation.'

To which Elizabeth had replied : 'But I don't want to be repatriated. I want to stay on here and fight.'

His response was scathing as he asked for her papers.

'I have no passport, and no papers. One doesn't escape from prison with one's papers and passport !'

When Elizabeth told him her name was Haden-Guest, he immediately looked up, searching her face, turned around in his swivel-chair, and reached for his *Who's Who* and *Debrett*.

'Related to the MP?' he asked casually.

'Yes,' she replied. 'Daughter-in-law.'

'Well, Mrs Haden-Guest,' he smiled, as he rose from his chair, hand out-stretched. 'That changes everything of course.'

In answer to his hidden bell in came the one-armed Jimmy Langley.

'Ah! Jimmy!' exclaimed the Major, all smiles and affability. 'I believe you've got a nice little place in the Rue de Belloi . . .'

'Yes, sir,' replied Jimmy, always one who knew how to head for the best people at the best addresses, wherever he might find himself, and useful contacts wherever he went.

'Well, I'm afraid you'll have to find somewhere else and let Mrs Haden-Guest have it. You see, she's got a small child. You'll be happy to do that, won't you, old boy?'

'Yes, of course, sir,' Jimmy had replied, looking anything but happy: livid in fact.

And adding insult to injury Major Dodds, in front of the impecunious junior officer, pressed 20,000 francs into Elizabeth's hand, and patted the small boy on the head as he went by.

To Elizabeth Haden-Guest, seated at a table outside a bar in the town, came Captain Ian Garrow within a short space of time. Anthony, legs dangling, was munching radishes when the tall good-looking, undeniably British officer asked if he might join them. Without time to waste, Garrow introduced himself, and was clearly well aware that Elizabeth spoke English as well as French. Her story had surely been passed to him, and he launched at once into the possibility that she might care to involve herself as a courier with the organisation.

'But you will know that the child will have to disappear,' was the first of many orders she was to receive from Garrow.

She was fortunate that via the Rodocanachis she was introduced to a young Frenchman waiting to get to England to join de Gaulle's forces. His name was Jean Fourcade, and he took the little boy up into the mountains above the town, where they lived close to a wild fox amongst the rocks. Twice a week they came down to the splendours of her base at Hôtel de Noailles on the Canebière, when Elizabeth could see the little boy, and give them food to last until the next visit. This arrangement worked quite well for a time. But the child became ill, and once again Dr Rodocanachi was called to attend him.

To many who spent those unreal wartime years in Marseille, there remains to this day the vivid memory of a young woman, small and of dark complexion, whom some remember as looking like a little gypsy. Others say that she had Eskimo features. But all agree that she was often to be seen trailing a small boy around the town. Some remember that the little boy invariably wore a large Mexican-style hat which made him very conspicuous, whilst others claim always to have seen him topped by a tartan beret – 'Which is what he did wear,' declared Elizabeth, 'since it was given to him by his good friend Captain Garrow.'

Whatever he wore, there were those who had good reason to fear the conspicuous mother and son, who made no effort to blend into the crowd. Rather, they seemed intent on attracting attention by their flamboyant dress, to their comings and goings . . . '*car elle était toujours extrêmement agitée*', say some who still remember her – always very excitable.

CHAPTER THREE

The Nouveaus on the Vieux Port

Autumn 1940 – Spring 1941

Renée and Louis Nouveau, living five floors up, at number 28a Quai de Rive Neuve in a modern apartment, overlooking the Vieux Port. It was an impressive flat, with elegant rooms tastefully furnished, and embellished with works of art. There was also a fine library. From a large window with its cushioned window-seat in the salon, they enjoyed a panoramic view of the quayside and the shabby elegance of the old buildings that fringed the port.

Crossing the entrance from the sea and suspended almost level with the window was a famous landmark, the Pont Transbordeur, which connected with the Bassin de la Grande Joliette where were berthed the great vessels that traded with the world. These ships were the life-blood of this commercial city. Many nationalities were involved in commerce, banking and other entrepreneurial activities. Amongst these were a thriving community of Greeks, some of whose ancestors had left Greece, its islands and Turkey in the nineteenth century when they had been persecuted by the Turks.

Horseshoe-shaped and sheltered, the old harbour cradled within its protective arms the many yachts, fishing vessels and pleasure boats that were moored there. Under the German occupation some familiar yachts and dinghies at anchor were lovingly cared for, though not allowed to put to sea. Others simply rotted away. No fishing boats were permitted to leave port, after the occupation of the southern zone on 11th November 1942, other than those commandeered by the occupying forces. Even the meagre fishing from the rocks along the Corniche was forbidden, since it and the entire sea-front were by then out-of-bounds. To add insult to injury, the Germans sold their own catches to the locals at extortionate prices on the black market.

In peace-time the Vieux Port had been a favourite spot with holiday-makers, and boats left the Quai des Belges at the top of the harbour for the Château d'If, made famous by Aexandre Dumas, and others,

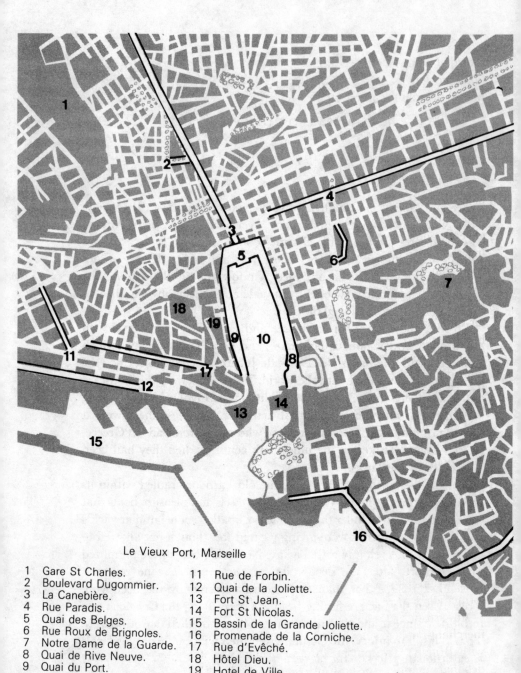

Le Vieux Port, Marseille

1	Gare St Charles.	11	Rue de Forbin.
2	Boulevard Dugommier.	12	Quai de la Joliette.
3	La Canebière.	13	Fort St Jean.
4	Rue Paradis.	14	Fort St Nicolas.
5	Quai des Belges.	15	Bassin de la Grande Joliette.
6	Rue Roux de Brignoles.	16	Promenade de la Corniche.
7	Notre Dame de la Guarde.	17	Rue d'Evêché.
8	Quai de Rive Neuve.	18	Hôtel Dieu.
9	Quai du Port.	19	Hotel de Ville.
10	Vieux Port.		

crowded with visitors headed for other destinations. Now those pleasure boats no longer ran; instead they ferried the new masters to various places of military importance, and the two historic fortresses at the narrow entrance to the harbour, the Fort Saint-Jean and the Fort Saint-Nicolas. They had been commandeered and pressed into use as prisons by the Vichy authorities.

With the Battle of Britain, since the beginning of the Luftwaffe's onslaught on 10th July 1940, now in full swing, practical and supportive help for the British war effort escalated within the Resistance. The blitz, and all-night raids on London which began on the night of 23rd August gave an added impetus to the determination of Resisters to keep harrying the Germans. Allied troops and aircrews, more aware than ever now, that they were needed back in the UK became desperate to return to their units. They were also plagued with anxiety and longed to know that parents, wives, children, and sweethearts were safe, after news of air-raids had reached them through various clandestine ways. They also heard details of aircraft losses, and longed to be back on the job.

Louis and Renée were acutely conscious of the bleak future that immediately faced their friends and former allies the British. Never for one moment could they forget about them, since their drawing-room window looked straight across at the Fort St Jean. The hasty armistice had caused them great personal distress, and their one desire now was to do something to ease the lot of the British officers and men they saw in difficulty around the town. But how, they asked themselves, did one get involved in such matters? What, as civilians, could they do to help?

Louis, a 46-year-old man of ample means, speaking fluent English, was now looking desperately for any opportunity to contribute in one way or another towards helping to undo the damage done to Britain.

He personally had only the most cordial of feelings towards the British, and felt that France's armistice had been a grave injustice to her former allies.

An artistic, sensitive and cultured man, he was also a successful merchant-banker, stockbroker, and entrepreneur who had strong ties with Britain. His immaculate and fashionable style of dress, and his debonair manner, for both of which he was well-known in Marseille, reflected his taste for the English life, its distinctive quality Savile Row clothes, and all things British.

He was violently outspoken about his disgust at the armistice, and made it his business to leave nobody in doubt about his own fiercely pro-British sympathies. This was a dangerous attitude to take at that time, and few local people shared his opinions. For a man who with his wife Renée was to become a key figure in the line, it was disconcerting for other members of the organisation to see him walking about Marseille in such a provocative manner. Later, when the Nouveaus' flat was almost always full of escapers or evaders in hiding, it was enough to put the fear of God into his colleagues whose chances of survival were indissolubly linked with his. He was larger than life, as indeed, in retrospect, was every member of the line. At their highest level such individuals were uniquely outgoing, fearless, flamboyant, and at times even outrageous. They lived dangerously, courting disaster daily, and they did it with style and panache.

He had never failed to show his admiration of Britain in the past, and nothing that he saw around him in the demeanour of the British troops under duress, caused him to deny, or conveniently alter his previous attitude. On the contrary, he was, however dangerously, more inclined than ever now to maintain his loyalty to Britain and his support of her courageous decision to go on fighting : and he longed to become involved in this fight himself. But he felt bound to respect Renée's anxiety for him : for he had been badly gassed in World War I, and although he had been decorated for bravery, he had been left with a devastating cough, and knew that this time he must try to find other ways to make his contribution. He settled for approving his precious only child's departure for London early in 1941 to join the Free French Forces under General de Gaulle, and did all that he could to help Jean-Pierre to get away. But by that time he was already taking an active part in the organisation himself. In his memoirs he wrote:

Then came the German raids on London, and I trembled. The Battle of Britain from August 8th to September 6th, the London Blitz from September 7th to October 31st, a massive raid on Coventry on November 14th, and the most devastating bombing of the City of London on December 29th.

But these raids began to weaken, and the British anti-aircraft guns and fighters proved wonderfully successful at shooting down the enemy.

People in Marseille were becoming more Anglophobe and Pétainiste, and I ever more Anglophile and anti-Pétain. I had violent altercations, and I can remember my amazement and fury at seeing everyone I knew, all my old pals, and my few intimate friends, cover England with abuse whilst displaying their whole-hearted admiration for the old Marshal, and even for Laval. . . .

In August I had the idea of joining de Gaulle . . . but my attempts came to nothing. The days went slowly by. I sold a hundred tons of beans [he had an import-export business with England]. But I did not know what to do with the proceeds, some 400,000 francs, as I feared they would be confiscated by the new government.

Something was to happen, however, that was to result in a total change in his depressed state of mind. He was invited to tea with some Greek friends, a Monsieur and Madame Nicolopoulos, to meet some of the British officers who were interned at the Fort Saint-Jean.

'I would have gone there on my hands and knees', Louis has recorded in his book *Des Captaines par Milliers*.

At tea he met Captain Ian Garrow, the Canadian Tom Kenny, Jimmy Langley, and a fourth whose name he forgot. He invited them all to spend an evening at his home, and two days later they all came.

They still had some whisky left, so he decided that every Monday evening should be reserved for their meetings, and he asked them to bring along anyone they liked, as he wanted them to have somewhere where they could feel at home, a sort of little informal club, open once a week in that big town where the atmosphere was distinctly hostile.

Since he was scarcely on speaking terms with anyone in the town, he couldn't see how it would be possible for him to achieve his ambition and undertake to do something definite.

He and Renée decided that they would invite one of the British officers to lunch each week, and this they duly did, and all accepted. Milk, butter and eggs were like gold-dust, but occasionally they could obtain fish, perhaps a precious *Dorade* or *Rouget*, filched from the sea somehow, somewhere, under the noses of the authority. But their guests didn't appreciate or enjoy them: they found those local fish too bony.

Meanwhile, Louis and his son Jean-Pierre became aware that something was afoot, and that those British officers were planning on getting some of their companions out of France. Louis immediately offered his services to Garrow : they were politely declined.

During the late summer and autumn of 1940, the situation became progressively more hazardous, and those who had made it to Marseille were rounded up and imprisoned at the Fort Saint-Jean. By November and December 1940 it was also proving much more difficult to persuade Spanish guides who had hitherto been prepared to risk being caught by the Milice, not only to tackle the journey across the Pyrenees, but to run the gauntlet of the increased vigilance of the authorities. They began to demand higher prices for the men they guided to safety, charging extra for the increased risks they ran.

Garrow finally confessed to Louis Nouveau that he was in need of money, and Louis was quick to realise that this was not for Ian's own use, but to facilitate the escape of British officers and troops to Spain.

Business had been brought practically to a standstill for many months, and the substantial credits he had in England were blocked and therefore useless. Louis managed to lend Garrow 15,000 francs, and also to find him two or three other reliable financial supporters who raised 25,000 francs between them.

News of the air battles raging over Britain filtered through the jamming of BBC broadcasts and the censorship of the Vichy press. Britain's stoicism and the courage of her people did not go unnoticed in French homes. She had fought off the invasion threat; on 13th November the RAF had attacked the Italian fleet at Taranto, and on 9th December Wavell's desert forces began their successful offensive in North Africa.

Ian had confided to Louis the details of their escape link via Toulouse to get men across the frontier with Spain. He told him he was in touch with the British Consul in Barcelona, though his method of communication with England was still primitive. It consisted of handing a message to one of the neutrals acting as couriers, who hopefully would see it as far as Lisbon. From there it was passed to London : a cumbersome and leisurely way of keeping in touch with MI9 and a method of communication that simply must be improved if the line was to succeed and expand.

Ian was still without any regular dependable funding. Such money as Louis had managed so far to procure for him simply was not going to be enough. More crews than ever before were crashing and baling out all over France during bombing raids. The need for these men to be returned promptly to base was being emphasised by MI9.

A French factory, Le Fil à la Châine, owned by the British firm M. & P. Coats, had provided five or six million francs. Louis was sent off by Garrow to collect one million francs from a Mr Gosling, an ex-manager of the French factory at la Coquille, a small village in the Perigord district.

This was the first of many such trips made by Louis on behalf of the organisation. But Mr Gosling, living in a small hotel in this village of some two or three hundred inhabitants, though he received Louis politely enough, was not prepared to hand over the agreed one million francs before his head office in London had received a corresponding sum from the War Office. Fortunately it was still at that time – late 1940 – possible to send a telegram to England, and the money was forthcoming.

This system guaranteed reimbursement from the War Office, and it was practised thereafter on innumerable occasions by Louis Nouveau. It made it possible for Garrow to continue with his work until such time as MI9 became regularly government funded.

Things did occasionally go wrong : and the bombing of offices in London, and in other towns up and down the country did from time to time cause poor Louis much concern and frustration : the more so, since he was always one to become emotionally involved with people.

In his memoirs an entire saga emerges from the telegrams he sent and received during his quest for ever more financial support from patriotic firms in Britain, who loyally sent money to him in Marseille.

His cables were not only to the point, but often poignant too :

TO COPPIN/LONDON 159 'THE HIGH' HIGH STREET STREATHAM 23/12/40. THANKS WIRING GOOD WISHES FOR CHRISTMAS NEW YEAR GOD SAVE OLD ENGLAND AND OUR COUNTRY – NOUVEAU.

And on New Year's Eve 1940 :

TO COPRA DEALERS COMMERCIAL SALE ROOM MINCING LANE LONDON: HOPE EVERYTHING ALRIGHT NOTHING DESTROYED IN YOUR OFFICES AND PRIVATE HOUSES I KNOW YOU KEEP STEADY STOP THINK VERY

MUCH OF YOU RELY UPON YOU GOD SAVE ENGLAND AND OUR COUNTRY
HAPPY NEW YEAR — NOUVEAU.

Why had there been no reply to the following telegram? Because,
unbeknown to him, the Commercial Room had been destroyed by
bombs. On 19th January 1941:

LONDON COPRA ASSOCIATION LEADENHALL STREET 84 LONDON.
WHY NO REPLY MY TELEGRAM 31/12/40 ADDRESSED COPRA DEALERS
COMMERCIAL SALE ROOM WANT NEWS YOUR MEMBERS GOD HELP AND
BLESS YOU ALL — NOUVEAU.

In response to news of bomb damage in Copra Association's Commercial Sale Room in Mincing Lane, Louis sent the following telegram:

HOPE ALL MY FRIENDS AND FAMILIES AND STAFF ALRIGHT GOD HELP
YOU THINK EVERY DAY OF YOU ALL WILL SEE IT THROUGH I KNOW
YOU ARE PATIENT AND STEADY AS YOU ARE BRAVE HEARTILY —
NOUVEAU.

*

By the spring of 1941 Georges Rodocanachi was concerned about the
deterioration in the conditions under which British officers were being
detained at the Fort Saint-Jean. This might have been the result of
German pressure since, contrary to the armistice agreement, they had
begun to infiltrate into the south.

The presence of British officers free around Marseille had for a long
time been a source of irritation to the German and Italian Armistice
Commission. All those officers living loose about the town, and who had
not found a safe house to hide in, together with all inmates of the Fort
Saint-Jean, were to be sent to a mediaeval fortress called Saint
Hippolyte du Fort, about thirty miles north of Nimes. This was an old
barracks which, according to Donald Caskie, who was allowed to visit
there once a month upon his clerical duties, was diabolically filthy, and
had been used for housing the sons of former servicemen, or Arab troops.
Living conditions were entirely different there, with no opportunity for
going out for the men. Officers were permitted to walk about the town
on parole as a special privilege.

Dr Rodocanachi was much concerned about the health of men under his care at that time, who would be facing such pitiful conditions.

Ian got wind of this removal and was alerted to the limitations that would be put upon officers allowed out only in the Nimes area, and failed to report back to the Fort Saint-Jean for the last roll-call. Since he had no intention of deserting his expanding escape line, he went to ground at the Rodocanachis. Thus one day Séraphine opened the door to him, and exchanging the torrid brilliance of the Marseille streets for the sombre cool of the flat, he took tea with my uncle and aunt, and settled into a room at the back of the building. From then on it was his heaquarters.

The other POWs all left Marseille for Saint Hippolyte de Fort, and formed a very rowdy convoy yelling 'Tipperary' at the top of their voices all the way down the Canebière in full view of an astonished and apathetic crowd of onlookers.

Two of the officers who had been lodging in semi-concealment at the Hôtel Nautique on the Vieux Port just before this change took place, were winkled out. Like all the others they too were driven away, though both were in a poor state of health and under the medical care of Dr Rodocanachi who was treating their wounds.

It was in April or May 1941 that Louis first heard of Madame Catala. In January his son Jean-Pierre had urged him to seek Garrow's help in getting him to England, and on 7th March he had left Marseille. It was Madame Catala who had helped Jean-Pierre to cross the border, and her house was used as a regular staging-post. She was in touch with a number of Spanish guides, made all the necessary arrangements with them, and had already succeeded in getting several evaders into Spain before Ian had got to know her.

She put him in touch with a man named Aguado, who was living at her house with his wife at that time, and he linked Ian with Vidal,* a Spanish anarchist who had some half-a-dozen excellent guides working under his orders.

At first, all convoys were organised through Madame Catala. She took charge of the funds, paid her guides, and kept them moving, with men who sometimes crossed at Andorra, but more often via Perpignan. Booted in white to be more easily followed at night, the guides led them

---

* Vidal, the head of the Spanish guides, was eventually betrayed, tortured, and in 1944 executed by the Germans. Some say that he was burned alive.

along footpaths and goat-tracks to cross the frontier somewhere remote in the mountains.

Madame Catala's husband, a scientist, was working in London, which naturally made her an object of suspicion. But the fact that she had four or five children and a niece living with her helped to divert attention from her activities.

By the spring, Ian was sending Louis on ever more responsible business, and thanks to his experience with finance and communications, his invaluable contacts with local and more distant residents in the south of France and to the generosity of French friends who joined him in the drive to raise even more funds, he was proving himself an invaluable member of the small team. He recorded :

> There was a continual drain on our funds at the rate of roughly 100,000 francs a month. With a view to building up a kind of reserve fund for emergencies, I had gone to see André Vagliano at his works on one of the islands in the Seine, near Puteaux.
>
> Though people engaged in the kind of work we were doing were not always welcome visitors, Vagliano, whenever I applied to him, always gave me a warm and understanding welcome. He never failed to grasp the position at once, and told me that I could always count upon fifty thousand francs in case of need. [He was] the son of one of my father's oldest friends and put me up in his Paris house and I spent several blissful days in his beautiful house in the Rue du Général Appert in luxurious comfort.

There had come the day when Louis had very little money left, and needed to be able to reimburse their agent Jean de la Olla, who had himself had to borrow from someone else to pay helpers.

'I decided to ask Vagliano for the fifty thousand francs he had promised.' They dined at the Café de Paris, and Louis explained that he had telephoned because he had something to ask him. As they sat in a remote and secluded part of the restaurant, Louis felt Vagliano's hand touch his leg gently, and putting out his own hand, felt a bundle of notes. Such thoughtfulness and discretion touched Louis greatly. By taking the initiative, André Vagliano had spared him the asking for financial help.

'I understood at once what was in the wind, when you telephoned,' his friend said.

He was reimbursed subsequently by the British Services at the Palais Royal in 1946 at a time when, unfortunately the franc had already slumped considerably. Pat O'Leary himself had come to return the money and to thank him. But Vagliano wouldn't hear of accepting it, and at once donated it to some charity.

British residents along the Riviera, with the Duke of Westminster as chairman, formed a committee to raise funds to help their own nationals. They came up with loans against promises of repayment by the War Office, which were guaranteed and confirmed in coded messages over the air. Money lent in this fashion was not charity. It was money to be risked, gambled, in support of Britain's hopes and prospects for a successful war. It became a good investment, and was returned with interest after victory.

Nubar Gulbenkian, so wealthy that he was considered unlikely to attract attention, not only helped with money, but also acted as a link with Spain, and just happened to be the holder of a neutral passport. Thus he was able to act as a go-between, and two trips that he undertook, supposedly to visit his father, Calouste Gulbenkian, who also just happened to be in Vichy, required Nubar to travel via Lisbon, Madrid, and Perpignan, in the autumn of 1940. This resulted in the setting up of a useful link with London. Up to the time of Pearl Harbor neutral couriers were chiefly Americans, but thereafter things became more difficult for them. Another valuable courier in the early days was Madge Holst who was the wife of a Norwegian businessman. A Yorkshire woman she had known the MI9 agent Donald Darling before the war, and meeting him in Lisbon agreed to become a courier.

The London End
MI9 had not wasted time in establishing their agents after the fall of France. In Spain there was Michael Creswell, code-named *Monday* at the British Embassy in Madrid. He dealt with the Spanish side of escape and evasion affairs. In Lisbon there was MI9's Donald Darling, code-named *Sunday*, who in July 1940 had been sent by MI9 to Lisbon officially to the Repatriation Office, and secretly to create underground links with France.

As Vice-Consul in charge of repatriation at Lisbon, he had opportunities for meeting people who were travelling to and from Marseille. Through contacts such as Gulbenkian he began to be in communication with Garrow, and to send him money.

Donald Darling, who acted as the line's terminal, dealing with men arriving along any of the several escape lines set up by MI9 during the winter of 1940–41, also acted as inquisitor. He vetted all escapers and evaders, confirming their authenticity and good faith, before allowing them to proceed to Britain by sea or air. In early 1942, once firm links had been established with Marseille, he was transferred to carry out the same duties at Gibraltar.

In March 1941 evader Jimmy Langley was repatriated by destroyer, and was posted to MI9 in London, where in due course he was to be joined by Airey Neave, code-named *Saturday*.

Jimmy had been examined and pronounced unfit for further military service, at the Mixed Medical Commission at the Military Hospital Michel-Levy in Marseille by Dr Rodocanachi in February 1941.

At first London had not in the early days been in a position to help Garrow on an organised and regular basis. But with the return to England of Jimmy Langley, and Airey Neave's arrival there in May 1942, this team of experienced escapers was able to provide the right back-up for the line.

*

In the north of France Lille became the collecting point for airmen ditching or baling out. Here they were regularly picked up and escorted south by a member of the line. This was Sergeant Harold Cole, better known as Paul Cole, an evader from the British Expeditionary Force, who made a name for himself up there as a man of great gallantry and resourcefulness.

Shepherding his men with experienced daring, he managed again and again to steer them across the hazardous demarcation line, speaking on their behalf, covering for their lack of French, and generally jollying them along until they reached Marseille. There he would present himself in front of Ian in his room at the back of the Rodocanachis' flat, give a good account of himself, and collect payment due to him, and money for his next trip. He appeared a first-class operator, but before long his value was to come under scrutiny.

(Left) Georges Zarifi. Arrived in England along his own escape line, and serving with the Forces Francaises Libres. *(Right)* Ian Garrow.

Ian Garrow 'somewhere in France'.

Sue and Tom Kenny on the ?
of their engagement on 29th
April, 1941 on the terrace of
Hotel Martinez in Cannes.

Mrs Haden Guest shows ho?
she guided her son Anthony
they crawled across the
demarcation line by night in
unoccupied France.

Meanwhile, on his travels for Ian, Louis Nouveau was locating safe-housing, and recruiting couriers capable of prospecting a new district themselves, of establishing genuine contacts with all sorts of people, and who promised to be imaginative and enterprising enough to help spring prisoners, and keep their nerve.

Louis himself escorted men to and from railway stations, and to get photographs taken, and hair cut by known sympathisers. He visited regular helpers, making sure that all was working as arranged, heard about any problems or suspicions that might have arisen, and settled for expenses incurred. If a cover had been blown, then it was agreed that no more parcels would be delivered or collected.

'We were continually busy organising convoys, and establishing contacts with Spanish guides at Toulouse,' Louis records, 'for more airmen were escaping and arriving than it was possible for us to drain into Spain.' And this despite their agent Jean de la Olla's many new hiding-places and recuperation centres in the Paris area, and others in Lille – all crucial delaying points along the line.

By 1941 airmen in the UK were briefed that on the run in enemy territory, they should steer clear of built-up areas, and using a spire or tower as a guide, make for the local *curé* or 'brother'. Opposed to Nazism, no priest is known to have betrayed Allied men on the run, and convents and monasteries had saved many an Allied life. Railwaymen, or porters returning home after a shift on duty, were another possibility. Though teachers may hold strong political views, and be swayed by interests in job-security or preferment, or be sympathetic to the new régime, they too might hide a man on the run.

Compass-guided and travelling south, many an escaper or evader soon made good use of the telephone-box maps : for these were to be found on the backs of the local directories, each one covering the area of that postal region.

Arrived in Marseille, some made straight for a small bar on the Boulevard Dugommier, Le Petit Poucet, Tom Thumb. This was where many British men made their first contact with those who would hide them in Marseille. And it was to this bar that Louis Nouveau would stroll, elegantly sauntering towards a table, and ordering a drink, as he chatted with the patron, before collecting his parcels.

It was in May 1941 that the Nouveaus began to fill their own flat with men. And by the time that MI9 had advised them from London that they must close their Safe House down, in November 1942, they had had no fewer than 156 Allied officers and men hidden on the premises.*

Whitehall, judging that the morale of airmen would be improved if they knew that ditched crews could reappear at their stations in the UK as quickly as was now becoming possible, gave priority to escape networks out of Europe.

Thanks to the courage and determination of helpers in the field, the prompt return of men to base was miraculous, and led to an undying affection and gratitude for the thousands who in time became involved in the escape *réseaux*.

Donald Caskie told me that many soldiers and seamen found the orders from London to return air crews first unacceptable. This departure from the first come, first served policy was hard to come to terms with, and he himself often felt extremely sorry to have to enforce it.

In all, some 17,000 officers and men had disappeared after Dunkirk, unaccounted for. They were not taken as POWs at the time, but dispersed, and tried to escape. Most were caught, and remained interned in POW camps for the duration. But a considerable number having lost touch with their units, lingered on in hiding in the north and in other parts of France. Many settled down with French families helping on farms, becoming reasonably fluent in French, attached to their hosts, and they to them, and anxious to make themselves useful in return for hospitality and the risks run. According to Louis Nouveau:

> Peasants fell into two classes when it came to harbouring airmen. Those who took a strong liking for their guests, retained them as long as possible, and soon came to regard them as practically members of the family. When their presence at a farm became known, and we arrived to fetch them, it was almost as if the MP had come to arrest a deserter! ... The other kind immediately concerned themselves with the best means of facilitating their escape.

Some stayed forever, and married French girls. But most made the long

---

* Louis Nouveau's list of 'secret visitors' and members of the line who stayed at their home, is in the appendices.

trek south, as did Resistants in the north for whom the chase had become too hot, and the ever-increasing number of crashed aircrews from bombing raids all over Europe.

Since it cost some £10,000 and took several months to train a bomber pilot, the Air Ministry decreed that aircrew must have automatic priority over anyone else, for return to the UK.

The Nouveaus' first visitor was one of four survivors whose Wellington had crashed after running out of fuel over the Mediterranean. After drifting for nearly nine days on an inflated rubber raft with no food, and only two pints of water, they were picked up by a French cargo vessel. Landed in Marseille, they were locked in cells reserved for wounded men undergoing disciplinary treatment, or awaiting court martial at the Military Hospital Michel-Levy nearby.

Garrow was planning their escape, and Louis had himself done some reconnaissance under the barred windows of the hospital. Eventually Ian succeeded in making contact with the men inside, and the Nouveaus were asked to hide one of the three men a sergeant, and the second pilot of the plane who was in a bad state of health and needed nursing.

Sergeant Herbert, who had managed to give the slip to the sentry, found himself free, and having been supplied with civilian clothes hastened to Donald Caskie. Garrow had him collected at once, and sent him to the Nouveaus.

'He and Peter Jones are the only two of our first twenty-five or thirty names I remembered when I began, a little later, to note these in the Voltaire in my library,' wrote Louis.

'I remembered him because he was our first visitor, and because we had him for about a fortnight, and he was alone with us in the flat.'

Thereafter Louis kept a record of everyone who stayed with them, inscribing their names, units, and details of their circumstances and the history of their escapes or evasions in fine pen and ink lettering the length of the hinge of the book. In this fashion the Gestapo or Milice flicking casually through it, would surely fail to spot them in volume forty-four of his complete edition of Voltaire's works in seventy volumes.

He estimated that 156 visitors, of whom only 11 were French, were secretly harboured at the flat. In the same book he noted the 42 journeys he undertook in 1941, and up to November 1942 on instructions first from Ian and subsequently from his successor Pat O'Leary.

Sergeant Herbert was in pretty poor shape. So every day Louis took him out for a little gentle exercise, avoiding the busier streets and building up his strength by slow degrees. Sergeant Herbert was in fact the only man hidden at the Nouveaus ever to be allowed out of the flat, other than for the indispensable visit to the photographer for photographs to be affixed to forged documents.

He had arrived wearing plus-fours supplied by Ian from a little stock of clothes he kept, and which was later transferred to the Nouveaus' flat.

Sergeant Herbert slept in Jean-Pierre's bedroom. Soon the flat became a regular camping-ground. But at that time Herbert's presence had simply reminded the Nouveaus of a peace-time visit from a friend from England. He did in fact remain hidden with them for fifteen days.

Fortunately there was little risk of their receiving unexpected calls from friends for they had quarrelled with more or less everyone, and none of their old acquaintances who, in the past might have turned up without giving any warning, ever thought of doing so now.

Nouveau had taken care to instruct his maids always to say 'Mrs Nouveau and the Master are out.' These splendid girls were perfectly aware of what he and Renée were doing, and were prepared to play their part in anything going.

After twelve days the Nouveaus were to part with their first visitor. There was a convoy leaving for Toulouse, one of whom unbeknown at that time to the Nouveaus, was coming from the Rodocanachis. From Toulouse they were to go by train to Perpignan, a rallying point near the frontier and the guides.

They were all starting out from the Seamen's Mission. But nobody turned up as expected to fetch their visitor. Louis fearing something had gone wrong, hurried round the Vieux Port to the Rue de Forbin to find out what had happened.

It seemed that one of the Englishmen whose job it had been to wake all the others, had overslept, and failed to do so. And further to Louis's annoyance, he was upbraided by Elizabeth who had just arrived at the Mission in a tearing hurry. She was furious that Louis had by coming in person to the building, allowed the Padre to know that Sergeant Herbert had been staying with them. He had as she saw it blown their cover unnecessarily.

Louis was equally angry. And he told her in no mean terms that he only took orders from Garrow, and most certainly not from her. He was then required, since the journey was cancelled, to collect his parcel and return home.

There the visit was extended by three more days, until the Sergeant was successfully delivered into the care of a remarkable man who had just arrived from St Hippolyte du Fort.

His code name was *Joseph*, or sometimes *Adolphe*, but he was better known as Pat O'Leary, and was before long to give his name to the Line. He was in fact a Belgian doctor, Albert-Marie Guérisse, and he had served with a cavalry regiment during the eighteen days of a campaign at the beginning of May 1940. When the Belgian Army capitulated on 28th May, and King Leopold surrendered, Pat O'Leary sailed from Dunkirk on 31st May and landed at Margate. He remained in London for a few days whilst the Belgians sorted themselves out, after which the officers were sent back to France, disembarking at Brest on 8th June.

In the ensuing chaos, on 20th June, Pat joined a re-grouping centre for the Belgian army in the south of France, and by the end of June set off for Gibraltar with about twenty other Belgian officers and a Czecho-slovakian contingent, sailing from Sète. In Gibraltar he joined the crew of a small trawler registered with the French Paquet S.S.Co. of Marseille, the SS *Rhin*, soon to be taken over by the British and renamed HMS *Fidelity*.*

She was an armed trawler by this time, operating secretly as a 'Q' ship conducting clandestine operations on behalf of SOE† in the Western Mediterranean with a mixed crew.

During an operation at Collioure close to the Spanish frontier, a motor launch was lowered from the *Fidelity* in connection with clandestine sabotage operations on the south coast of France, and it capsized during a sudden squall.

Pat O'Leary, appointed second in command of the *Fidelity*, with the rank of Lieutenant Commander RN and wearing Royal Naval uniform, nearly drowned, but was eventually picked up and arrested by French coastguards. He was interned at the camp for British prisoners at St Hippolyte du Fort near Nîmes.

---

* See Appendices.

† Special Operations Executive, London, the organisation formed in the summer of 1940 for secret sabotage operations in occupied Europe.

Pat was a man of exceptional fearlessness and total dedication to whatever he undertook. He became at once a popular leader who gave the impression of having great physical and spiritual reserves, cool, ingenious, and ideally suited to the clandestine life he was soon to face.

> His sense of humour [wrote Donald Caskie] led him to enjoy situations so nerve-racking that they might have stopped the stoutest heart. But he was strict, kindly, and protective towards those under his command.
>
> Fighting the enemy he was ruthless. He knew the methods of the Gestapo, and he hated them.
>
> A cultivated man, one felt that he had set everything aside, the things he enjoyed and loved in peace-time, all that makes life worth living, until victory was won.*

He was a slight man, frail-looking even, and not very tall. He moved with the svelte agility of a cat on velvet paws. His comings and goings inconspicuous, so that he seemed just to manifest himself in that he didn't so much walk into a room, or towards a bar in a café, or a table at a restaurant, as simply arrive there. He had suddenly come amongst you. It was disconcerting for those with anything to hide or fear. Yet his presence in itself brought a sense of all being well and under control, and engendered confidence amongst his friends and war-time colleagues, both in and out of prison. But when he was around there was also invariably a feeling of urgency and purpose. His presence stamped authority and dedication on whatever matter was being planned or discussed.

His hands were strong, his fingers sensitive and fine as befitted those of the doctor he was not at that time known to be – except to Elizabeth Haden-Guest. She recalls that Pat gave himself away to her early in their relationship within the Line.

'It was really very unlike him, but he happened to be with me when Jean Fourcade brought Anthony to see me from his hiding-place in the hills above Marseille. The child was ill: and it was the way Pat handled him, putting one hand against his back, and the other gently pressing against his belly. He turned to me and said thoughtfully . . .

* *The Tartan Pimpernel.* Oldbourne Book Co. Ltd. 1957.

' "Elizabeth ... *rachitisme* ... rickets ... *Faites attention*, be careful!"

'I knew from that moment that he was a doctor. That transient instinctive flicker of concern and diagnosis. It was the only unguarded moment I ever knew in him. The only mistake I ever saw him make. But it was also the reason why I took Anthony to see Dr Rodocanachi at the flat in the Rue Roux de Brignoles.'

CHAPTER FOUR

Pat O'Leary moves into the Rodocanachis' Flat

Summer 1941

Whilst out on parole from St Hippolyte du Fort, in June 1941, Pat O'Leary had a rendezvous with Ian Garrow. It was through Donald that Ian had got wind of Pat's arrival there, though Ian kept in regular touch with the inmates at St Hippolyte through two British officers who had volunteered to stay on there as POWs maintaining a link with the network outside. They met at a flat occupied by some friends of Ian's, an American married to a French wife, who lived close to the fort at Nîmes.

There were over a thousand men at St Hippolyte, and Donald made regular visits there, holding a service, and taking with him comforts of various practical kinds amongst which were compasses, files, and ropes, hidden amongst the hymn books. The place was run efficiently, and he judged that it would be difficult to escape from its ancient stone walls. As was his practice, he talked with officers and men, and received news of recent arrivals, and took Garrow's instructions, and what war news he had been able to come by, to the men inside. Though the prison was a hard nut to crack, men had been known to escape from it, and would surely do so again.

This meeting between Ian and Pat was to be the first of many, and they got down to business straight away. Since officers were allowed out during the day on parole, it hadn't been difficult for Pat to meet Ian. It was also useful for officers planning on breaking out, to be able to make contact with one or two people in the town, to know the geography of the place, and to be able to envisage what they would do immediately they were free.

Once plans were agreed, Ian returned to the Rodocanachis, and thereafter he kept in touch with Pat via Elizabeth who had been present when the escape plans were laid, and who sat at a table outside a café opposite the gates of the prison. There she lingered over cups of acorn coffee until Pat joined her. Conspicuous to officers out on parole, she was able to give and receive messages for the line, and any last minute instructions from Garrow were passed by word of mouth.

Pat was to make the first move at the prison which was to talk to his companions about the escape itself, and the importance of withdrawing their parole immediately. This was simply done. It was just a matter of notifying the senior British officer of their intention. But time would be needed. The escape committee, which had selected Pat as their leader, had well rehearsed the plan of escape. In ones and twos they rushed the walls and stole away, with the enthusiastic help of all the British soldiers at the fort who created a monumental diversion at the critical moment.

Once free, Pat had no difficulty in reaching Marseille and locating the Safe House Ian had recommended. Being Belgian, he was able innocently to ask for instructions in French, and to board public transport to the Rodocanachis' without attracting any attention to himself or their home.

Through the massive carriage entrance he strode, which led into a covered driveway, and to doors to flats on the ground floor. A vintage wrought-iron lift was flanked by the concierge's cubby-hole in a dark recess. He didn't need to ask for instructions but made purposefully for the stairs, and on up to the second floor.

He rang the bell and the door was opened by Séraphine. Recalling that incident, Pat said she looked to be between sixty-five and seventy years of age, and wore a maid's uniform.

He asked her if he could see Mrs Rodocanachi, and was asked who he was. Knowing that Ian Garrow had already spoken to her about him, he introduced himself as Pat O'Leary, and was given a very warm welcome.

And that was it! He had arrived at what was to become his home for some long time.

She took him to the large twin-bedded room which he was to share with Garrow. It had its own bathroom, the one access to which was in the room. The bathroom faced inwards away from the street with tall frosted windows opening on to an inner courtyard. This remote suite supplied all their needs, and Ian now lived there all the time, out of sight. Pat used the flat whenever he was in Marseille, for he was to travel widely for Garrow from the beginning.

Séraphine took the two young officers under her wing, washing, ironing, mending, and keeping their clothes well brushed and pressed.

Another room far removed from the front-door and busy medical part of the flat was an even larger double bedroom. Here men were hidden away for varying lengths of time, if necessary receiving care from their doctor host.

'Parcels' these men were called by some. Or 'guests', 'packages', 'footballers', and sometimes by their kindly hosts, affectionately, *'les enfants'*.

The Nouveaus were full to overflowing, and the Rodocanachis too had a steady stream. Two or three other flats around the town could be relied upon to find a bed for a man for a night or two. One such was the flat belonging to a New Zealand girl Nancy Fiocca. Hers was a luxuriously appointed flat, with a room which was used as a bar, and a couple of rooms which could accommodate one or two men for the odd night. It was not a Safe House in the sense that numbers of men remained hidden there for any length of time.

Nancy was a freelance journalist who had arrived in France in 1939, and who whilst staying in Cannes met a Frenchman called Henri Fiocca at a party. In November of that year they were married. He was a wealthy man, a good deal older than she was, and he idolised her and would give her anything she asked for.

For a few precious months they lived happily and luxuriously together in Marseille. After the fall of France and the débâcle at Dunkirk, with the division of the country into two zones, her husband's French identity card couldn't protect her since her French identity card showed that she was a British subject, as it gave her place of birth. Because they lived in the unoccupied zone, however, she was safe enough, just so long as she didn't do anything politically dangerous to attract the Vichy police.

But Nancy Fiocca (née Wake, and now Forward), was not the sort of girl to be told what she might or might not do. And what she did do was to invite a number of British officers from the Fort St Jean to enjoy the hospitality of her home. She was also free with her drinks, and gifts of cigarettes, soap and other black market goodies that were beyond the means of most people.

'She was an extraordinary person,' Louis has recorded. Others remember her for her outrageous hats, and style of dress, and men flocked round her like bees round a flamboyant honey-pot.

Soon after they were married, Henri was called up. Nancy with an abundance of energy and patriotic fervour, and no domestic commitments, embarked upon a course in heavy goods driving, and volunteered to drive ambulances all over France.

After the armistice, she and Henri returned home. They were both of them extremely generous, and lent a lot of money to the line when it was most needed.

One of the officers frequently to enjoy their hospitality, and a regular visitor to Nancy's home near the Palais de Longchamp, was Ian Garrow who often had the Canadian, Tom Kenny with him.

Kenny too was very generous to the budding escape line. A peacetime resident of Marseille, he lived an easy-going, comfortable life as a business man in the town. He was engaged to the daughter of the Martinez family at Cannes. He was a good and enthusiastic supporter of Ian Garrow's from the very beginning, though he had no political leanings or affiliations.

Nevertheless he was naïve, and had no previous experience of clandestine activities. At the bar of the Hôtel de Noailles where Nancy was lavishly offering drinks, parcels were regularly collected and there were amongst the few local civilians involved, anxious moments as tongues were loosened and voices raised.

Just a handful of these pro-British enthusiasts were treading on egg-shell, their homes full of hidden men, their commitment irrevocably made.

But many had at least one asset. For well-to-do Marsellais could still count upon the loyalty and natural gut-reaction of servants who would answer door-bells in their absence. For unlike their counterparts in Britain whose servants had all been whisked away for war work, France no longer at war, left domestics where they were.

In time Nancy developed a conscience about the dangerous way in which by her involvement with Garrow she might threaten her husband's business, and even his life. Since she was by this time filling her days with escort work, and her home with visitors, she asked Henri if he would give her a flat of her own where her work would not compromise him. And this he duly did.

Henri like Louis had considerable trade links with Britain, and a flourishing import-export business in fruit and vegetables amongst other things. And like Louis's, his business was at a standstill at this stage of the war. He too had financial assets accruing to his account across the

Channel. Both of these highly successful entrepreneurs put their brains and expertise to work for Garrow in the early days, backing the escape line with money guaranteed by the War Office.

Henri, infatuated by his lively, enterprising, young wife, took delight in involving himself with her in the work of the burgeoning escape line. He soon became an escort himself, as well as a financial adviser. But his marriage was destined to be cut short. For he was denounced, arrested and tortured by the Gestapo who executed him on 16th October 1943. He proved himself a courageous and loyal husband who despite prolonged and merciless torture refused to reveal the whereabouts of his wife, or her involvement in resistance work.

Both Henri and Nancy regularly led parties of escaping men to points along the route, and delivered mysterious parcels the contents of which they preferred not to know. Nancy became ever more involved in Ian's line, acting as a courier between Toulouse, Nice and Marseille, and taking parties as far as the guides who would see them across the mountains. And her flat, close to the Palais de Longchamp, was used for meetings of the network.

At Dr Rodocanachi's flat baths were taken cold, and food had become extremely difficult, the more so since Fanny Rodocanachi was not the sort of person readily to tap the black market. Even cats had begun to disappear from the streets, and cats and pigeons were served in restaurants as 'rabbit'. Meals at the doctor's home were frugal and monotonous. Yet they continued to be brought to the table and served by Séraphine in her maid's uniform.

It was no mean task to manhandle back to the flat, and up in the lift enough food to feed the enlarged household. With only three of the five now permanent residents possessing ration cards, it was nothing short of a miracle that all were adequately fed – especially when the large bedroom at the back was also full of hungry young men.

Fanny Rodocanachi was extremely grateful for considerable quantities of macaroni, supplied to her by her nephew Georges Zarifi, whose father Theodore's macaroni factory must have been the saving of many a distraught housewife.

She developed a system of doing her marketing more than once a day, so that had she been stopped and followed home she should not have been found with an improbably large quantity of food for her small household, nor led the police to her perilous flat.

Her home was by this time well organised for the sudden receipt of visitors. Pat was immediately allocated not only his room with its adjoining bathroom, but the soft-soled slippers that were *de rigueur* : as was strict adherence to a few house rules.

Baths and lavatory plugs were to be pulled as infrequently as possible. English or American cigarettes were never to be smoked on the stairs outside the flat, nor their stubs left lying in ash-trays or waste-paper-baskets in an identifiable state.

Séraphine would attend to the opening and closing of all shutters and curtains at all times. These should never be disturbed. All visitors passing through had to be told never to stand close enough to the windows to be seen from the busy street below. There were many pedestrians, most of them local, who might chance to look up, and none of them was now to be trusted.

The aim of all whose daily lives were not quite what they seemed, was to avoid attracting attention and interrogation. 'Keep away from the windows' was the eternal cry as the men, especially those shut away in the back room and just passing through, were tempted to sit for hours watching the world go by.

Renée and Louis Nouveau repeated the same refrain and had even established an imaginary 'line of demarcation', beyond which their visitors must never stand. The wonderful wide modern window overlooking the Vieux Port was a great temptation to men held captive there for weeks on end.

Fanny Rodocanachi had the gravest misgivings about the dark figure silhouetted in a small window of a flat that backed on to their block. Significantly, it stayed at its post day and night, yet no light was ever switched on during the hours of darkness. The fear of betrayal was always present but they remained free of investigation by the police.

Donald Caskie, who had had the same anxiety, was relieved of it when his lone watcher was found in the early hours one morning, his body riddled with bullets, the matter settled by a friend or friends unknown.

In the large bedroom Fanny Rodocanachi's darts-board was a great success. Nevertheless she felt it necessary to thicken the floor covering beneath it.

Playing-cards, games and the piles of old books and magazines in English became more and more shabby. Unbelievably, contributions for this kind of entertainment would from time to time be left in the doctor's waiting-room. It was impossible to trace the donors, and none of these gifts was ever reclaimed. Wisely she determined never to try to identify who it was who had thought that those things might be of use.

*

The first evening of Pat's arrival, he discussed with Ian the matter and manner of his own return to England. The contacts Pat had established with Garrow from St Hippolyte du Fort had been made primarily with this in mind. But Ian had other ideas, now that he had met Pat and realised what an excellent partner he would have in the bi-lingual and delightful Pat O'Leary, if only he could convince him that he could do invaluable work by remaining in Marseille.

In the meantime, at the appointed hour of eight o'clock the day he arrived the Rodocanachis, with Ian and Pat, crouched over the wireless set in the drawing-room to hear the news from London.

The summer of 1941 was appallingly hot. Along the avenues of the town, pollarded planes and palm trees hung limp and dusty in parallel lines. Trams trundled along red-hot rails and had an easy time of it careering along streets that carried few cars. Many vehicles bulged grotesquely with bags of the new butane gas. A bombing raid on Marseille had just brought death to a number of civilians, and shocked the populace who were, after all, no longer at war. Across the crackling of ether, and through the jamming of the enemy, came as always the reminder . . .

'*Baissez vos postes** . . . *Baissez vos postes* . . . *Baissez vos postes* . . .' Then followed the familiar tune of *La Cucaracha* . . . *La Cucaracha* . . . to which were sung those catchy words . . . *Radio Paris ment†* . . . *Radio Paris ment* . . . *Radio Paris est Allemand.* Then came the drum

---

* Turn down your sets . . . Lower the volume . . . This announcement was followed by *S'il y a lieu* . . . If need be.

† Radio Paris lies . . . Radio Paris lies . . . Radio Paris is German.

beating the haunting rhythm of 'V' for Victory, and ... *Ici Londres! Les Français parlent aux Français* ... Voici les ouvelles ...*

Twice a day after a brief surge of Beethoven's Fifth Symphony, from the European Division of the BBC a confident voice spoke to France from a bomb-proof underground studio in Bush House, London.

This for the listeners at my uncle and aunt's home in Marseille, was their life-line, and like countless others around the world, they heard avidly, up-to-date news of the progress of the war. They also listened for the coded messages in French that meant so much to those who awaited them : and were so amazing and even amusing to the millions who heard them, knew them to be important in a clandestine way, but who could not decipher them.

Pat was soon haunting the large drawing-room twice a day, awaiting the message from London that would determine his immediate future. For it hadn't taken Ian long to convince Pat that there was an important job for him to be doing in Marseille. It wouldn't be too difficult to replace a naval lieutenant commander, but it would be hard indeed to find a better qualified colleague at this critical time.

'You, like myself, are an officer,' Pat said to Ian, 'and you know that I can't just make this decision for myself. I need orders now that I've escaped, and I'll abide by them.'

In desperation Ian reminded Pat that there were fourteen aircrew imprisoned at St Hippolyte at that very moment, and more men were arriving there every day. All highly trained, and destined to be lost to the RAF until the war was over, unless rescued and returned to base as quickly as possible.

They decided to send a message to London, and if the War Office approved, Pat would stay on.

As one of Pat's code names was *Adolphe* it was agreed that the message of consent should run thus : '*Adolphe doit rester* – Adolphe is to stay.'

'It will take about a week to reach London via the British Consul General in Barcelona : and after that we mustn't miss a single broadcast,' Ian said.

* This is London ... The French speak to the French ... Here is the news ... Radio Paris broadcast from the former Normandy Cinema in the Champs-Elysées, under the leading broadcaster Jean Hérold-Paquis, whose Collaborationist refrain was the need for England, like Carthage, to be destroyed. He was executed after the Liberation.

And, like a small miracle, as they were all together around the radio, through the enemy's jamming, a crackling voice from London said, and repeated : *'Adolphe doit rester – je repète – Adolphe doit rester.'*

Their request had been received all those miles away, deliberated, and granted; and Pat, free now to throw in his lot with these new friends, joined them in the celebratory drink of champagne brought in by a beaming Séraphine.

All the men hidden at the Rodocanachis had the run of the flat, but never went into the medical area during surgery hours. Security was at no time relaxed, and if anybody called at mealtimes the dining-room doors would be folded across by Séraphine so that the extra places set at the table should not be seen by an unexpected visitor.

Pat and Ian were very conscious of the danger that their presence, if caught in the flat, would mean for their hosts and Séraphine, who did so much for them. Removing tell-tale labels from the clothes of men passing along the line, she stitched badges and chevrons, and French money into the thickness of shoulder-pads. These credentials might be crucial if the men were caught, and had to prove their POW status. Later on, as a result of treachery, many British troops secreted the length of the O'Leary escape line were captured, and those unable to produce proof of their status were executed.

Along with badges, Séraphine also transferred magnetic buttons and buckles from service tunics, to the civilian clothes in which the men would be crossing the Pyrenees. Some of them had magnetic safety-pins, cuff-links, and pencil-clips : never had the old woman seen so many fascinating novelties !

They repaid her in the only currency they had. With concentrated Horlick's Malted Milk tablets and boiled sweets from their survival kits.

One day Netta Zarifi arrived burdened with a pile of excellent clothes which had belonged to her brother-in-law, recently dead. With simple innocence she said that Georges would surely know of any needy families who might make use of them. They would certainly come in handy for *someone*, and already Fanny was running a practised eye over the garments, and sizing them up. What a windfall for her visitors to be kitted out for their journey home in such superbly-cut quality clothes !

Netta herself was fully occupied with her own large house and family. Staffing and running the Red Cross canteen at the station kept her busy.

(*Above*) Jean de la Olla.

(*Right*) Pat O'Leary snapped by a
street-photographer in Marseille,
only a few days after he had taken
over control of the line, following
Ian Garrow's arrest. His
expression shows that he is
displeased at being committed to
paper by anyone at such a critical
time.

(Left) Jimmy Langley in France in 1940. *(Right)* Nancy Fiocca, Ian Garrow, and Henri Fiocca. Part of a group taken as a small snapshot.

Harold Cole, gangster and traitor shot by French police in Paris. (From an original photograph marked from Press reproduction.)

And she was also involved in the administration of the Dispensaire des Enfants Malades, a day-centre for sick children where her brother-in-law was senior consultant paediatrician. So there was no shortage of conversation when Georges joined the two sisters for his precious afternoon break and the cup of Earl Grey tea brought in by Séraphine. The war news from London was a continual topic of conversation, as was the difficulty of finding food.

Yet Netta had no idea that the Rodocanachi household was not any longer what it seemed, and that her sister's problems over food were incomparably more difficult even than her own. Nor could Fanny share with her sister the hair-raising story she had just heard of a doctor in a small town not far from Marseille. Whilst seeing patients, his consulting-room was suddenly invaded by the Milice, hot on the trail, and scenting blood, literally.

An American airman known to have been shot down in the vicinity had survived, since his parachute too had disappeared. And since the cockpit of his plane was spattered with blood, he was surely by now seeking medical aid within walking distance of the burnt-out plane.

Following a trail of gory droplets that led straight to the doctor's surgery, the Milice were ready to catch him in the act of treating, feeding, or sheltering this member of the Allied forces – a crime well known to be punishable by death. Fortunately for the doctor no patient of his had come bleeding to his door that day, and the drops of blood were traced to the meagre piece of meat that his wife had not yet stowed away. Innocent and bloody, it still sat upon the kitchen table.

At Dr Rodocanachi's surgery-home, such an exhaustive search would undoubtedly have resulted in total disaster.

One evading airman delighted his English-speaking hosts when he told of his success in avoiding detection throughout his journey south, by asking at every bar for *deux bières*, two beers – thus avoiding having to use *une* which, as an Englishman, he found it particularly difficult to pronounce convincingly.

Couples running Safe Houses, whose marriages had run uneasily on parallel lines never destined to converge, now found themselves enjoying a secret life of harmony and unity such as they had never before achieved. Shared danger gave an edge and brittle brightness to their lives, and many reached a pinnacle in their shared commitment, often finding in one another exciting, unsuspected heroism and resource-fulness.

Renée Nouveau, only a mile or so distant from the Rodocanachis, was like Fanny busy secreting below floor boards, between joists, and behind skirting-boards, those tell-tale army and RAF boots and shoes, the rucksacks, and other compromising oddments the men had brought with them all the way from Dunkirk and other parts of northern France.

No wonder that both these Safe Houses never permitted their visitors to go out unless to get their hair cut or photographs taken for documents, when they were invariably in the care of a courier. For these men, who became accustomed in time to the limitations of the dreaded slippers, would have needed to have handy boots or shoes equal to their numbers in the flat and all to be properly concealed again in a hurry in case of a raid by the Milice or Gestapo.

Lady Airey told me that, to his dying day, her husband Airey Neave felt trapped in underground restaurants, and began immediately to investigate and establish exit points in any room that was new to him. He said he had always felt vulnerable and threatened by living in bedroom slippers at the Nouveaus' : not knowing where they had so wisely hidden his shoes. Had the enemy come knocking on the door he could never have made a run for it with those slippers flopping all over the place, liable to trip him up, fall off, or at the very least be noticed and questioned by any passing member of the Vichy police.

In his book *Saturday at MI9** Airey Neave wrote :

The slippers were hairy and too large for me. They made a soft, shuffling sound as I moved round the flat.

They had amused me at first, until they became a symbol of my helplessness . . . As I came shambling up to the table, Louis Nouveau laughed.

'How do you like your slippers?'

'They are very comfortable, thank you,' I replied without conviction.

'Everyone has to wear them. The people in the flat below may be pro-Vichy.' . . .

* Published by Hodder and Stoughton in 1969.

I understood. Gestapo agents were well established in Marseille, and I had been on the run long enough to know the need for these precautions. But somehow the slippers made me feel afraid. If the police should raid the block, it would be hard to escape from the fifth floor.

But I did not show my irritation. I was in the hands of the Pat O'Leary Escape Line. Who they really were, or how they worked, I did not know.

And who was their legendary chief Pat O'Leary?

Still, it was never dull in that extraordinary flat with its many small precautions and its comings and goings. Neave and Woollatt* soon became familiar with 'our special knock', and came to recognise the series of quick rat-tat-tat-tats on the door which announced the arrival of a welcome friend such as Mario Prassinos, a suave and sophisticated Greek member of the Line, carrying his mahogany walking-stick and leather gloves with style.

He had been charming on the occasion of their first meeting. The accent attractive and mellifluous, with just the suggestion of rolling R's, and the soupçon of a Greek intonation to match the warmth of his personality, and his gesticulations. During Pat's absences, Mario handled the organisation's affairs in Marseille, and Louis records that he habitually dined with them about twice a week. 'He was a very cautious man, rather lacking in initiative.'

But Renée tells me that it was usually Mario who was sent to meet visitors arriving by train. Urbane and charming, he greeted them like diplomats at a reception.

'Léoni Savinos,' Louis records, was 'one of the cleverest and most courageous men I ever met : a cold, calculating realist.' Like Prassinos, Savinos, a Greek Marseillais, called regularly at the Quai de Rive Neuve upon the business of the Line.

Soon, the atmosphere would become thick with continental smoke, bottles would be produced by Louis from his excellent cellar, and glasses kept generously filled as an unreal peacetime conviviality pervaded the drawing-room. It was even possible then to forget for a little while the nightmare in which they all were involved. A short

* Captain Hugh Woollatt, MC, Lancashire Fusiliers. Killed in action July 1944.

interlude and happy occasion to be treasured to the end of all their days.

The Battle of the Atlantic was raging now, with staggering losses to British shipping. Collaborationist press reports made the most of these. The BBC didn't conceal them, but tried to minimise them since Britain's food supply, and hence the outcome of the war were at stake.

The radio was the most important piece of equipment in many homes, and at the Rodocanachis and Nouveaus their visitors were able to live through their ears, keeping in touch with Britain via the nostalgic voices of Alvar Liddell, Frank Phillips, John Snagge, Freddie Grisewood, Stuart Hibberd and Wilfred Pickles. They were fortunate that, as at the Seamen's Mission, their 'hosts' spoke English.

But on 24th May, Empire Day 1941, the news from London was traumatic. HMS *Hood* was sunk with only three survivors, sent to the bottom by the German battleship *Bismarck*.

In agonised revenge, the *Bismarck* was pursued, and sunk off Brest on 27th May.

In the Mediterranean the Luftwaffe had delivered a terrible blow to the Royal Navy which lost in a single engagement, two cruisers, and three destroyers, its aircraft carrier HMS *Formidable* being severely damaged and put temporarily out of action.

Living covertly by the BBC, they suffered and shared with their people at home the nadir of their wartime fortunes. It was at times like these that ennui and impatience at their impotence and dependence on others known and unknown, most distressed them.

CHAPTER FIVE

Paul Cole and the Northern Link

1941

By the autumn of 1941, the morale of the French people had dropped to an all-time low. Only a handful of Marseillais knew that the head-quarters of the escape network was at the flat in the Rue Roux de Brignoles, and that Ian and Pat lived there. Those who did were the Rodocanachis, Pat, Ian, Bruce, the two Greek friends of both households, Mario and Léoni, Elizabeth, and the British courier Paul Cole.

Cole worked from Lille, and regularly, and with conspicuous gallantry, brought men down to Marseille. There he delivered them as instructed. Such rendezvous were often cafés, bars, restaurants, newspaper kiosks, or a bench in a public place. This enabled the next link in the chain to collect expected parcels without either link coming to know who the other one was. Needless to say when escorting men to Marseille, Paul never delivered them to the highly secret headquarters itself. But he would turn up there between trips, reporting to Garrow, and in due course to Pat O'Leary, saying how many men he had managed success-fully to winkle out of their various hide-outs in the north, and how they had fared during the hazardous crossing of the demarcation line.

At the Rodocanachis he would expect and received, in return for the smart little mock-salute and deferential bow with which he imparted his news, the approbation and funding that were his dues, the mission having been satisfactorily completed. This was also when Garrow briefed him for his next convoy, and sorted out any problems or diffi-culties he might have encountered with the many new helpers now working for the Line in the north.

Cole was born on 24th June 1906, and christened Harold though he chose to be called Paul in France. Trained as an engineer, by the time he was in his twenties, he had a record of convictions for house-breaking and false pretences, and was known at Scotland Yard as a con-man. He joined the army in 1939, and in April 1940 before the invasion of France, he absconded with the sergeants mess funds whilst they were in his charge.

When France was occupied after the Dunkirk evacuation, Cole was hiding in Lille, masquerading as a Captain in the British Secret Service, very much the ladies' man. With his military moustache and regimental tie, he was living expensively on his wits and his ill-gotten gains.

His French was far from good, but he had the sort of cheek that had got him out of tight corners, and had been known when this was to his advantage, to produce a letter certifying that he was deaf and dumb, and to use sign language to support this.

He had first appeared on the Marseille scene in November 1940, bringing with him a party of evaders from Lille. A noteworthy achievement for someone who had no authority or experience in such matters. Thereafter he continued to round up hidden men all over the north of France, and with astonishing daring to escort them south across the demarcation line to the point of departure for the Pyrenees.

There were those in Marseille who did not like him – Donald Caskie for one, who seemed to react against the man even before he set eyes on him. But when they met, Donald, in his book *The Tartan Pimpernel*, recounts that he liked the look of Cole even less. There was something about him that greatly disturbed the Scottish Minister, and he was not alone in this instant reaction to the sandy-coloured, heavily freckled young man with the close-set eyes. He had an ingratiating manner, and a tendency to call colleagues 'old man' or 'old chap', which epithets didn't go down too well in a hyper-sensitive Marseille.

Pat, newly established in the headquarters, was present at one meeting with Cole. Checking in with Ian after bringing down a further convoy, Paul was introduced to Pat by Garrow.

'Paul', Ian said immediately, 'this is Pat O'Leary who has just joined us and is staying on to help. He speaks fluent French and will be working with me from now on.' He then continued to debrief Cole, checking on the number he had escorted south, and generally putting him through his paces.

Ian told Pat that two or three girls had come south with Cole, and helped on the journey. It was always useful in fact to have the odd extra person to make light desultory conversation in French when guards or other officials on trains or buses were within earshot. And a girl who was coy and flirtatious often sweetened the guards, who were distracted from the men on the run. Anything to keep things running smoothly, and to cover for the men's total lack of fluent French by speaking up for them if they were asked a question.

Cole then said that everything was going fine, but he needed money. Ian was undismayed, and prepared for this routine request.

But on this occasion Pat recalled, it was for a staggering 50,000 francs, which clearly shook the usually unshakable Garrow. Pat alert as always to atmosphere, and with his well-developed sense of smell for what was false, dangerous, or misleading even when all appeared normal, says he 'smelt a nasty smell'.

'I heard the way this man spoke to Ian : and the way he presented his case. To me from the first moment I set eyes on him at the Rodocanachis', he was a nobody. No good at all. And most certainly not the sort of person for us to be in harness with.'

In private and with the utmost urgency, Pat warned Ian to be very careful.

'It's just that you haven't yet had the chance to see how invaluable he is to us,' Ian said.

'He has this uncanny ability to get the men through. No other courier is as successful as he is. Lots of chaps swear they owe their lives to him. He amazes them with his outrageous, cheeky schemes for outwitting the guards along the way. You'd never get any of them to question his . . .'

Pat let Ian go on extolling Paul Cole's virtues. He was clearly totally convinced he had the ideal courier in their man in the north. However, a disquieting message had reached the headquarters from Elizabeth who was under temporary arrest in a Marseille prison at a time when rumours about Cole's trustworthiness were circulating. She had been arrested at the room at the Hôtel de Noailles on the Canebière, which had been rented (at Tom Kenny's instigation), to be used as an office, for picking up orders or messages, and for distributing funds for use by various agents/couriers. It was neutral territory, but was always seen by her as highly dangerous, since she reckoned that the hotel staff must be aware that nobody ever slept there . . . and so – why the room? This is Louis Nouveau's account of how several of them came to be in prison at that time.

'Now and then when I hadn't seen Garrow, Kenny, or Elizabeth for some time, I used to go up to that room number 530 on the fifth floor, where I sometimes took tea,' he records.

There came a day when by some merciful providence he had been prevented from knocking on the door of that room. Perhaps someone with whom he had had an appointment downstairs in the foyer had failed to turn up. Or was it because the concierge had been looking at him too closely? He could no longer remember.

'At any rate,' he has recorderd, 'it must have been common know-ledge amongst the staff that that room was not being used for sleeping in, which must have caused some surprise and talk.'

Instinctive caution and self-preservation had made him decide not to risk going up as usual on this occasion. They all remember them-selves as living in this way like animals then, with an extra sense : 'We could actually smell danger, and recognised the difference between a "good" and a "bad" smell about places, situations, and people.'

Thus warned, Louis had promptly and discreetly spun the revolv-ing doors, and left the hotel immediately, and so wasn't caught as five of the others were that day, in the trap that was set for every person calling at room number 530.

'It happened like this,' Pat told me, recalling how he, along with Mario Prassinos, Tom Kenny, Francis Blanchain, and Elizabeth Haden-Guest had all sprung that trap, and fallen into the hands of the police.

'At about 11 o'clock that morning, I had gone on Ian's instructions, to our office at the Noailles. Elizabeth had money for us, Ian had said, and would I collect it from her. Within two minutes of greeting her, there was a telephone call, and she lifted the receiver. It was just a brief message, and she excused herself, saying : 'Somebody is waiting for me downstairs. I'm so sorry : but I'll be back as soon as possible.'

When she hadn't returned by 12.15, Pat knew that something was very much amiss, and that he was in peril if he remained in that room.

'I had to get out at once : and I reached up above the wardrobe,' he says, 'and took down an empty suitcase that just happened to be up there.' Deciding that it would look better in a hotel if he was seen to be carrying something like a piece of luggage, he left the room hurriedly, and fled silently down the deeply carpeted stairs to the ground floor. There he checked his speed, and walked purposefully towards the revolving doors, and out into the Canebière.

Unbeknown to Pat at the time, Elisabeth had been arrested on the spot in the hotel hall, and had gone to join Tom Kenny in a prison cell: and the same was about to happen to him. Scarcely had he left the Noailles than he felt a heavy hand on his shoulder from behind, and he was swung round to be confronted by a man in civilian clothes.

'French Police,' he called out in a staccato voice, and flipped back the lapel of his jacket to expose the dreaded badge.

'And just what were you doing in room 530?' he asked. 'And what have you got in that suit-case.'

'Nothing at all,' Pat answered, all affronted innocence. 'Absolutely nothing!'

Over and over again he repeated this reply, as he was frog-marched as far as the Evêché, now the police headquarters. Arrived there, the case was set down, and the anti-climax of its total emptiness revealed.

'Needless to say, they were even more angered by this,' Pat chuckles today.

'But since it was clear that they knew that I had been in that particular room, and had got to give some plausible explanation for my presence there, I hurriedly came up with a passable story.

'I said that I'd been desperate to get to England to join de Gaulle's Free French Forces,' Pat continued, 'and had thought that perhaps the Englishwoman in that room might be able to help me to get over there.'

In the event he, like the others was locked in a cell there for four days, during which time they simply never ceased to question him and try to trip him up. It transpired that they had suspected that room 530 was being used as a recruiting centre for some clandestine work for the Allies.

They were undoubtedly alert to anti-German activities going on in the town, and alarmingly, they were also aware that several Greek names had cropped up in connection with these.

As Pat stood, time and time again in front of the desk at the Gestapo headquarters, whither he was taken, to his astonishment he read (upside down on the desk before him), ACROPOLIS, as the name given to that particular dossier. This 'Greek' filing system was not wasted on him, and he now knew that his Greek friends had been noted, and their activities were being watched.

Elizabeth, according to Pat today, being the professional and courageous person that she was, had not mentioned his presence as being still in that hotel room when the police had picked her up. She had been trying to give him time to get clear of the dangerous place he was in. Had they known that Pat was still up there, they would have had over an hour during which to go up and arrest him.

'But Pat had good papers,' Elisabeth says today, 'so he got out after four days. I had already admitted to being involved in some British escape work, having heard that Tom had, in his inexperienced way, and being unusued to clandestine work, confessed about there being a "line".

'But it was really Garrow they were after. He was the one they were trying to pull in. And I just prayed that he would keep well away from us all. But I ought to have known better! For suddenly there he was, to my horror, swinging along with his bouncy walk, and bounding up the steps to get me out.

'They had got nothing they could actually pin on him, and he insisted that I had got nothing whatsoever to do with any sort of escape work.

'How could she possibly? Now I ask you : when she has got a little boy of two years old, who has not been at all well, how could she be involved in any sort of secret work?'

Mario Prassinos had managed to wriggle out of the net by saying that he had gone to call at room 530 in order to congratulate Tom Kenny on his engagement to the Martinez girl, which had only just been announced. And if they didn't believe him, then they could check this for themselves!

Francis Blanchain too had managed somehow to clear himself, but Elizabeth, Pat, and Tom had all been endlessly interrogated at the Fort Saint-Nicolas, and put to considerable discomfort, and varying spells of solitary confinement before being released.

Elizabeth was anxious to let it be known at once that one of the secret police who had interrogated her, had taunted her with the name of the person who had betrayed her.

'Do you know who gave you away?' the inspector had delighted in asking her.

'Not a Frenchman, not a Greek, not a Spaniard, but – believe it or not – one of your *own* people.'

Pat was not inclined to discount these stories. And he was no more impressed when Cole arrived with his next convoy, and a dramatic description of the desperate mishaps, and miraculous escapes they had all survived – thanks, it was implied – to his own cunning and experience. He was most certainly not one to minimise his successes. His lack of modesty, and ingratiating manner irritated and frightened Pat in a way that they did not affect Ian.

Over France, Allied air crews crashed or baled out with £600 worth of francs, a forged ration card (stamped up to date), two spare passport-sized photographs of themselves in civilian clothes, a pair of wire-cutters, knife-pliers, a collapsible water bottle, tablets for sterilising water for drinking, a tube of condensed milk, Horlick's tablets, energy tablets, French cigarettes and matches, and an 'L' or lethal pill, the size of a pea. And all was packed in a waterproof escape-pack, and stitched into their flying jackets.

They were by now also sporting the new flying boots. These had been supplied in response to requests from escapers and evaders who reached home safely and described what was needed for survival in enemy territory.

The old flying boots had been too conspicuously what they were, and hard to disguise. They wouldn't stay tucked under trousers, and men had had to swop them with helpful civilians, who had given them walking shoes in exchange.

The new boots had perforations at ankle-level, so that a cut along these with a knife* would free the top, leaving an innocent walking shoe, with a stable, non-fraying, patterned edge around the top.

One evader, typical of Cole's parcels, was a young airman, Denis-Crowley-Milling†. He was brought down by Cole at about this time with papers supplied at Abbeville, and delivered to a small bistro on the edge of the Vieux Port, beneath the Pont Transbordeur. The parcel was promptly checked out, collected, and delivered to the Rodocanachis' flat.

Sir Denis Crowley-Milling told me that he arrived in time for a civilised cup of Earl Grey tea and wafer thin sandwiches. He stayed one night at the flat, along with three other men, one of whom was a Pole who spoke no English. The following day they were all escorted to the station one stop beyond the Gare St Charles, and took the train to

---

* In some cases the small knife with its razor-sharp blade, was not in the escape pack, but inserted into a little pocket inside the boot itself, where it nestled within the thickness of the sheepskin lining.

† Now Air Marshal Sir Denis Crowley-Milling, KCB, CBE, DSO, DFC, Vice-President of the RAF Escaping Society.

Perpignan, passing safely through all the checkpoints on the way. A taxi up to the mountains kept them intact and unmolested, and they were handed over to the Spanish guides who had already been paid to take them across.

When they eventually reached the top of the pass, the man demanded more money, and when this was not forthcoming he abandoned them. Inevitably they were picked up by the Guarda Civil, the local Spanish Police, and imprisoned at Miranda de Ebro a vast concentration camp forty miles south of Bilbao. This was a hutted camp into which had been dumped the flotsam and jetsam from the Spanish Civil War and the world in general. Those who found themselves imprisoned there were often deeply affronted, for Spain was supposed to be neutral.

Anyone found by the Guarda Civil to be loose around Spain and not in possession of the correct documentation, was automatically imprisoned. In Miranda there were escapers and evaders of various nationalities. Any fugitives who could not claim and prove themselves to be British subjects, and many also who *could* in fact prove themselves so to be, were nevertheless also liable to be deflected into prisons such as Figueras, Gerona, Caldas del Miravella in Catalonia, or other gaols or camps.

In these miserable places languished many wretched people who had succeeded in escaping from France. Only after prolonged and complicated negotiations and determined efforts on the part of Embassy and Legation personnel, were they eventually released. Here it was that *Monday*, Michael Creswell, was active and effective.

Denis Crowley-Milling spent three months in his Spanish prison, but finally made it back to England to rejoin his unit at a most critical time for the RAF during the war.

Another parcel to sing Paul Cole's praises to Pat was a squadron leader by the name of Higginson,* who was credited with thirteen German aircraft and who had been shot down near Abbeville on 17th June 1941.

Hobbling along on one flying boot and using money he had unstitched from his jacket, Higginson had bought a can of beer from a café to slake his thirst after a long walk under the hot French July sky. He then tried to thumb a lift from a passing car.

---

* F. W. Higginson, OBE, DFC, DFM.

'It stopped', he says, 'and the Germans inside took a look at me, but they didn't offer a lift. Then the proprietor of the café where I had bought my beer came and picked me up : and they hid me in their home for two days and nights.'

At Lille he had met up with Cole who took him to get faked papers made for him by the Abbé Carpentier : and he joined a party of two other RAF officers, and two flight sergeants, and they set off for Marseille in Cole's care.

'We stayed a night in a brothel in Paris,' he told me, 'because you didn't have to register there.'

He locked himself into his room overnight, and for added safety he slept with his belongings in his bed with him. In the morning he visited the lavatory, and to his horror suddenly realised that he'd dropped all his money down the hole in the floor of the *Siège Turc*, or squatting plate.

He had great difficulty in retrieving the sodden banknotes which, after washing them as best he could in the violent flushing of the timed upsurge, he was able to dry in the merciful sunshine.

He recalls that at one point Cole opened his briefcase and he is still convinced that he was carrying plans of the Schnorkel submarine, together with a Russian railway timetable.

In December 1967 Squadron Leader Higginson gave Airey Neave an account of the last part of his journey south, during which they crossed the demarcation line in July 1941.

'Cole had ginger hair, with a freckled face, and spoke French with an atrocious accent,' wrote Airey Neave in his book *Saturday at MI9*.

He was dressed in plus-fours. He carried a briefcase in which he had a revolver, and a mass of information on troop train departures from Lille to the Russian front. He carried a false identity card, and a French soldier's discharge papers which showed that he had been discharged 'as of unsound mind'.

We had crossed the river which preceded the demarcation line, and it was a very hot July day, when we were stopped by a German officer and a sergeant. They began to question us. Cole did the answering. He told the officer I was simple-minded.

I had a briefcase with a change of underwear and a large slab of French chocolate.

The sergeant pointed at me: 'He's an English soldier: he's not speaking'.

The officer then asked for my identity card. It had been made for me by the Abbé Carpentier, the priest at Abbeville, with a Pas de Calais stamp.

He seemed satisfied, but threatened to take us to the Kommandatur for questioning.

Cole became aggressive. He said he had seen the officer come from a café. His aunt lived at this café, and he would report both of them for drinking on duty! But the sergeant still pointed at me.

'I'm sure he is English. He is not speaking.' The officer told me to turn out my biefcase on the road. By this time, because of the heat and excitement, the chocolate had spread all over the contents of the briefcase and looked an absolutely frightful mess. Cole, with tremendous presence of mind, said:

'Look, I told you he was out of his mind, look what he has done in his briefcase!'

The officer turned away in disgust and told me to clear off, which I did and hid in a copse.

About a quarter of an hour later, I was joined by Cole and crossed the demarcation line that night.

'Was Cole a double agent at this time? . . . We shall never be sure', continues Airey Neave.

Though the evidence suggests that he first began to work for the Abwehr after his arrest by them on 6th December 1941. What was he doing during the quarter of an hour that Higginson was separated from him? There were many reports reaching MI9 at this period, of his coolness and skill in saving airmen from German controls, and many French people, especially those in the Lille area, worshipped him as a hero of the British Secret Service.

Higginson himself still maintains that he owes his life to Paul Cole. And on hearing, whilst he was in gaol at the Fort de la Revère, that Pat was out to kill Cole, said, 'Over my dead body!'

He had arrived safely in Marseille where he spent two nights with the Rodocanachis. To his great delight he was present there on the night London transmitted the vital message *Adolphe doit rester*. Before he reached Spain, however, he was arrested, to be imprisoned once again.

But this was not to be the end of the story, as we shall see.

One endearing and enduring picture lingers on from his short visit with the courteous elderly Greek doctor and his charming wife, who both spoke such perfect English – and that was their serenity. They had retained an almost Victorian style of dignity and coolness in the face of danger. Madame Rodocanachi insisting on dressing for a meagre dinner, and being escorted to the table : a kind of defiance which worked wonders for his morale. Arm-in-arm they moved from the drawing-room, through an ante-room, and into the dining-room where the polished mahogany table was sparsely spread. Only one largish platter, prettily garnished was shared between them all, but the table was beautifully set, and the conversation good.

Another evader who eventually reached Marseille safely was a Flying Officer Jean Nitelet of 609 (Belgian) Squadron RAF. He had succeeded in shooting down a German aircraft : but not before he had himself been hit a number of times.

One bullet removed part of his right eye, and he had had to crash-land his Spitfire. He was fortunate to be picked up near St Omer by one Norbert Fillerin, a stalwart and active member of the line, who lived at Renty. Beekeeper, philosopher, reader of Plato, the son of a wholesale butcher, Norbert always wore workman's overalls, had perfect manners and a calm smile that radiated confidence, and he delighted in finding 'little girls fallen from the sky', or hidden in the neigbourhood.

Fillerin took the wounded Nitelet to a local pro-British Dr Delpierre, whose wife was English. He remained hidden with them, and under medical care from the doctor until fit to continue his journey.

At the next safe house, the home of a man called Dideret, he was supplied with forged papers by the Abbé Carpentier of Abbeville, and made his way south to a regular rendezvous, the Petit-Poucet bar on the Boulevard Dugommier in Marseille. There he sat at a marble-topped table, secluded by window-boxes of oleander, until retrieved by Louis Nouveau. Adjusting to the loss of his eye, Nitelet remained hidden at the Quai de Rive Neuve under medical care from Doctor Rodocanachi for ten days. As we shall see later, he had arrived at a dramatic moment for the future of the line.

The Petit-Poucet, a modest undistinguished little bar, was ideally placed as a receiving depot for parcels on their way from the Gare St Charles to the Vieux Port.

A quick message sent via Bensi, a Greek who acted as runner for *le patron*, Monsieur Dijon, saying that he had just taken delivery of so many parcels, soon resulted in the discreet and casual arrival of a courier. Before showing interest in parcels awaiting collection, these could be viewed in a leisurely way through the greenery, and further investigated over a glass of *pastis*.

Only when proof of identity led to total confidence and satisfaction did the courier take them in charge.

After his convalescent stay at the Nouveaus, the airman with only one eye took a train along the coast via Arles, Montpellier, Perpignan, and Banyuls, and was en route for England. Unbeknown to him at that time, he was to return to the Marseille area as a wireless operator.

It wasn't long before Pat, having seen Nitelet on his way, began again to be plagued with doubt about Cole.

Through Elizabeth, there came disquieting rumours.

'I received a message in prison,' Elizabeth said, 'tapped out to me by this friend Collette : be careful of your man up north.'

That was three months after she was arrested, Elizabeth said. And she made it her urgent business to see that this message was given to Gaston Defferre when he went to visit her in prison. Gaston Defferre, who became Minister of Justice in France after the war, was himself running an escape line. He was therefore party to the devious and desperate methods that had sometimes to be employed to get information into and out of prison cells where Gestapo and Milice scrutinised prisoners before and after the departure of their visitors.

Elizabeth, an experienced clandestine worker, contrived to send Gaston Defferre* out of her cell with precious information of this and other kinds, scribbled on scraps of paper, and stowed in male contraceptives supplied by the brothels in which she regularly spent the night.

At one time, whilst her cell-mate, a known stool-pigeon, was out emptying latrine buckets, she was able to copy material hidden beneath the girl's palliasse, and get it out in this way. Many women were driven to hiding and carrying vital information within their vaginas or rectal passages.

Gaston Defferre was a man who dressed impeccably, and invariably

---

* Gaston Defferre. French lawyer, journalist and politician. Mayor of Marseille from 1944–45, and from May 1953 to the present day.

wore fine glacé kid gloves. Not the ideal way to have to handle material kept against his expected visit, in moist places as secret as was the information popped in there.

'He handled it literally with kid gloves,' Elizabeth told me, 'dropping the poor little package in its rubber container into his beautiful leather briefcase, whilst fastidiously averting his gaze.'

The Gestapo were well aware of these secret hiding places, and frequently stripped and searched every woman who might be a threat to them. It was not uncommon to hear of women who were thought to be in the business of helping or hiding escapers, having been shot up through the vagina. These devastating injuries most certainly destroyed every shred of evidence: but they caused grievous damage to the women, since there was no limit to the extensive havoc caused to vital organs and structures.

At about this time Pat happened to be dining in a Marseille restaurant, where by chance he met up with a woman friend of Cole's mistress. He invited her to join him at his table, and plied her with drinks and small talk, so that in time he had her chatting freely. Then nonchalantly, he brought the conversation around to Paul.

'Fancy your mentioning Paul,' she said, laughing.

'Well, I had a feeling that you might know him, since you are so friendly with his girl-friend,' Pat said innocently.

'Do you ever see him these days, or is he always up in the north?'

'It's funny your asking that,' she said, accepting another drink. 'Because we're all meeting up tonight for a party. You know – just the usual crowd – Paul and Françoise, and the girls who came down from Lille with him this time. They seem to love this big wicked city! It makes a change from a small country town, I suppose.'

'It ought to be quite a party,' Pat said, visualising Paul's reputation with the ladies up and down the country.

'Why don't you come along and join us?' she said? 'It's going to be one hell of a party! You know what Paul's parties are like!'

'Well, I don't actually know Paul all that well,' Pat mumbled, but confirmed where and when this famous party was to take place.

'It'll be quite late tonight,' she said brightly, twinkling at him. 'His parties always go on for ages!'

'And Paul is sure to be there, is he?' Pat asked for good measure.

'Oh, yes, the party is for him and Françoise, while they are down here.'

Well, this was really just exactly what he needed, Pat decided, and was horrified by what he saw as indisputable evidence that his suspicions of Cole were justified.

The thought of such a man, and the fearful consequences of his knowing everybody in the network, and the whereabouts of the headquarters of the line . . . when Ian was convinced that he had left to return to Lille, and here he was, unbeknown to them, still in Marseille.

He passed on his fears to Ian and later that evening, remembering with alarm the large sum of the organisation's money he had only just handed over to Cole, Ian was shattered to find him at the centre of so much expensive gaiety. Confronting him immediately, and challenging him with his altered plans and deceitful behaviour, Ian told him that for a man who had undertaken such important and responsible work, this was quite unacceptable.

Cole, profusely and obsequiously apologetic, explained that he had been exhausted by the last strenuous trip down, that he hadn't wanted to disappoint the girls who had travelled with him, and that they would all of them be going north the next morning.

Alert now to sudden danger, Ian decided to send Pat to the Lille area to look into what was going on up there. Louis Nouveau records that the total sum entrusted over the months to Paul Cole was some 300,000 francs, 'partly for the general expenses of the sector, in other words for compensating people, often of very humble origin, who concealed and fed British soldiers and airmen, and often had to buy them clothes. And partly for the purchase of a lorry, which he (Paul Cole) had himself suggested, as it would facilitate the transport of escapees.'

Returning to the Rodocanachis and checking that he wasn't being followed, Ian made certain of getting back before eleven. He and Pat had always made a point of being in by then, so as to cause as little inconvenience as possible to the well-established and regular-as-clockwork routine of the three elderly members of the household.

Séraphine was always up and about to answer the door until ten o'clock. But from then on, until his bed-time at eleven, the doctor himself dealt with anyone calling at the flat medically or socially.

Neither Pat nor Ian had ever for one moment considered accepting the front-door key offered by the Rodocanachis.

'We simply did not want to have *any* key on us at any *time*,' Pat told me. 'Certain unwritten rules of security had to be obeyed. Keys, telephones, concierges, and lifts in which one could be caught and held like a rat in a trap, were all highly dangerous.

'A key found by the Gestapo or Milice was a nightmare. Where did it come from? What house? What flat? What hotel room? We could, and surely would have been tortured to divulge such information. Not to have a key on one's person was just one less thing to be tortured for. To have accepted the Rodocanachis' key would have been too dangerous for them, and for us.'

Shortly after the escape of Nitelet to England, and the alarming scene at the night-club with Cole, Ian tackled Pat and asked him if he would go north and try to find out what Cole was up to, and what company he kept.

Enormously relieved that the matter of Paul Cole was to be investigated, Pat set off prepared to call on Monsieur Dupré, an agent in Lille who had agreed to act as the organisation's 'banker' in the north. He had a family business in the town, and knew the helpers in the area to whom money would have to be paid from the funds sent to him from Garrow.

Together with another agent for the line, Maurice Dufour, Pat travelled first class as they always did, since this afforded greater privacy and seclusion, though the trains without any heating made travelling a bitterly cold business. He had intentionally taken only a small amount of money with him, which would give him reason to call on their 'banker', and at the same time introduce himself as a new member of the *réseau*, now working with Captain Garrow in Marseille.

Both Pat and Maurice had satisfactory forged papers to take them as far as the river Allier. But there were two crossings of the demarcation line to be coped with on the journey, and the border crossing at Amiens was bound to be difficult. The river Somme would be heavily patrolled, and the organisation had not by this time succeeded in forging good enough replicas of the special new passes, to satisfy the police.

After the comparatively low profile being maintained in Unoccupied France, the German presence in the north was overpowering. Those sinister grey-green uniforms, and the easily identified over-long rain-coats, and the pork-pie hats of the Gestapo plain-clothes police were everywhere.

It was an adventurous journey with a number of near disasters, but Maurice knew the district well, and had useful contacts at various check-

points, and they were soon knocking at the door of a house in the Rue
de la Gare, La Madeleine. At first they were told by Madame Dupré
that her husband was not at home.

'But that,' Pat said, 'was probably not true. He didn't know me,
and nor did his wife, and he needed time to decide who I was.'

Madame Dupré was a short woman with fair hair and a full figure.
She was clearly worried by their arrival and nervous. Pat tried to
calm her, and hoped that by mentioning in casual conversation the
names of Ian Garrow and Paul Cole, she would feel secure. She knew
that these two men at her door might be plants, well-briefed and therefore highly dangerous, and she needed corroborative information.

Pat began to talk more of the man who knew them best, Paul Cole,
indicating by the tone of his voice the dislike he himself felt for their man
in the north.

Only then did Madame Dupré, driven by relief and an urge to
unburden herself of a deep-rooted dislike and fear of what Cole might
do to them, invite her visitors inside.

'I do not like that man. He is not to be trusted,' she said, enormously
relieved at last, that these words had actually been said.

A man with an artificial leg, whose disability debarred him from
military service, and who desperately wanted to support the Allies in the
only way that he could, came limping into the room.

'I am here, *Monsieur*, from Marseille, on behalf of Captain Garrow,'
Pat said. 'And I shall be needing to draw money from the organisation's
funds to pay helpers whilst I am up here. Would you be so kind as to
make this available to me?'

'He looked at me,' Pat told me, 'with an incredulous expression, and
said : But, *Monsieur*, I have no money belonging to the organisation.
What money are we talking about, may I ask?

'Why the money that Paul Cole brings you from Captain Garrow
when he returns from his trips south. What has become of those funds,'
Pat said, tentatively, his worst fears apparently about to be confirmed.

'But I assure you, *Monsieur*,' Dupré said, 'I have never received any
money at all from Captain Garrow via Paul Cole. I know the man
of course since he lives in the district and escorts our airmen on their
way to you. But he has never handed any money over to me for banking
in the name of the line.

'He's not got a very good reputation round here, that one. He spends money like water, which doesn't go unnoticed by the local people who know him as one of the organisation's couriers. People round here are usually of modest means, and to be honest with you, *Monsieur,*' he continued, 'they have been surprised and not a little irritated at the extravagant and flamboyant life-style of the captain with whom they have to treat, over the escape work that they too are involved in. It has struck them as unreasonable that they should be hiding and feeding British troops on money raised by charity locally, whilst Cole has been living in comparative luxury in the neighbourhood.'

Paul had been in trouble too with a man called Roland Lepers, early in October that year. Lepers, a bright lively young Belgian student, had been working for the line from its earliest days, with his girlfriend Madeleine Dammerment and had spent much time escorting men from the far north.

The Chope du Pont Neuf was a large brasserie close to the main fruit and vegetable markets in Paris, Les Halles. There the tall distinguished-looking owner, a Monsieur Eugène Durand, was goodness itself to British troops and airmen, feeding them and allowing them, compromising as they were, to rest and refresh themselves on his more remote benches at the back of the premises.

Never did he or his courageous wife, who not only acted as cashier, but also did all the cooking, insist upon payment. Lepers was well aware that Paul had money for this purpose, but became incensed at the non-payment for services supplied by his good friends the Durands. He knew how much was asked of people who risked being incriminated by sheltering anyone connected with the work of the line, without further adding to this debt expenses that were not being reimbursed.

In fact, the money had never been paid over at all, and Roland Lepers had complained to Pat that he himself had never been able to see Captain Garrow in person. Any communication had always had to be made through Cole, who, correctly as it happened, would not divulge the address where Garrow might be contacted.

Whilst in the north Pat was disgusted to learn that on the last trip Cole had supposedly made, it was Lepers and not Cole who had brought a convoy to Marseille. Cole had simply told him the contact, address, and then appropriated both glory and money.

There was only one thing to do under these disastrous circumstances, Pat decided. He must try to persuade Monsieur Dupré, who was clearly speaking the truth and whose witness he would need, to accompany him back to Marseille. Only in this way could Ian who had so much confidence in Paul Cole, be convinced of his treachery and dishonesty.

'He lodges with a Madame Deram in the town,' Monsieur Dupré continued. 'No doubt she could tell you more about his life-style and activities than anyone else. But she may well be unwilling to get him into trouble. He has a very persuasive way with women as you must surely know ! I can tell you this much though. He is to be seen in all the more expensive bars and restaurants in the town, and he's always treating girls to his generous hospitality. He also makes frequent long-distance journeys all over the country, often enough accompanied by one or more female companions. All these are expensive habits which must surely have been funded by Garrow's money.'

'The information you have given me, *Monsieur*, leads me to ask you,' said Pat, 'if you would do me a very great favour. Would you be willing to accompany me to Marseille, and confirm the shocking news about the line's financial situation, when I return to our headquarters to report back to Captain Garrow? He has always had such a high regard for Cole that he is going to find it almost impossible to believe what only you could positively tell him about Cole's failure to deliver any money at all into your care.'

'I do understand your predicament, *Monsieur*, and it strikes me too, that we ought perhaps to be wondering how it comes about that Cole seems to lead a charmed life, and has not been arrested by now,' Dupré replied.

'That,' Pat agreed, 'is a very good question.' But it made Dupré's presence at the headquarters all the more urgent.

Pat, unable to persuade Dupré to travel south with him, using his own secret crossing-points, had to accept that just as soon as he could manage it, Monsieur Dupré would visit Marseille, and would call on Ian Garrow by appointment.

'And so,' Pat said, 'I moved about the area of Lille, seeing various people on Garrow's behalf, and asking discreet questions about the way that Cole spent his money and his time in the town. And then, using one of our latest crossing-points, I started on my journey south.'

Madame Deram, herself to become a victim of Paul Cole's treachery, was running a safe house. One of her 'parcels' was Flight Lieutenant George Barclay who recorded in his diary :

One of the first things I noticed on entering the house was a photograph of Taffy Higginson on the mantelpiece. I was astounded. Apparently he had stayed 12 days in the house after he was shot down. . . . Madame Deram supplied me with a clean shirt and a smarter suit than that I had been wearing, and also some shaving tackle, which I hung on to and brought home. She had one English book, *Sorrel and Son*, so I spent the day reading and enjoyed the diversion. . . . Madame Deram was always talking about Monsieur Paul, an Englishman, who I gathered was the mainstay of the organisation getting bodies out of France. Everyone seemed to look up to him, he had a great hold over the Frenchmen who knew him, owing to his fearlessness and the splendid work he was doing. I was to meet him later on.*

In the meantime, whilst Renée Nouveau went to Toulouse 'to bring a couple of airmen home, and also to visit near Limoges the fiancée of a British officer who had stayed with us, and to cheer her up and encourage her to be patient,' records Louis Nouveau, he himself was sent to visit a Madame Arnaud. He was to investigate the possibility of discovering a new and convenient crossing point on the demarcation line at Les Tuyères, near Saint-Rémy en Dordogne. The one they had been using near Nevers had recently become distinctly unsafe, and the hope was that near the Arnauds' farm, a better place might be established.

I spent a whole hour with Madame Arnaud discussing the possibility of finding a passage [writes Louis]. In her opinion it ought to be comparatively easy, and she promised to help us to the best of her ability whenever we needed to use it. The best time to cross, in her opinion, was at dawn, she leading the way, as if going marketing with her bicycle. There was only one awkward moment, she said, at the spot where you had to cross the main road, which there runs parallel with the dividing line, about fifty yards away. At that point, as she had a pass, there should be no risk for her. The man following behind

* Fighter Pilot: A Self-Portrait. Edited by Humphrey Wynn. William Kimber, 1976.

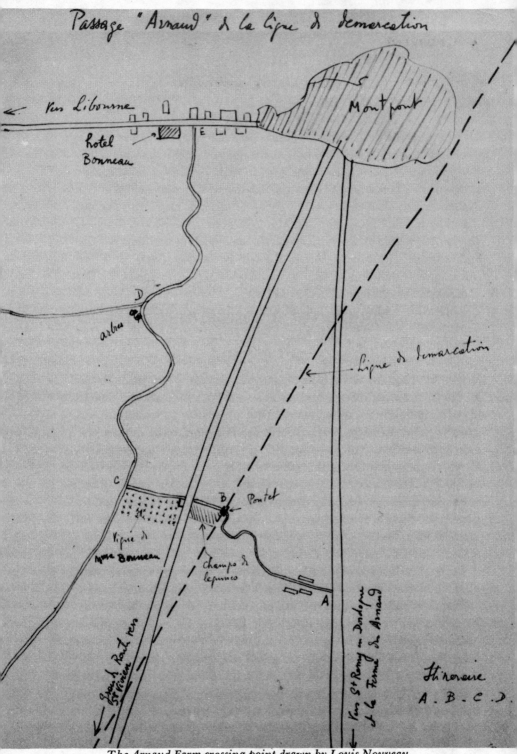

The Arnaud Farm crossing point drawn by Louis Nouveau.

her had only to fall back some fifty or a hundred yards behind some bushes until she had reached a foot-path running parallel to the road and to the dividing line. We settled all the details as definitely as possible. When I returned to my taxi, the chauffeur seemed inclined to talk. I told him some yarn about having come to inspect a plot of land with the idea of buying it.

Another member of the organisation was also away on business. Georges Zarifi had gone to Carcassonne to impress upon a contact of the Line, the necessity for holding her tongue. 'Paulette had been of some use to us,' records Louis, 'either at Perpignan or at Toulouse, but she had been gossiping too freely about our work.' Pat, anxious to put a stop to such dangerous talk, had asked Louis to investigate the rumour, but had then dispatched him elsewhere, and Georges Zarifi after visiting Carcassonne reported that 'Paulette seemed to be keeping quiet.'

In the meantime poor Louis had had trouble with one ill-disciplined visitor.

I believe this is practically the only Britisher who disobeyed orders. The day before the time fixed for leaving, after the question of clothes and boots had been settled, we always insisted on fellows shaving the evening before, so as not to waste any time the following morning.

The train was due to leave at 6.30 a.m. which meant arriving at the station at about 6.0, breakfasting at 5.0 and getting up at 4.0. Lockhart, however, insisted on shaving in the morning, but I forbade him categorically to do so, and nothing more was said about it.

I had forgotten all about this when next morning at breakfast, Lockhart turned up at 5.10, his face streaming with blood. In his hurry he had cut himself badly, and as he suffered from haemophilia, found it impossible to stop the bleeding. He had already soiled two towels, and his face was mottled with patches of blood.

As we were in a hurry, I ticked him off severely, and took him to the bathroom where luckily I had special stuff to cauterise razor cuts, and we finally succeeded in getting off without further incident, and reached the station by 6.10.

We learned later that Lockhart was quite an extraordinary fellow.

It turned out that he was light-weight boxing champion for the RAF, and Louis' son Jean-Pierre later saw him boxing to entertain the troops held captive in Miranda de Ebro gaol in Spain. One can only hope he didn't suffer cuts and bruises!

For Louis, the arrival at his home during his absence on a mission for Pat in Northern France, of a man called Barnabé, was disconcerting. For he had been sent to him directly by George Whitting-Hill, the American Vice-Consul at Lyons, to whom the line had reason to be grateful for many invaluable services rendered. He was wounded whilst trying to escape and Dr Rodocanachi called several times to attend to Barnabé.

But Pat was distinctly reluctant to take risks for people belonging to other organisations, doing entirely different work, and who ought to have their own machinery, including guides, for passing people across the frontier [Louis explains].

After all, it was impossible to know whether these fellows were not already being shadowed, which would of course have meant our taking far greater risks than those already involved in assisting airmen directed to us by our own people.

*

Arriving back at the Rue Roux de Brignoles from his strenuous journey to Dupré at Lille, Pat slipped into the building, up the stairs, and rang the bell.

Mercifully everything appeared normal. The concierge took note of his entry, the iron gates of the old lift clanged shut upstairs, and the lift passed him going down . . . empty . . . of whom, Pat wondered? It was dark, and the timed light-switch didn't quite last until Séraphine opened the heavy mahogany door to him. He therefore remained for a minute or two in total darkness, alone on the landing with nothing but the metallic clanking of the lift to break the silence.

The entrance to the flat smelt vaguely medical as usual. And Séraphine looked distressed as she said in a hushed voice:

'*Entrez, Monsieur. Madame voudrait vous voir tout de suite.* Come in, sir, Madame wants to see you immediately.'

'I exchanged my shoes for slippers at the entrance, and I went towards the drawing-room as Séraphine opened the door for me.

'The room was yellow and heady with mimosa, and Fanny Rodocanachi, so strong and unemotional, was weeping as few would ever have seen her weep.' And Pat was shattered.

'It's Ian,' she said. 'He's been arrested.'

'When?' Pat said in horror.

'Yesterday,' she said.

'How did this happen? And when yesterday?' Pat pressed her, intently.

'We simply don't know,' she answered.

'So there I was,' Pat told me, 'having only just arrived home with so much to report to Garrow : and he had been arrested twenty-four hours earlier. I simply couldn't take it in. I stayed with Fanny Rodocanachi for some time, late into the evening, as her husband had been called to visit a sick child.'

It appeared that nobody had heard Ian leave the flat. Neither Fanny nor Séraphine had seen or heard anything unusual. Some message must have caused him to depart from his usual practice of remaining in the flat, and he had simply gone out and not returned.

In the evening they had begun to be anxious, as both he and Pat had always been most considerate and conscientious about not being late for meals : an inconvenience for Séraphine, and a waste of precious food.

It was of course, the moment they had all known might come at any time of any day or night. Dr Rodocanachi had always told his nephew that Garrow daily expected to be arrested. But now that it had actually happened, the flat was full of foreboding, and London must be informed at once.

Pat, fresh from Cole country, was plagued with fears of treachery. Who had betrayed Ian, known where he lived, and might at that very moment be deciding who should be the next member of that household to fail to return? Danger was suddenly close enough to touch. Come to think of it, had one perhaps already touched it?

From all that he later heard, and odd rumours, it was probable that Ian had been arrested in the street whilst on his way to keep an appointment with one or other of two French reserve police officers. They were thought to be loyal to the line, trustworthy Resistance men, in whom Garrow had had much confidence – but of whom Pat had warned him on more than one occasion, as being unreliable, and likely to be corruptible.

Prassinos had come the previous evening to tell Fanny the awful news and rumours that Ian had been taken by the Milice. The flat was by then a hectically busy centre of an extended network, and she just had not known what to do. Nor was she certain when Pat was proposing to return.

It was too late to do anything useful that night, and it would probably be too dangerous in any case since they had no information to work on. He felt sure that Prassinos would come again in the morning : and that this would be the time when plans must be made.

And sure enough, between seven and eight the following morning, as well-groomed and charming as usual, he rang the front-door bell. Such information as he had, which was minimal, was discussed, and it was agreed that their situation was critical. Ian's arrest was a body-blow to the Line.

It was essential that London was informed immediately, and the matter of Garrow's successor be raised.

Having at last succeeded in catching him the Milice would never let him escape. But who was now to take his place? Pat was urged to do so, and was offered the total support of everyone concerned.

CHAPTER SIX

Confrontation with Cole

1st November 1941

When Garrow was arrested in October 1941 by the French Police, he was imprisoned in the Fort Saint-Nicolas within sight of the Nouveaus' flat on the Vieux Port. His health declined rapidly from the near-starvation diet, and Renée and Mario eventually managed to smuggle food in to him by the American Consul, and by one or other of the barristers Louis had promptly enlisted on Ian's behalf : Maître Bontoux, President of the Marseille Bar, and Gaston Defferre, known as a Gaullist and who was still practising at that time.

In due course Garrow was removed to another gaol, Meauzac in the Dordogne, and was condemned by a French court-martial to ten years' hard labour, for there was no shortage of evidence against him.

Pat O'Leary immediately agreed to take over command of the Line, at which point he himself ceased to use his former code names and became Pat, the network itself became known as the Pat O'Leary Line, or simply the Pat Line, or as PAO after the initials of its head. The founder of the organisation having now disappeared, Pat agreed that, subject to the approval and support of the Admiralty and MI9, he would carry on from where Ian had left off.

It was, compared with later and larger networks, not only the first of its kind, but composed of a particularly united team, all reasonable, intelligent, and enthusiastic people. They didn't stand on their dignity, expect ponderous explanations for what they were asked to do, and were given a fair measure of opportunity for personal initiative. They had always been aware of the very dangerous game that they had volunteered to play, and were able to like and to trust one another.

It was unfortunate that Pat, from the moment that he took command of the line (and on his own admission to me, there were many things that Ian was involved in at that time that Pat knew next to nothing about), was already committed to a direct confrontation with Cole.

Dupré duly arrived as arranged, and as it happened only two or three days after Garrow's arrest. And Paul Cole too was back in town with another convoy. His parcels delivered, he would soon be checking in at the headquarters and collecting his money for distribution up north, as well as his own remuneration.

Never had a routine visit from Cole been more poignant and momentous. Did he, the others wondered, know about Ian's arrest? Had he perhaps betrayed him?

It was agreed that no mention would be made of the disaster that had just befallen the line. Pat would simply say that Ian had been called away on urgent business to Perpignan and had asked Pat to take his place during his absence.

Fanny Rodocanachi in the account she left with her son Kostia after her death, described the scene as she so vividly remembered it :

As an example of what this secret, intensified life meant, there remains the memory of All Saints' Day, 1st November 1941, in the bitterest of cold weather.

In Dr Rodocanachi's consulting-room waited a Monsieur Postel-Vinay who had arrived that morning from Paris with certain plans. He wished to contact our chief, of whom he had heard speak by Dr Rodocanachi's nephew Georges Zarifi.

The latter did most useful work in the organisation, until he became too suspect by his activities, and his height, and whom we were able to send into Spain by our last convoy. He was interned in Spanish prisons for six months, before being able to get to England.

In Dr Rodocanachi's bedroom were hidden three escaped airmen.

In the big spare-room inhabited by Pat, were also Bruce, Mario [Prassinos], Léoni [Savinos] and Dupré (a receiving agent from the north), who were conducting a tribunal against Cole, the traitor, who was being convicted from all sides.

In the drawing-room were having tea, three placid ladies. [One of whom was Netta Zarifi. Being unaware that her sister and brother-in-law were hiding men in their flat, she suspected nothing of the goings-on in the other rooms.]

The scene with Cole became violent, but unfortunately he was not killed, for fear of the noise, and he managed to escape when left under the guard of Bruce.

He later betrayed many of our agents in the north, as well as poor Bruce who has never been heard of since.

Séraphine had to admit patients to the waiting-room for the doctor to see when he had finished dealing with Monsieur Postel-Vinay. Dupré, when he arrived, was shown into the bedroom used by Pat and Bruce, now that Ian was no longer there. As soon as he had been introduced to everyone, he was told of the plan agreed amongst the other four, and that Cole was not going to be told about Garrow's arrest. In order that Dupré should hear the story that Cole was telling, for himself, and to ensnare the suspected man, Dupré would be settled in the bathroom, and would be party to the conversation that would take place once Cole arrived.

The door-bell rang, and Séraphine, who knew Cole as a regular visitor to the flat, admitted him.

She too had been briefed not to mention Ian's arrest, but simply to take Paul along the corridor to the bedroom, once the door to the waiting-room had been closed, and patients thus unsighted.

On arrival, Cole was greeted in the normal way. Vincent Brome* sets the scene :

It was a cold November day with the curtains drawn and the air thick with cigarette smoke from five men in varying states of tension. Four sat in the living-room and Dupré, unknown to Paul Cole, was concealed in a back room. In the armchair lounged a remarkable young man called Bruce Dowding – known in the organisation as *Mason* ... who loathed violence, and was even more perturbed by the scene than Paul Cole himself. . . .

'Listen carefully, Paul,' [said Pat] 'I've been to the north and I've found out one or two things which don't make me particularly proud of you.'

'What on earth are you talking about ?'

* *The Way Back* by Vincent Brome. Published by Cassell in 1957. This account was given to the author by Pat O'Leary himself.

'I found out that you haven't paid the organisation's money to Dupré.'

'Who told you that?'

'And I have reason to believe that you squandered it on yourself and women.'

"I swear it's not true. I did pay Dupré.'

'He says you did not.'

'He's a liar!' Words began to pour from Cole. He worked up a fine indignation, throwing himself into the part with considerable effect until Pat walked to the door, opened it, and Dupré himself came into the room.

Paul Cole's sudden pallor was emphasised by his red hair. He literally staggered back a step or two, but what happened in the next few minutes remains somewhat confused.

It is possible that Cole intended to escape and took a menacing step towards Pat. Whatever the precise nature of the provocation, Pat suddenly hit him and he fell to the carpet and lay there a moment, his mouth bleeding.* Then he rose to his knees, tears came into his eyes and he began pleading, his voice broken ...

'I've done something terrible – I admit it – terrible – it was a moment of weakness – I'm sorry – sorry – sorry ...'

There was a silence. Dowding and Mario had come to their feet, Dupré and O'Leary stood guarding the door.

'We cannot trust you any longer,' Pat said, controlling his fury. Cole crawled a pace forward on his knees, his hands in supplication.

'Oh, I know it's terrible – terrible – but I've done some good things too – I did bring men down from the north – you know that.'

Again there was silence. Cole's babbling burst out afresh. He seemed utterly broken, and the spectacle emphasised his weakness to O'Leary, who had already determined that weak men were a danger to an organisation which must from now on be run with military precision.

'What do you think, Bruce?' he asked. Bruce hesitated a moment. Then said quietly :

'I think we should kill him.'

* I have seen Pat O'Leary's hand which is misshapen to this day from the blow he gave Paul Cole. The small bones were not properly set, for he was not willing to let Dr Rodocanachi see and treat him. Pat feared this might lead him to betray his medical status, and destroy his official cover story.

The only photograph of allied soldiers ever taken in the 28a Quai de Rive Neuve – from left to right Achille (Francis Blanchain), Mario Prassinos, Hugh Woollatt, Airey Neave, and Louis Nouveau, at Marseille 1942.

Doctor Georges Rodocanachi.

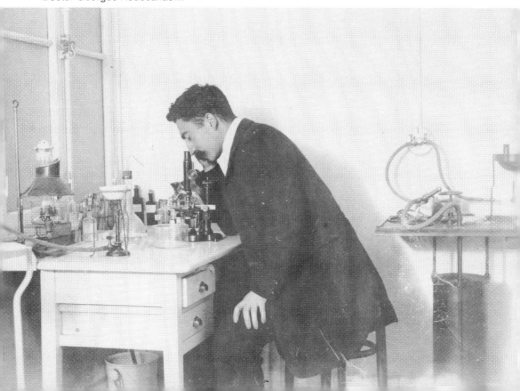

(Right) This small photograph taken for Doctor Rodocanachi's wartime identity card shows him as he looked at the time of his arrest by the Gestapo.

(Below) Mme Rodocanachi's identity card.

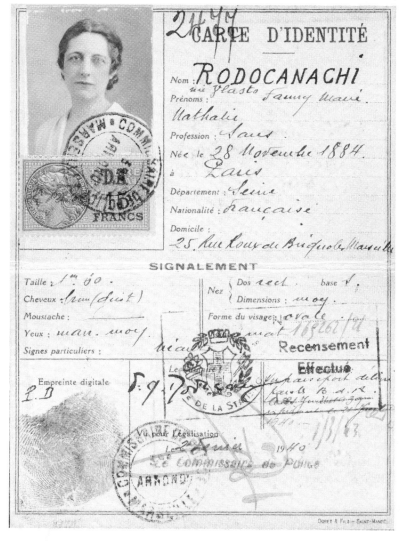

An extraordinary combination of the aesthete and man of action, he knew, and the others knew, that the weakness revealed in Paul Cole was a danger to them all. Quite clearly he meant what he said.

Mario threw up his beautiful hands – 'Oh no,' he said, 'we can't do that.'

Every civilised susceptibility was outraged.

Pat thought for a moment.

'I could send him back to England and forget what he has done,' he said.

'He'd be safely out of the way.'

Unaware that Cole already had a criminal record in Britain, they were surprised when he did not seize upon this but began pleading all over again until Pat broke in abruptly.

'Put him in the bathroom while we talk.'

The bathroom door was locked behind him and Bruce Dowding stood against it.

The conference which followed was brief. There was no evidence that Cole had yet played the traitor and it seemed extreme to condemn him to death for a momentary burst of embezzlement, but releasing such a man as this, armed with a detailed knowledge of the organisation and a considerable capacity for corruption was – well – unwise.

Suddenly Dowding heard a noise from the bathroom.

Swiftly unlocking it, he was in time to see Paul Cole stepping across from the minute bathroom window to a window opposite in the main building of the flat.

Lit only by the little daylight that came through the frosted glass Bruce could see the bathroom window open, and Cole's leg perilously straddling the short distance as he smashed the other window open. Below him the courtyard descended deep and dark to the basement. Had he fallen they would have had him caught like an animal in a huntsman's pit.

Today that window and courtyard look unscalable. But Cole in desperation had made it, and instantly the chase was on. Using the familiar corridor on the opposite side of the flat Cole made a headlong dash from the front-door and street below.

Bruce rushing after him realised that a chase through the streets of

J'imagine leur joie à l'arrivée. J'ai l'impression que les marchands de whiskey feront des affaires.

Veux-tu me faire le plaisir de remettre à Paula ou de faire suivre la lettre ci-jointe.

P.V. t'a certainement raconté son histoire ; elle est édifiante !

Si Dieu est juste, mon cher Donald, c'est entre mes mains que ce salaud de Paul tombera ; je te jure que je le soignerai.

Je t'envoie encore quelques boissons pour toi et les amis, les colonels et ce vieux Jimmy.

Au plaisir de te lire ou mieux de te revoir. Reçois mon cher Donald mes amitiés les plus cordiales. Mes respects aux Colonels et une bonne poignée de mains aux amis.

Doing !

Très perso/.   Pat.

Extract from Pat O'Leary's letter to Donald Darling concerning Paul Cole.

Marseille was dangerous and unwise. The safety and privacy of their headquarters were paramount. And there were the patients in the waiting and consulting rooms, and Fanny Rodocanachi's guests to consider. With three airmen on the run in the spare room, they dared not draw attention to themselves.

With hindsight : Bruce had been right to advise killing Cole. But even then they had appreciated the impossibility of getting a body downstairs and past the concierge. And after that : what to do with it once out in the street? The doctor's car was not being used, and the police presence in the town was daunting.

Louis Nouveau takes up the story : at the end of the corridor Paul made a quick agile swerve to one side, hurled himself at the front door of the flat and rushed headlong down the stairs. Bruce, trying desperately to catch up with him without drawing the rest of the household's attention to the drama, was brought to a halt as Cole slammed the door in his face.

Bruce, after a moment's agonising hesitation, Nouveau recorded, gave up the chase and returned to join the others for a hurried conference. It was agreed that Paul was likely to have returned to his hotel where no doubt he had left his money. But though Bruce reached the hotel at break-neck speed, he found that his quarry had indeed returned to collect his things and had only just checked out.

'We were never to see Paul again,' he writes, which was true as far as he was concerned. But Pat at any rate was to see him just once more at the end of the war.

The whole dramatic story of the afternoon's events at the Rodocanachis' flat was discussed that evening at the Quai de Rive Neuve where Mario, Pat and Bruce foregathered with Louis in his kitchen before Bruce and Pat left for the north. Mario was enjoying the gizzard of a chicken – his own special treat, a tit-bit reserved for him by Renée. He was a gourmet who could always be relied upon to do justice to the remnants of a good meal. Pat and Bruce were tucking into what they could pick off the carcass, and their urgent conversation was conducted in subdued voices as Renée kept a group of airmen chatting in the drawing room.

One of them was Jean (Alex) Nitelet, another Flight Lieutenant George Barclay who had arrived in the same party as Nitelet. On 29th October Barclay had 'bicycled to Marles . . . where we picked up the

Abbeville train. On board were Paul, Roland (guides), a friend of Roland's, Oscar, Ken, Bill, Joseph, Patrick, Alex [Nitelet] and about four other Scottish Tommies. . . . Help from priest at Abbeville.' They had arrived on the morning of the 1st at the Nouveaus' flat 'with its "lovely view", as Barcley remembered. There he met Pat O'Leary and other members of the organisation – a meeting not without incident, as he cryptically recorded in his notes: "Argument with Belge [Nitelet] over Paul. Meet O'Leary and others. Swollen hand in fight. Slept on floor. Changed shoes and doctored feet. Left behind tinned food . . ." '*
Clearly even now Cole had his supporters.

Pat decided, Nouveau relates, that Bruce and Jean de la Olla must take over the area in the north where Paul Cole had been working. They also all agreed that without any further funding from Garrow, it was almost certain that Cole would immediately sell himself to the Germans. It was therefore essential to warn at once the thirty, and perhaps even as many as fifty families who were regularly having dealings with Cole not to have anything more to do with him.

That night, Pat, with Jean de la Olla and Bruce Dowding, set off for the north, sending in addition agents Debaume, Dufour, Pierrot Lanvers and Dauffes. It was hoped that by saturating the northern area in this way, word would more quickly be spread to reach the many unsuspecting families who were now in imminent danger of betrayal. Bruce, Louis says, was wearing only a thin rainproof coat, and he managed to persuade him to take with him a heavier and warmer coat of Jean-Pierre's. It had been agreed that Bruce would stay at the headquarters in Lille, whilst Jean de la Olla went on to Paris : both were to keep in close contact with each other. One of the first Pat warned was Raffarin, the chef on the Paris-Marseille express who was an invaluable courier between the two zones. Next, Pat's primary task would be to warn their chief agent in the north, the Abbé Carpentier, the priest at Abbeville to whom Barclay referred in his diary.

Functioning in the far more dangerous forbidden zone north of the Somme, he was under ever more rigorous control by the Germans, and was at the heart of a network of priests helping in that area. It frequently happened that crashed airmen made their way to the nearest farm or local priest. In this fashion did the Abbé come immediately to know the

---

* *Fighter Pilot* op cit. Edited by Humphrey Wynn.

whereabouts of practically every Allied airman in the district. This heroic man forged passes and false identity cards. A true craftsman, he produced work of a very high calibre on his own printing press. And now, though he didn't know it, he was a marked man.

So was Monsieur Dupré with whom Pat had pleaded that he should change his name and move away from Lille before the net cast by Cole should get him too. Pat offered (now that he was receiving regular funding from London) to make Dupré a paid agent of the line in the south, if this would enable him financially to give up his job in Lille. But Dupré would not desert his family or his work, though he knew that it was probable, as indeed proved to be the case, that Paul had gone straight back to the north, and might well betray him.

After a visit to Paris, Paul returned to the safe house run by Madame Deram in the Avenue Bernadette in the la Madeleine area of Lille, where Barclay and Higginson had been but two of the many evaders sheltered. There Paul Cole was arrested early in December together with Madame Deram. On the same day the Germans arrested Monsieur Dupré at his desk in the Mayor's office. The effects of Cole's arrest were tragic and swift in their repercussions for the line.

It seems that it was within a few days of his removal to prison at Loos* that Cole was persuaded to turn traitor. For however unsavoury a reputation he had made for himself as far as loose-living and financial indiscretions were concerned, he had not until this time been positively accused of treachery.

Nobody will ever know exactly how Paul Cole was persuaded thereafter to betray his friends up and down the country. Nor whether this was a direct result of beatings or torture from the Abwehr. But it is probable that he was encouraged by the notorious Alsatian, Richard Christmann,† who worked as an agent-provocateur for the Abwehr. He had already penetrated several Resistance groups and escape organisations. Helped by Cole, he thereafter sent some of his men along the line as 'escapees' and in this way learnt the names and addresses of many members of the Pat O'Leary Line.

Not everybody however believes that Cole's decision to act as double

---

* A suburb to the WSW of Lille.

† Airey Neave says (*Saturday at MI9*) that 'Sonderführer Richard Christmann of the Abwehr had penetrated several SOE circuits in France, using a bogus escape line. He also worked on the "North Pole" deception under Colonel Giskes, head of the Abwehr in Holland.'

Not everybody however believes that Cole's decision to act as double-agent dates from this time. Pat, along with others, reckoned that Cole had always from the very beginnings of the line been disloyal and untrustworthy, and had surely been working for both the Germans and the British.

Whatever the true explanation of this monstrous decision, within two days of his arrival at the prison at Loos, Cole's co-operation whether voluntary or under duress, resulted in the arrest on 8th December, only two days days after his own arrest, of the Abbé Carpentier.

On this, the morning following the Japanese attack on Pearl Harbor, and two days before the sinking of HMS *Repulse* and HMS *Prince of Wales* off Malaya, and scarcely a month after the fracas in the Rodocanachis' flat, Cole turned up at the house of the Abbé Carpentier.

Pat and Bruce hastening north from Marseille had warned of Cole's treachery and advised the Abbé not to have anything to do with him. But the Abbé was not easily to be deflected from his self-appointed task. Nor could he as a Christian be persuaded instantly to accept such terrible truths about someone with whom he had done good work over many months.

The number of parcels that Cole was handling on the day he called for the last time on the Abbé Carpentier is uncertain. In the room in which the Abbé kept hidden his forged documents, his photographs and his dozens of engraving stamps ready and awaiting modification and adaptation, Bruce sat talking with the priest of whom he had heard so much admiration and gratitude.

Suddenly there came a knock on the door. Vincent Brome in his book says*:

Paul Cole stood there with three British airmen. Showing them into the drawing-room he, the Abbé, returned to Dowding, and they held a swift consultation.

Was Cole out to betray them, or was he simply resuming work to expiate his past? For two agonised minutes they debated what to do, and then while Dowding, as they agreed that he should, remained hidden in the back room, the Abbé went on to talk to Paul Cole again.

* *The Way Back*. Published by Cassell & Co. in 1957.

Dowding at least must be free to escape if there was any trouble, and warn the others.

In the drawing-room one of the airmen spoke to the Abbé with an unmistakably English accent. It seemed proof enough. He decided that Cole was genuine.

Listening in the next room Bruce heard the sound of a drawer opening, of papers being shuffled, and then suddenly: 'Put your hands up!'

Immediately Dowding opened the French windows and ran for it across the garden. Back in the house two of the airmen revealed themselves as disguised Gestapo agents.

Extraordinarily, the third man, who had first spoken, was a genuine British pilot, and no one ever knew how he came to allow himself to play the part of dupe.*

The Gestapo turned the house upside down, took the seals, the photographs and the printing press, searched the cellars, terrorised the maid, but found no trace of Dowding.

All that day he wandered alone from place to place, too distraught to speak to anyone. Then at last, galvanised into action, he set out to warn everyone in the area, and that was precisely what the Gestapo expected him to do. On his third call they were waiting for him.

When he undertook to work for the Gestapo, Cole did so with accuracy and a sinister devotion to his new duty.

Ten other agents whose names, addresses, and individual activities were supplied by Cole, together with the Abbé Carpentier were all imprisoned in dreadful conditions awaiting a horrible death. The gentle Abbé, Monsieur Dupré, and the gallant young Australian Bruce Dowding – all three were in the end to be brutally treated, and later executed: victims of treason.

Louis Nouveau records the detailed indictment of Paul Cole, sent out from his prison cell at Loos by the Abbé Carpentier, using the good offices of a friend he had made there amongst the gaolers. . . . It is signed in his own strong hand, this last communication with the outside world, and dated 3rd March 1942, P. Carpentier.

* Airey Neave in his book *Saturday at M19* says that this was the first Abwehr operation using the traitor Cole and bogus British airmen. There were to be several more.

I declare that I was ignobly betrayed by Sgt Col(e) in the following circumstances on the 8th December 1941 at about 14.30. Sgt. Col(e) presented himself to me with five other persons who had come to cross the Line secretly with him. He introduced these persons in the following fashion, two Belgian pilots, one English soldier, one RAF Captain, and a Polish pilot. The two Belgians spoke French, and it was easy for me to verify that they were authentic. The English soldier spoke a little French. The Captain of the RAF spoke French correctly, was the 'perfect English' type, and appeared to be a *beau soldat*.

The so-called Polish pilot spoke neither French nor German. I therefore put in hand the procedures to produce the necessary papers. Having got them I started to make all the necessary false identity papers : it was at this moment that a German policeman in civilian clothes arrived and took us away, hands raised, to a nearby barracks. The British pilot was immediately taken on one side. The Belgian tried to escape, but was caught. The Captain of the RAF had understood from looks that Col(e) (sic) had denounced him, and was calling him names under his breath. Col(e) was soon taken on one side also, and I was taken to Loos. Two days later I was taken to Lille to the Bureau of the GFP in the Rue de Tanremonde, and I was interrogated. I found in this office the so-called German pilot in the grand uniform of a German sub-lieutenant. He is the head of this bureau. He came to taunt and mock me about my arrest. During the interrogation the judge declared to me, as he did to Dupré, that Col(e) had shamelessly betrayed us, not only by handing us over, but in revealing in his declaration many things that he need not have said, and this to aggravate our case, and to be sure that we would not be able to catch up with him.

During the interrogation I was able to ascertain these revelations made by Col(e). He revealed things, (hidden arms in my home and at the homes of my friends) that he alone knew about. It was he who denounced Adolphe (alias *Joseph**) and *André Mason*.†

The Abbé was beheaded by the Germans at Dortmund, as was also Bruce Dowding. Madame Deram spent agonising months in a concentration camp. And those were only the first of Paul's good friends to whom he brought disaster.

* Pat O'Leary.
† Bruce Dowding.

The Rodocanachis were losing *their* good friends and most welcome wartime visitors at a distressing and alarming rate.

And Pat was wishing with all his heart that they had followed Bruce's instinct and advice, and made an end of Cole in the Rodocanachis' flat. Could it really have been only one month ago?

After Cole had escaped from Marseille Pat had sought permission from London to kill him. However, London was not convinced. Permission was refused, and Cole remained at large to carry on his treacherous career.

Donald Darling, MI9's agent in Gibraltar, recalled:*

Before I had left Lisbon, O'Leary had mentioned in a recent message his conviction that Cole was not only an embezzler but more than possibly a traitor as well. He told me that he would liquidate him when next he had the opportunity.

The information did not please Colonel Dansey [in London] who told P15 [Darling's MI9 contact] to inform me that he did not agree to Cole being killed and to pass that message to O'Leary in Marseille. I did not know how to obey this instruction and water it down.

After much thought I sent a note to Marseille in as ambiguous a was as possible, referring to the need to forgive human frailties, which I hoped O'Leary would read to mean Colonel Dansey's own soft attitude to Cole ('give him a run for his money'). It was all very well, I thought, to sit in London and issue instructions covering a situation only understood by the man on the spot, who was in danger! Luckily for Cole he had gone once more to northern France out of O'Leary's immediate reach, but O'Leary's next communication on this subject was adamant.

A month or two later Pat was to meet P15 face to face and show him the letter the Abbé Carpentier had smuggled out of prison, 'proving that he and others had been betrayed by Cole'. No further efforts were made by London to dissuade O'Leary from his resolution. But now it was too late. The opportunity never arose again.

What Pat did not know was that Ian Garrow also had had similar

* *Secret Sunday*, William Kimber, 1975.

after much thought, that Coté
needed killing & I was the
man who had to do it, in
spite of the certainty of sub-
-sequent court martial.

Not knowing Pat's medical
qualifications – (I suppose such
hugger-mugger is unavoidable
in clandestine activities? –
I consulted Dr Rodocanachi
& told him my difficulty.
I had to kill a man in
such a manner that it wd
not invite a police enquiry
& investigation which)
might reveal our
organisation ie it wd
have to appear death from
natural causes. His
solution was a massive

7.

injection of insulin, sufficient
in a non-diabetic person
to produce coma. Thereafter
a gentle push into one of
the side basins of the old
Port, Marseilles ((I had chosen
the spot, unfrequented &
in the shadow of Fort
St Nicolas) All was ready,
& we awaited Paul's return
from the North.

However "L'homme propose
et le bon Dieu dispose" &
in the interval I was arrested
& put in that same Fort St
Nicolas. You know the
sequel.

Extract from Ian Garrow's letter to Donald Darling, 4 May 1965.

plans before his arrest. In a letter he was to write, also to Donald Darling, on 4th May 1965, he said :

> Returning to Cole. It was kind of you to think of shielding me, but as the following will show, the shielding (except for the will of God) was unnecessary.
>
> I did not warn [his wife] because my solution was far simpler, and would have protected [her], the Abbé, Dupré, Dowding, and all the other victims of Paul's treachery. I had decided to kill Harold Cole alias 'Paul'. I had discovered in my solitary wanderings, all with a purpose, sufficient of Cole's activities, to be convinced of his potential danger.
>
> I stress 'potential' – because that was all it was at that time, but no less dangerous for all that. So I decided after much thought, that Cole needed killing, and I was the man who had to do it, in spite of certainty of subsequent court-martial.
>
> Not knowing Pat's medical qualifications, I suppose such hugger-mugger is unavoidable in clandestine activities? I consulted Dr Rodocanachi and told him my difficulty. I had to kill a man in such a manner that it would not invite a police inquiry and investigation which would reveal our organisation, and it would have to appear death from natural causes. His solution was a massive injection of insulin, sufficient in a non-diabetic person to produce coma. There-after a gentle push into one of the side basins of the Old Port, Marseille (I had chosen the spot, unfrequented, and in the shadow of Fort Saint Nicolas).
>
> All was ready, and we awaited Paul's return from the north. However – *'l'homme propose, et le Bon Dieu dispose'* – and in the interval I was arrested, and put in that same Fort Saint Nicolas.

When Bruce was arrested, Jean de la Olla bravely hurried to Lille, and at great personal risk, did his desperate best to make contact with every single helper known to him in that area. But for many of them he arrived too late. They had already been betrayed by Cole to the Gestapo, arrested and taken away, never to be seen again. Some of the others, Louis Nouveau has recorded, were by this time totally disillusioned, and many had lost all confidence in the *réseau*.

Soon, Pat was once again making the long cold dangerous journey from Marseille to Paris. This time it was to warn Jean de la Olla that

André Postel-Vinay had been arrested, and must be offered every help possible. He must try somehow to make contact with him, to see if he needed money, or what could be done to encourage and support him. But despite his efforts a terrible ordeal faced Postel-Vinay.

According to Fanny Rodocanachi, Cole was again to cast a shadow over their flat when her husband was faced with a request which professionally he could not refuse.

A young French girl, who had been a brave and stalwart courier with the Line, and who he understood had married Paul Cole, paid the first of five or six ante-natal visits to Dr Rodocanachi. Was she still in touch with Cole, he wondered. She was not in fact; she had remained loyal to the Line.

Via London, Georges Rodocanachi was able to provide her with funds to enable her to live modestly until the birth of her child in October 1942. It was the doctor too who made arrangements for her confinement in a local clinic, and finance to settle her account there. But in January 1943 the baby died in a bitterly cold bedroom in a small hotel: and once again it was Dr Rodocanachi who was called to establish that the child had died, and to fill in all the necessary documentation.

CHAPTER SEVEN

Parcels on the Move and Radio Operators

1942

Louis and Renée Nouveau were by now running an almost continually full house. Alerted to Cole's treachery, they were appalled to learn that he had betrayed some fifty helpers. In time he was to deliver into German hands many of his own countrymen, secreted along the escape route – who were shot as spies because they were wearing civilian clothes.

During those intensely busy and anxious days, the Rodocanachis and Nouveaus did not meet at all. Pat did not want any communication between one Safe House and another, and he himself made this easier by never mentioning one establishment to the other. Yet had they pooled their experiences, they might have been able to help each other out.

Fanny, who like Renée had been only too delighted to give her visitors the run of the flat, had by now been forced to forbid her visitors the use of her grand-piano in the drawing-room. She, like her guests, missed the music. But she did not usually play Chopin, and certainly not morning, noon, and night, and she dared not allow them to continue. The greatest threat were close neighbours. It just didn't do now to be too familiar with them. Far better to keep oneself to oneself, and avoid informal comings and goings amongst friends and acquaintances who lived close enough to pop in on the spur on the moment.

Those who sported pictures of Pétain, and there were many homes of the *bourgeoisie* who did at that time, were sure to be against their activities. Fortunately such people were unlikely to want to risk being seen in the company of, or known to fraternise with, anyone whose activities would be likely to attract the interest of the Milice or Gestapo.

A further weak point in their security which it seems probable that neither Fanny nor Georges appreciated at the time, was the increasingly hostile attitude towards Dr Rodocanachi amongst his medical colleagues in the town. They must have known that through his pre-war links with the American Consulate, and his excellent command of the English language, as well as Greek, he had been chosen as the ideal person to examine the hundreds of Jews waiting, and hoping to emigrate to the USA.

No doubt the French doctors saw him as having by this appointment been put in the way of earning himself a substantial income in fees and back-handers, or gifts in kind from Jews fleeing the Nazis.

In point of fact Georges Rodocanachi used nearly all of his personal fortune for the cause he so fiercely supported. It was a mercy that his widow had money of her own in England, for at the time of his death he had only some £500 in his account. He could so easily have made a fortune during the years 1940, '41, and '42 had he chosen to charge for false certificates for which his patients would willingly have paid him generously in cash.

It is highly probable that Fanny and Georges, both of them proud Greeks of patrician families, of conspicuous long-standing integrity in Marseille, must have had their enemies at that time. The Greeks themselves had a word for this kind of pride. Hubris, they called it. A kind of insolence or arrogance perhaps, resulting from excessive pride or from passion. The penalty exacted by the Gods for this hubris, was the disaster of Nemesis.

Did Dr Rodocanachi's stoicism, his refusal to bend, literally or spiritually to his enemies, turn against his own best interest at this time? Were his enormous strength of character in adversity, and his uncompromisingly passionate loyalty to the cause he had espoused, to create tragedy for him? It is possible that those very qualities and strengths became unacceptable to a number of his colleagues, once the Allies began to triumph. The outcome of the war was still undecided. But now that the USA had joined the struggle it was beginning to look as though, against all the odds, the Rodocanachis had backed a winner when nearly all his colleagues had backed a loser.

Did the medical fraternity now turn against him, even to the point of informing against him? There was much that they could have said regarding his assistance given so freely to the Jews. And his attitude to the armistice, and the Allies, and his Gaullist sympathies were no secret.

Fanny herself left a telling account of the situation at this time. With hindsight it is possible to see in it the self-sown seeds of the harvest her husband would reap.

Until August 1942, the German interests at the Mixed Commission of the Military Board were represented by a French doctor. But from that date he was replaced by a German military medical officer.

He first appeared as a civilian. But the second and last time, it was a German officer who acted as medical examiner. This was a typical Prussian officer with a scar on his face, and extremely correct.

He introduced himself to the four French doctors, offering to shake hands. Dr Rodocanachi alone affected not to see his gesture, but the other three shook hands very cordially with him.

The examination started. This time there were only civilians to attend to – none interesting in any way – but the German was anything but lenient : to which attitude he had a perfect right.

In one case which seemed a dubious one, Dr Rodocanachi observed that in this circumstance it would be normal to declare the patient unfit for military service.

'Not at all,' said the German. 'In Germany a duodenal ulcer is considered curable if it is attended to, and anyway it can be operated on.'

Dr R.: 'I represent British interests here, and neither in England nor in France can a man be operated on against his will.'

German Dr: 'We pay no attention to personal opinions in Germany, and a duodenal ulcer is an ordinary operation.'

Dr R.: 'Whatever the operation, there is always a risk to be incurred by the patient, and no one has the right to inflict that risk without his consent.'

German Dr: 'In Germany this operation always succeeds because we have excellent surgeons.'

Dr R.: 'Germany has not alone the privilege of making good surgeons. In France too we know how to operate !'

The three other doctors, who were not of Greek blood like Dr Rodocanachi, did not even turn a hair at this insolent German thrust at the medical profession.

At the end of the meeting, the German doctor did not attempt to shake hands with Dr Rodocanachi, but did so warmly with the other three doctors.

(Left)
Whitney Straight.

Prisoners of war at St Hippolyte-du-Fort in December 1941. Such group photographs were taken so that prisoners could be seen to be in good condition according to the requirements of the Geneva Convention.

Marseille, January 1943.

Marseille, January 1943. Note the child being hurried away from the German troops.

When the German had gone Dr Rodocanachi, in spite of the control he usually kept over his opinions and feelings, could not refrain – in view of the complacency of his craven colleagues – from saying to them :

'Gentlemen, I think I am the only one who does not need to wash his hands.'

Not one of the three doctors took an exception to this scathing and unwise criticism of their attitude, but one of them in his ignorant and *bourgeois* provincialism, remarked :

'You are right – it was most incorrect on his part to shake hands with us without removing his gloves !'

Renée and Louis, though they knew Ian so well, were not aware at the time that he had made his home and his headquarters in the flat of their old friends, the Rodocanachis. They too were appalled at the ten-year sentence passed on Garrow. But they could not know what a personal sorrow his departure was to the Rodocanachi household.

The Nouveaus kept two splendid pro-British maids,* so there was always someone around to answer the phone or open the door to callers. Visitors were warned never to go near that door if the bell rang or anyone knocked, and to disappear at once if the maid went to answer such a summons.

To this day parcels remember how soon the novelty of creature comforts wore off. They suffered from an overwhelming feeling of frustration, depressed as they soon became at their own uselessness and indebtedness to total strangers who owed them nothing.

It helped to be a compulsive reader at the Rodocanachis and the Nouveaus where both homes had good libraries which their visitors were welcome to use. Many escapers and evaders say to this day, that their sanity was preserved by the excellent selection of books in English which they greatly appreciated.

Derrick Nabarro† said that his tastes were to a great extent formed and stimulated by the reading that he did at the Rodocanachis. But that even then he was much troubled, and feared for his hosts, should the Gestapo ever investigate their flat. The rows of English classics, and modern paper-backs would surely have interested them, and inclined

---

* Both received citations from the British Government.
† Author of *Wait for the Dawn*, Cassell, 1952.

them to look more exhaustively into the Rodocanachis' attitudes and activities.

Music on gramophone or the wireless passed many restive hours. But the sound had always to be kept very low. Neighbours would soon have noticed a sudden change in the listening habits and musical taste and preferences of the people above or next-door to them.

Curfew made clandestine activities increasingly hazardous. Only doctors, nurses, midwives, nuns and vets were allowed petrol and passes to permit them to be out and about during curfew hours. The penalty for breaking the curfew was arrest, deportation and sometimes death.

At the Nouveaus', departures by convoy for the station nearly always took place between 5.00 and 6.00 a.m. Either Louis, or Renée in her Red Cross uniform saw the men as far as the station. The streets would be almost empty, tyreless bicycles clattering over cobbled alleyways, their metal rims making a grating sound unless swathed and muffled in strips of rag for nightly post-curfew opportunism.

Since there was no Mazout* to be had for love nor money, there was no central heating, and all water for baths or other purposes had to be heated on the stove. For those on low incomes, life had become extremely difficult, and thin dogs with rib-cages like basket-work had the same hungry look as their owners: and soon they were all gone. At the Rodocanachis and the Nouveaus water was supplied and lavatories were flushed by tipping buckets of water into the pan.

There was little that willing men could contribute to ease the lot of their busy hosts. They would gladly have helped with the chores, but at the Nouveaus and the Rodocanachis these were dealt with by the maids.

'The men's big moment came,' Renée Nouveau told me, 'when the petit pois were in season. Then they all got down to podding peas for our large party!'

At least the presence of maids protected their visitors from the well-recognised hazards of causing marital friction, and from breaking one of the strict rules of escaping.

Group Captain Frank Griffiths gives a good example in his book *Winged Hours*† when he writes about one of the Safe Houses in which he passed some time.

* The oil required for central heating.
† Published by William Kimber in 1981.

When we had finished the meal, Madame Roche started to clear the table and carry the crockery to the sink to start washing up.

Automatically I started to help, but remembered that I was about to transgress one of the cardinal rules of escaping. This was not to do anything which might make a husband jealous.

Whether it was a clash of cultures or just unusual circumstances, but many RAF had discovered that on the continent the men seemed to expect their women to do the washing up, and their consciences were quite untroubled to see a woman stagger into a room with her arms full of firewood for the stove. The hiding of an RAF crew was a great event in their lives, and the wives would show especial favour to the poor downed aviator who might be injured, and possibly suffering from shock.

In every Safe House there was the familiar routine, the house-rules of a near-prison existence, the local agents of the line coming and going, then the news that tomorrow was the day for moving on, and the men must shave that evening ready for an early start.

Our flat [wrote Louis Nouveau] continued to be almost always full, sometimes two, four, or six staying there for a day or two, or in some cases for a fortnight at a time.

I generally did not take them in charge, but merely accompanied them to the station when they left. And I still have a vivid recollection of rising early in the ice-cold flat, making tea on an electric kettle in the kitchen, breakfast without butter, the fellows as cool and cheerful as if they were just starting off for their day's work, and finally the slight feeling of apprehension as we went out by the front-door, as there were always two customs officials, and sometimes even two policemen, sheltering from the wind beneath the porch.

It might have been expected that leaving an ordinary middle-class block of flats at half-past five in the morning, three men – two of whom at least, looked a bit out of the ordinary – would have aroused suspicion. It never did.

To them via the Gare St Charles and the Petit Poucet* had come on

---

* Louis Nouveau records that 'one address was fairly often given to air crews before they left on flights over Europe. The Petit Poucet was quite an easy place to remember and to find.' He was told this by two or three pilots who stayed with them.

16th April 1942 a Lieutenant A. S. M. Neave, aged 26, who had escaped from Oflag 4/C (Colditz) near Leipzig, and had reached Marseille via Switzerland. To the end of his life Airey Neave, like countless others, was to remember the name of that modest little bar. For it was there, feeling desperately conspicuous and vulnerable that so many of them had sat toying with a glass, and waiting to be picked up by someone they did not know, and in whom they must blindly put their trust.

Lady Airey tells me that her husband said that it was always a complex, and often slightly distressing feeling that you owed so much – perhaps even too much – to your hosts. The gratitude that you felt for their unselfish bravery and generosity in housing and feeding you in their own homes, at the risk of their lives, often sat heavily on you.

Why, after all should they take you in? Who, in fact were they? You never quite knew. And since they weren't British, you couldn't find out. Could you – should you – even entirely trust them? Might they be acting as double agents – out to trap you? Mighty they, under duress, hand you over to the enemy? Complicated pressures resulted, and a sense of guilt and stressful gratitude.

The Nouveaus, as Airey was soon to find out, were transparently honourable people. But as he himself had said to his wife, 'Safe Houses were *very* dangerous places!' In addition to his dislike of confined spaces, for the rest of his life, he also hated handling passports and papers generally. They had hauntingly disageeable connotations for him.

After reaching neutral Switzerland, he and Hugh Woollatt had received orders from MI9 to proceed to Marseille. Airey Neave had arrived from Berne, and Hugh Woollatt (escaped from Oflag Vc at Biberach in southern Germany) had travelled from Lausanne. Their rendezvous had been a bookstall in Geneva.

After a safe re-entry into France, they had reached the penultimate stage in their journey back to England. Gibraltar was their next goal, and the Safe House in Marseille would apparently see them on their way to crossing into Spain.

Airey Neave in his book *They Have Their Exits** describes the situation:

* Published by Hodder and Stoughton in 1953.

It was a small neat place with a row of painted tables down each side of a sawdust passage. A waiter came towards us, motioning us to a table. Beyond was a pair of double-doors with frosted glass. As we sat there, I could see a young gendarme* walking slowly past the entrance.

He seemed to be looking into the café. The customers, working people wearing caps, spoke in low voices, eyeing us over their glasses. This worried our French escorts. I turned to the waiter and softly asked for Gaston. He looked at me in terror and disappeared.

Then came a small bald man who ushered us in silence from the table to a room, behind the double doors, at the end of the café. It was a square room with a large skylight and ancient furniture upholstered in green satin. It looked like an out-dated photographer's studio.

We sat down obediently, and the bald man turned to us and peremptorily demanded the password. We both repeated it perfectly like a catechism.

He seemed satisfied and tapped on a side door. To our consternation, a youthful gendarme entered and saluted sheepishly. It was the same gendarme that I had seen outside.

'Who is this?' I cried, fearing a trap.

'Who is this?' the bald man said sourly. 'Mind your own business. This is Jacques. He will fetch someone to talk to you. I regret the suspicious way in which all four of you barged into my café. I am not certain of your identity . . .'

We waited uncomfortably for the new character to make his appearance. The bald man, relenting a little, sent for coffee and drinks until we were in a mellow mood. Slowly I realised he had been deeply embarrassed by our clumsy arrival.

There was a knock on the frosted glass. A slim man of middle-age dressed in a smart grey double-breasted suit and green pork-pie hat entered the room. His keen grey eyes surveyed us anxiously for a moment.

'The password please,' he said in English. His accent, though French, had a flavour of Throgmorton Street and of London clubs. We repeated the password obediently in our best French.

* Monsieur Boulard. Police Inspector, and member of the Organisation.

In *Saturday at MI9** Airey Neave said :

Louis amazed me as soon as I saw him. He was slightly built, and wore a light grey suit and suede shoes, a silk shirt and dark red bow-tie with white spots. He looked – and was – a successful merchant banker and stockbroker, well-known in Marseille ... He checked my false papers ... my identity document ... his English was perfect.

'Follow me at thirty paces. Stop when I stop,' he told us.

Woollatt and I followed him home from the café, down the Canebière, and along the quayside of the port. Through the cluster of masts we could see him approach a modern block of flats on the Quai de Rive Neuve. Then he turned back, motioning us into a shop doorway.

'I think there's someone watching the flat. Hide here until I give you the signal,' he whispered.

He sauntered slowly to the door of his apartment house, studying a newspaper. A uniformed gendarme passed by. Louis lifted his hat, wiped his brow with a red silk handkerchief.

'False alarm,' he said as we climbed the stairs to the fifth floor. Next morning I went to the window of the flat and looked out over the Old Port of Marseille.

It was just like a fairy story.

'You must stay in the flat and keep your slippers on. Don't open the door to anyone. We will be back for lunch.'

And so saying, and after helping the maid to clear away the remains of the breakfast things, Renée Nouveau had left the flat in the company of her husband.

'That window is our sentry-box', he had said to the new arrivals. 'Keep it manned!'

But there was, nevertheless, a strictly defined imaginary line beyond which it was dangerous to be seen looking out.

After the hazards and exciting sense of individual achievement of escaping from Colditz it was, thought Airey, going to be claustrophobic and something of an anti-climax to have to remain like a parcel in a sorting office awaiting collection and delivery.

* Published by Hodder and Stoughton in 1969.

At the Rodocanachis' their visitors in the large bedroom overlooking the courtyard at the back, were also living vicariously via their open windows. But the shutters there must always remain closed across so large and dangerous a space. The buildings opposite looked straight at them.

Along the parquetted corridor, Séraphine was everlastingly filtering drinking-water in her pantry. It looked like a laboratory, with retorts, tubing, filters, funnels, and winchester jars fixed to the wall.

'The doctor,' she managed to explain to the visitors, 'insists that all water to be drunk here, must be filtered. We have always had many visitors from England, and they soon get ill from the water unless it has been purified.' It wasn't simply that foreigners mistrusted the water in Marseille specifically. 'Continental tummy' was well-recognised as a hazard to travellers.

Shoes were collected from outside the bedroom doors, wonderfully polished, and returned there by the morning. The visitors' bedroom slippers gave Séraphine no work : but the men often enough took it upon themselves to retrieve any shoes they could find, and clean them before she could get to them. As they so often said : it was the least that they could do.

Donald Caskie, who in January 1942 was ordered by the Milice to close down his Seamen's Mission building, had been active up to that time and even after it.

Like Georges Rodocanachi, he paid regular visits to hospitals, camps and prisons in and around Marseille. Combining his clerical duties with passing information, identity cards, passes and the occasional sawing or cutting device, he was a vital link in the chain of escape.

It was on just such an innocent pastoral visit to St Hippolyte du Fort that he chanced upon a certain Captain Whitney of the RASC who had arrived there on 9th August 1941. This information was promptly passed to Pat who immediately alerted MI9.

Whitney Straight, a member of the celebrated American family of Whitney, American by birth, but educated in England, was already a racing driver of international repute, and a dashing and intrepid aviator.*

Shot down whilst attacking E-boats near le Havre on 31st July 1941,

* Later Air Commodore, CBE, MC, DFC. Died in 1979.

he was at that time a dark, strongly built man of thirty years of age. He crashed in a field in the north of France, beside an unsuspecting farmer, and having failed in his attempts at blowing up his aircraft,* he determinued to avoid capture and headed south on a zig-zag course towards the Mediterranean.

His French was good, and he was soon using his silk map of France, his compass, RAF survival kit, and French banknotes stitched into the lining of his flying jacket.

His was a famliar face to readers of such journals as *The Bystander*, *Vogue*, and *The Tatler* who knew him as a glamorous figure in society drawing-rooms, and a successful racing driver often photographed in overalls in the pits. Fortunately for him – though his fame as a dangerous adversary in the sky was well established, he was not so immediately recognisable to the enemy. For there was a high price upon his head.

After hair-raising near-misses, he continued to evade capture until he gave himself away to a German agent. Unaware that ration cards were required in Vichy, he ordered a meal.

Three gendarmes picked him up, and on 9th August 1941 he was sent to St Hippolyte du Fort where he was known as 'Le Capitaine Whitney'.

In no time at all he was busy planning his escape. Had his captors known who he really was, his chances of getting away would have been remote. For news of his having been shot down over France had been given over the wireless.

With another pilot by the name of Gibbs, they launched a well-synchronised attack on one of the guards, and in the confusion managed to make a run for it. But Whitney Straight was forced to surrender at gunpoint.

Since London now knew where Whitney was spending his impatient days, an early attempt was planned to try to get him repatriated on medical grounds. On 9th September 1941, Dr Rodocanachi, not for the first time, squared his sensitive medical conscience and successfully

---

* Air Chief Marshal Sir Lewis Hodges, KCB, CBE, DSO, DFC, says that as a Flying Officer in 1940, he himself crashed in Brittany in a Hudson, and found it extremely difficult to set light to a plane as instructed. He had run out of petrol (the reason that he crashed) and his box of matches and all his maps and charts were not sufficient to feed the flames. He is now President of the RAF Escaping Society, and of the Special Forces Club, and a life Vice-President of the Royal Air Forces Association.

État commotionnel labyrinthique —
— vertigineux avec bourdonnement
avis de spécialiste —

Commission du 9 9ᵇʳᵉ 41

Monsieur le Consul,

J'ai l'honneur de vous rendre
compte que le Capitaine Willer et
WHITNEY ~~aviateur anglais~~ a été
présenté à la commission médicale
mixte ~~réunie~~ à l'Hôpital (Médical
Militaire)
Lyon le 9 9ᵇʳᵉ 1941 et a été reconnu
après examen par le spécialiste
d'oto-rhino-laryngologie, atteint de
état commotionnel labyrinthique —
État vertigineux avec bourdonnements
~~(crossed out lines)~~
~~(crossed out lines)~~
~~(crossed out lines)~~
~~(crossed out lines)~~
~~(crossed out lines)~~ la persistance
de ces phénomènes sans amélioration
~~(crossed out)~~
appréciable doit faire porter un
et faire craindre de voir s'installer un syndrome à jamais
pronostic très réservé — Il serait très
important que le Capitaine ~~Whitney~~ Whitney
soit le plus rapidement possible mis
dans des conditions physiques et morales
qui permettent de lui donner tous les
soins que nécessite son état, et qui
sont seuls capables d'améliorer

Part of Dr Rodocanachi's draft report to the Repatriation Medical Board
on Whitney Straight.

cleared this dashing young airman as being unfit for further military service.

As the American Representative on the Repatriation Medical Board, he used his considerable influence with his German colleagues. With subtle pressure, and a nonchalant and apparent lack of any personal interest or concern in the case, he was able to demonstrate good and sufficient reasons why Captain Whitney should be repatriated.

Coached and carefully rehearsed in the acrobatics of medical signs and symptoms, and by playing up an old wound in his back, and damage to his ear-drums sustained when he had been wounded in Norway, Whitney Straight was cautiously advised by Dr Rodocanachi for whom this duplicity was an agony of mind and conscience.

Demonstrating a convincing discharge of pus from both ears, the handiwork of the doctor who had mixed finely grated brick-dust with the proper proportion of Marseille soap, Whitney Straight was able to present himself before the Medical Board as suffering from damaged ear-drums and vertigo.

Counselling assumed deafness, and an unsteady gait due to loss of balance, Dr Rodocanachi was able to establish that the case was plausible enough. Yet another important member of the RAF was about to be returned to base – there to fly again with great distinction.

'The organisation had many concealed victories of this kind,' writes Vincent Brome.* 'Their true extent is difficult to determine ... but at this period Dr Rodocanachi reaped a rich harvest with no fewer than eight of these faked repatriations.'

Ever one to appreciate the good things of life, to have friends and acquaintances in all the 'best' places, and familiar with the French Riviera in its golden age, Whitney Straight took himself off to friends at Cannes – still apparently a British colony, whither such 'mad' English residents as had not left hurriedly along with Somerset Maugham in two coal boats for Gibraltar had now congregated.

There in the *ville des fleurs et des sports élégants*, at the club, he played conspicuous, dangerous and irresponsible tennis. Interested eyes would have found it rewarding to observe the agility and athleticism

* *The Way Back*. Published by Cassell & Co. 1957. A list of suggested ways of malingering convincingly, was put together in the form of a small book of matches. This booklet was for dropping over enemy lines – written in German for influencing German troops – by our aircraft. Later, the Germans reciprocated by dropping for our troops a translation into English of the identical advice for malingerers.

of this medically unfit British airman, as he awaited the call that would return him to England. Summoned to return to Marseille from *la ville fleurie* so as to be ready to leave at a moment's notice, he and a British soldier remained hidden at the Nouveaus'.

'He must have been quite a handful,' Elizabeth Haden-Guest remembers. 'He was so impatient, and pretty cock-sure too! He always knew what he wanted, and usually saw that he got it! There wasn't much humility about the man' – which no doubt accounted for his fearlessness in the air, and his reputation as the intrepid aviator the Germans would have given anything to capture or destroy.

I wondered if, on the whole, these airmen had been grateful for the enormous risks that people like Elizabeth and her fellow-couriers were daily taking on their account.

'Some were,' Elizabeth recalls today.

'But some just didn't realise what was happening to them. After all everything was shrouded in secrecy, no names were given, and all plans were kept from them. Nothing was said about what would happen. It was safer that way.

'So – one minute they were up in the air, loaded with bombs. And the next, there they were dressed up in other people's clothes, slopping around in somebody else's bedroom slippers, eating strange food, confined in what after ranging around France must have seemed a small room, and told by strangers to keep quiet.

'Remember, they were just ordinary, very young chaps who often enough had been having breakfast in England only three or four hours earlier. Many of them still had that morning's newspaper on them. And some were inclined to see themselves as the important people.

'Hot from England, and flying with the RAF, just a few of them reckoned that *they* were the ones whose lives counted most. After all it was they who had just been shot down, and were escaping. The civilians who now had them in charge should perhaps be grateful to them.'

Pat too recalls one incident in which disaster was a hairsbreadth away. Once, when he was escorting three airmen to Paris, he decided, as they had had nothing to eat since that morning, to take them to the buffet-car, although this was obviously risky. The tables were all for four, and they could only find two places free at one table, and two at another. They all sat down, the two airmen sitting opposite two German soldiers. As they were eating their sandwiches and drinking a glass of beer, one of the airmen, nervous at his first close encounter with a real live German, managed to upset his glass and spill the beer over the trousers of the soldier opposite him. In his extreme horror at what might come of this, and unable to speak either French or German, he simply roared with inane laughter ... which might have had disastrous consequences. But fortunately, the German did the same, and the whole crazy situation went off quite happily. When recounting this incident, Pat commented that it was often much easier, if not less dangerous to pass unnoticed among the Germans in the occupied zone, than amongst the Vichy Police in the unoccupied zone.

A better and more appreciative attitude to helpers was often found amongst escapers and evaders who had been a long, anxious and lonely time on the run.

To arrive suddenly, literally out of the blue into the clandestine world with all its intrigue and hidden perils, wasn't an easy situation to appreciate and instantly adjust to.

'The Brylcream Boys were the glamorous members of the armed forces,' Elizabeth told me. 'But for us the soldiers were easier to cope with. They had already walked themselves nearly into the ground, had travelled the length and breadth of France, and were at the end of their tether. Any accommodation or arrangements we made for them were acceptable. The pilots were men of the air, and difficult because they really only felt safe in the air.

'On the ground they shivered. To take them by train from Cannes to Marseille for example, with faked papers, was hell. They were totally lost and bewildered and it showed alarmingly.

'The air was their element. On the ground they were like fish out of water.'

The man who had been pronounced unfit for further military service, along with seven other repatriates, set off from the Rodocanachis under special surveillance, travelling by train to Perpignan.

The date was 4th March 1942. In no time at all, the train was halted. When it finally staggered into the station at Perpignan, the place was crawling with fully-armed soldiers. It transpired that the first massive air raid on Paris had taken place during the night before.

The Renault* factory at Boulogne-Billancourt at St Cloud on the out-skirts of the town, where tanks were being built for the Wehrmacht, had been reduced to smouldering rubble.

As a reprisal for this, the Vichy officials had decided to make things difficult for British prisoners-of-war. They were all turned back, and sent to the Pasteur Hospital at Nice, under detention in a security unit.

At the hospital Pat made contact with Whitney Straight via Francis Blanchain. London had emphasised that something must be done to get him back at the earliest possible moment. For some reason this man's escape must be given top priority.

Blanchain, living at a Safe House in Toulouse, Madame Mongelard's Hôtel de Paris, knew one of the nurses who worked on the ward where the British repatriates were being housed.

With her knowledge of the movements and routines of the guards, and the possibilities she had for doing so, she drugged the guards. Sleep-ing tablets in their lunchtime wine soon rendered them unconscious, and Whitney Straight and one other prisoner made a silent bolt for freedom in stockinged feet.

The external gate had been well-doctored, and Francis Blanchain perched level with the hospital roof on a hillside was waiting for them. Both men were given false papers, and were fortunate to be able to board a local bus just as the guards were waking up.

With Blanchain as spokesman and escort the three men lurched their way towards Juan-les-Pins, and the two parcels went into hiding for that night at the home of a Dr Levy. Blanchain continued his journey, hastening to report the job well-done to Pat at the Rodocanachis.

He was back at Juan-les-Pins the following day with fresh clothes, 'good' papers, and to accompany his two parcels to be photographed by a trusted photographer.

The three men, looking inconspicuous, boarded the train for Mar-seille, the parcels carrying flawless documents and photographs that couldn't be faulted.

In Marseille they were soon giving the familiar knock on the Nouveaus' door. Pat had arrived from the Rodocanachis, and both he and Louis were anxious to meet the man about whom London seemed so exceptionally concerned.

* Some 500 people were killed, and three times as many reputedly injured during that attack by 235 bombers, of which only one was lost. This was the first large experiment in using flares as guides during a bombing raid.

Nitelet's radio had already informed London that Whitney Straight was 'out'. And he had another piece of news to report.

The message ran : *Escape of Higginson and others from Fort de la Revère planned for six August* [1942].

Marseille resounded with German anger at the news when so many Allied prisoners escaped. The authorities instituted a massive search in and around the town, and the place was torn apart, as two at least including Higginson were lying doggo at the Nouveaus' for the next two weeks.

Then, suddenly, it was time to go.

They left by sea from Canet-Plage near Perpignan. Dressed in convincingly French clothes twenty or more familiar figures came dangerously together at a villa close to the Hôtel du Tennis on the beach.

In dribs and drabs they continued to arrive and pack themselves into a room intended for only four or five people. There were British, French, Polish, and Belgian travellers.

Whitney Straight was there, Léoni Savinos and his German-born wife, Pierrot Lanvers, Squadron Leader Higginson, and Paula Spriewald. Together they formed such a crowd that three trips were required to ferry everyone out in the small launch to where the *Tarana*, a trawler with a British crew, lay silent and unobtrusive.

Paula Spriewald, the daughter of a Socialist member of the Reichstag, came from a very anti-Nazi family. Soon after Hitler assumed power, she and her father fled from Germany, and reached Paris.

Her father went to the USA but Paula stayed in France, and became a close friend of Madame Emy Savinos. Both had been convinced anti-Nazis whilst in Germany. Paula settled into living with the Savinoses in Marseille, and rendered the organisation many useful services, including acting as Pat's secretary. With this first party to be shipped to England from Canet-Plage went Francis Blanchain, to whom Paula was later to be married in London.

This successful operation was to be the first of many that were to become ever more necessary if Marseille was not to become clogged with Allied airmen awaiting return to the UK.

London was by now mounting massive bombing sorties over Europe. Precious aircrews were falling or floating down as they crashed or baled out of crippled planes on to the fair but frightening fields of France. Pat, anxious to promote the obvious advantages of large-scale evacuation by sea, and with London's approval was already planning another for 5th October 1942.

This new method of departure with as many as thirty or forty leaving at a time, was soon to relieve the pressure on Spain and Gibraltar where accumulations of men had begun to present a major problem.

Louis Nouveau described how rapidly men could on occasions be returned to their units.

How uncertain and chancy things can be! On one hand some of the fellows spent six months from the day they were shot down, to the day of their arrival back in England.

For example, six weeks concealed in some peasant's house, a fortnight staying in Marseille or Toulouse, a week for the trip across the mountains, then if arrested in Spain, three weeks in Miranda Internment Camp, a week to reach Gibraltar, and another waiting there for a convoy, and finally a last week at sea to reach England.

Figures like these were quite normal. On the other hand one fellow who passed through our hands, from what Pat told me on his return from Gibraltar, was only a fortnight on the way between the day he was shot down, and the time he arrived back in England.

He was shot down somewhere in central France, in the Occupied Zone. With the help of his map, and probably from the information he obtained from signposts, he deduced what part of France he was in.

As he had a little French money on him, and could infer from the milestones that he was not far from a village on a railway, he walked a few miles, and reached the station.

Evidently having a good scent for people, he accosted someone at the station, saying simply in French, with a strong English accent: 'Please get me a ticket for –' either Bourges, or Châlons-sur-Saone, I'm not sure which, and took the train to a place a few kilometres north of the line. Then, without speaking to anybody, and guiding himself by his compass, he headed south, managed somehow to cross the demarcation line, went to another station where he repeated the same manoeuvre as before, giving someone a few French banknotes . . .

Each time the fellow he appealed to, though astonished by the speaker's accent, took a ticket for him. It was such infernal cheek on his part that the person he asked, doubtless couldn't make out who this fellow was, small and dark, and speaking French with such a perfect English accent! But how could it have been possible to imagine it was an English shot down pilot?

On arriving in Lyons and naturally feeling rather lost in the station, he got into conversation with someone (he must have been a pretty good physionomist, or else prodigiously lucky in hitting upon a decent fellow) and this man directed him to the British Consulate Offices. These were then in charge of the American Consul Whitting Hill, who sent him straight to Marseille, where he arrived less than forty-eight hours after being shot down.

The day after his arrival in Marseille there happened to be a convoy leaving for Toulouse, and the day after his arrival there, another one leaving for Spain. So he finally reached Barcelona only five days after being shot down.

His luck continued. He escaped arrest in Spain, was convoyed by British agents as far as Gibraltar, probably in the luggage boot of an Embassy car, which he reached about a week after he had been shot down.

His luck still held – for there was a convoy for England leaving that very day, so that he finally made it back home about a fortnight after his mishap.

Sometimes at the Hôtel de Paris in Toulouse, we were in a position to feed airmen in their rooms. Sometimes we took them to restaurants. I remember having often 'fed' some of them in a restaurant on the Place du Capitôle at Toulouse. It was crowded, which made things easier for us. We talked to them, speaking loudly, and they nodded in agreement. Of course it was essential that they should keep mum, or their accent would have given them away at once.

The fact that the Spanish Republicans, the only ones we could use as guides, all lived in Toulouse, compelled us always to keep a regular base there at the Hôtel de Paris, but for departures only.

Clothes, identity cards, and arrangements for journeys were all dealt with in Marseille at our headquarters.

If we had had several safe houses in Toulouse, as was later the case, when Françoise* took charge, this would have saved us many journeys backwards and forwards.

But the organisation had come into being in Marseille.

The line now had many active agents in specific areas. Guy Berthet†and Robert Leycuras (known as Albert) were two police inspectors who had served sentences for organising resistance amongst fellow police in Paris. They were tirelessly active as couriers and travelled widely for the line. Jacques Watterbled, Jean de la Olla, Norbert Fillerin and Costa Dimpoglou the Greek with the lively personality and quick wits – all functioned from Paris and the north on Pat's business.

At the Martins' house in Endoume‡ [wrote Nouveau] twelve men could be hidden without undue difficulty . . . Twelve was far too large a number to accommodate at the Hôtel de Paris, where it was hard to keep a close eye on them, and where they were also not so well fed. Still we were lucky to have this hotel, and to be able to count on the assistance of the worthy owner Madame Mongelard.

London was conscious that individual operations of escape networks, and members of SOE working in isolation, served little purpose unless acting as a cohesive whole, part of the grand strategy as conceived in Whitehall. Radio communication was the most vital and overriding necessity. The success or failure of every individual operation required a wireless operator, whose comfort and safety were paramount. Nobody was more perilously placed than the man whose trained ears and nimble fingers kept the lines of communication open. Others might, with cleverly forged documents lie and act their way out of tight corners.

But the man with the cumbersome set, capable of transmitting to England, his receiver forever tuned to the forbidden wavelength was inevitably burdened every single day by the visible and tangible evidence of his guilt.

---

* Françoise Dissart, in her late fifties at this time, suffered from poor health. She lived near the Gestapo HQ in Toulouse at No 12 Rue Paul Mariel. When Louis Nouveau went north, a new centre was established in her flat there, and she continued to send, and personally escort evaders as far as the frontier until the Liberation.

† Guy Berthet was to die a grim death at the Gestapo's hands.

‡ Less centrally placed than the other three safe houses down close to the Vieux Port.

In April 1942 Donald Darling, Jimmy Langley, and Pat met in Gibraltar. They discussed amongst other things sea evacuations, the desperate need for radio operators, money for the line, and the matter of Paul Cole, who known to be still in operation, was suspected of working for the Germans.

As an urgent priority it was agreed that they would change as many addresses, post-boxes, and cover names that Cole would know as possible. Orders were sent to all underground groups in France that he was a traitor and should be shot on sight. MI9 in London now agreed to warn SOE and other Intelligence services.

It was proving easy enough to receive the twice-daily messages from London, despite enemy jamming, but primitive methods of getting the ever more numerous and important messages *to* London were no longer satisfactory.

In response to urgent requests, Jimmy Langley had brought with him to Gibraltar a wireless operator for Pat, a tall thin Belgian called Ferière. From the start Pat was not impressed with what he saw of him, and mistrusted him as being unlikely to be a serious and dedicated member of the network. He said as much to Jimmy, once he had had a long talk with Ferière in Donald Darling's flat and had put him through his paces. Not only did Pat not take to Ferière as a person, but he remained obstinately unconvinced of the man's motives for returning to France in this capacity.

He did not sense any great patriotic fervour, or the kind of hatred of the enemy that would be needed to justify this chosen dangerous way of life.

'I just did not like the smell of him,' Pat told me. 'And when I asked him why he wanted to join us, he had no good reason at all. He said that it must be a very interesting way of life, and he seemed to assume that we would only be operating in the unoccupied zone in the south. But I soon undeceived him about that!'

'We function all over France. We shall most certainly be working in the occupied zone, too,' Pat told him.

'In Paris, too?' Ferière enquired, hesitantly.

'Yes, of course in Paris!' Pat replied. 'And the Gestapo are becoming increasingly competent with their detector vans. So it really is a most dangerous job, and I shall expect you to be adept at coping with such problems, and able to move quickly from place to place.'

'He seemed only moderately enthusiastic or interested in how we worked, and not motivated as he should have been, and as we all were,' Pat told me.

The man began to look distinctly uneasy, and Pat decided that a few whiskies might loosen him up a bit. He took Ferière away from Donald's flat, and made it his business to get the man well and truly drunk. Only in this way did he feel that he might find out what made this wireless operator tick, and why he had volunteered to leave the safety of Britain in order to join an escape line. There was still time for him to change his mind and go back with Jimmy to London. But time was very short.

Pat's scheme worked like a charm, and soon it all began to come out. The man was unmasked as a maudlin, blubbering, self-confessed inadequate. All that he had really wanted was to rejoin his wife Mimi who lived near Marseille, and from whom he had been parted when he was evacuated from Dunkirk with the BEF.

Taking this job had seemed to Ferière the only way to get back to Mimi in the middle of a war. But to Pat it was not a good and sufficient reason for taking him on.

'You can keep your wireless operator,' Pat had said to Jimmy the following day, and told him of his findings of the night before. 'I really do not need a chap like that! I simply cannot work with a man who is only motivated by a desire to return to his wife!'

But Jimmy, anxious to help Pat out and thinking that any sort of wireless operator must be better than none at all, pleaded with Pat to give the man a try. He explained that MI9 still came at the end of the line for priority in allotment of radio operators and that Ferière was all Pat was likely to get.

'So', Pat told me, 'I agreed to take the man back into France with me, though I already knew it wasn't going to work. And I felt angry that the security of our carefully built-up organisation might be set at risk by a lovesick husband, and his selfish sentimental desire to return to his wife in the middle of a war!'

A few days later, lugging a bulky canvas-wrapped package containing a portable transmitting and receiving set Type 3, Mark II, built into a small leather suitcase, and weighing $32\frac{3}{4}$ lbs, Pat and Ferière were put ashore at Canet-Plage in the early hours of the morning.

They had travelled on the *Tarana*, the disguised trawler used for landing and taking off agents and evaders; her ship's boat, with specially lagged rowlocks, had brought them silently ashore.

As the sun rose they crept towards the Hôtel du Tennis. The proprietress, Madame Chouquette, and her husband were already working for the line and they and their hotel were play an ever more important part in the escape line.

This hotel had many advantages. It was just large enough to accommodate the groups of passengers who would gather there, prepared to embark during the hours of darkness, and its remote situation on the beach did not attract too much attention from the Milice or Gestapo.

Pat noticed that already, even within the comparatively safe and secluded surroundings of the hotel, Ferière was showing signs of panic every time he was faced with strangers. Two days later, whilst it was still dark, Pat had him back on the beach helping to dig in the sand for the precious material they had buried on landing, after which they boarded the train from Perpignan to Marseille.

It soon became obvious who would be carrying the parcel through the various control points.

Vincent Brome in his book *The Way Back* gives a vivid description of how this was eventually achieved.

The thought of smuggling a wireless set through the dangerous area reduced Ferière to sudden silence. Quite clearly if anyone was to get it through successfully, it wouldn't be Ferière.

Suddenly a loud voice speaking in a broad *Marseillais* accent said: 'Why Pat! You here! I thought you were in . . .'

Pat gestured for silence. The irrepressible Gaston Nègre could never quite believe that the sphere of his influence did not extend from his home in Nîmes to the remotest corner of Marseille.

He seemed if anything a little fatter, his cheeks were pinker, and the inevitable cigarette remained screwed into the corner of his mouth. Lounging in the corridor he smiled as Pat explained his trouble with the canvas parcel.

Big, booming, without any regard for the elementary laws of secrecy, Gaston laughed.

'Don't worry, Pat, don't worry! I'll fix that!'

I'll fix that! With extraordinary consistency, Gaston Nègre always did. Whether it involved spiriting away secret documents from a gendarmerie, forging passes, smuggling prisoners into his house, or providing food for half a battalion of escaped British soldiers, he always did what he undertook to do.

Clearly the mere matter of getting a large transmitter through the controls in a huge station was to him child's play. Precisely how it was done, no one ever asked. Obviously he had some secret method of egress from the station which not even the stationmaster seemed to to know. He met Pat two hundred yards from the station, swinging the canvas parcel ostentatiously in his hand.

In Marseille they made their way to number 21 Rue Roux de Brignoles.

Pat was greeted with warm affection at the Rodocanachis', and not a little relief too. For Mario Prassinos, who had been deputising in Pat's absence, had been sent for from Barcelona to go to Geneva, and Louis had been holding the fort. Now Prassinos had returned, and Nouveau had taken his place in Geneva.

Pat resumed his duties at once, prepared to put his new apparatus and operator to the test.

Dr Rodocanachi, alerted to the fact that Pat would be returning with a transmitter and operator, had risked attracting the unwelcome attention and snide remarks of his neighbours.

'He installed a perfected antenna from the roof of the house to his bedroom, which caused comment from the concierges,' Fanny Rodocanachi has recorded, and continues :

From time to time transmissions were made from the flat* with necessary interludes, so that the Gestapo, whose headquarters in Marseille was just a few streets away in the Rue Paradis, should not not be able to locate whence they originated.

There were also the codes to prepare, and the messages to be decoded : and also the listening in constantly to know the answers, and notices about arrivals of the submarines and planes to fetch the men away.

What a hive of activity that seemingly innocent medical flat must have

* The Nouveaus' and the Nègres' flats were also being used for radio reception and transmission at this time. But of course none of them knew about the others.

been at that time. Fanny herself a frail-looking woman of 57, was soon to undergo major surgery for abdominal cancer in a hospital in the town.

'Now a pitiful scene took place,' Pat told me. 'The whole purpose of having a transmitter was so that we might ourselves call London on our own account, taking the initiative.

'But these contacts had to be made at specific times on specific days. It was a very precise business, and the air was alive with such communications, and every second counted.'

A really dedicated wireless operator was forever worried as to the whereabouts of his set, and whether it was properly and safely hidden. Constantly aware of the exact time of the day or night, his whole life geared to, and organised around his pre-scheduled times for transmitting and receiving messages, he lived in perpetual fear of detection by police listening sets.

'I had alerted Dr Rodocanachi to the fact that we would be calling London at 17.00 hours, and that his new antenna would be coming into play.

'Madame Rodocanachi was already tapping feverishly at her typewriter to muffle and blur any tell-tale staccato crackle of morse which might reach the ears of patients in the waiting-room. This was an important moment for us all. A watershed.'

It was hoped that the black Citroen, a car much favoured by the Gestapo, which had been observed cruising slowly up and down the street, was not in the neigbourhood at this time. For it was common knowledge that there had been talk of a transmitter in the district. A man had been seen standing on the running-board of the car wearing ear-phones and taking bearings, though so far it seemed that the Gestapo had not been able to locate it.

Ferière, who was by now well aware of Pat's mobility, his instant arrivals and departures, his volatile reappearances, and meticulous timing, knew that he would be with him in good time for the five o'clock transmission. Sure enough at four-thirty the sound of Séraphine's voice greeting him at the door, put Ferière in a state of near panic.

Already there had been angry words exchanged between the two men, when Ferière had told Pat that he wasn't keen on using the new external aerial.

'They taught us at college that in these conditions, it is better to set up an internal aerial,' he had said with all the authority of an experienced practitioner.

But Pat was simply not convinced. He suspected that for some obscure reason this man was conning him.

'How on earth can you transmit all that distance with a rubbishy little internal aerial?' he had snorted. 'When we've got a proper mast set up outside for this specific purpose it simply doesn't make sense. Anyhow, I'll be back in plenty of time and we'll start calling London at once. Like that we won't miss a minute of our time. And we'll see how well your internal transmitting system works!'

And so saying, he had stormed out slamming the door behind him.

Now as he moved into the flat exchanging his shoes for his carpet-slippers, he went towards the room at the back where the transmitter was to be set up. To his astonishment there was no sign of Ferière.

Instead, as Vincent Brome recounts, he became almost instantly enmeshed in a positive spider's web of wires which had been wound around the walls and furniture, carried up to picture-rails, stretched across the landings and festooned the length of the pelmets.

Led to the source of this tangled web, he found the set in the bathroom perched perilously on the edge of the bath, and Ferière anxiously manipulating the dials.

Pat saw red. But restricting his comments to a drily explicit 'so', he kept his disciplined mouth shut, whilst the petrified Ferière explained the elaborate positioning of his wiring for maximum efficiency, his rubber bath-mat to deaden the sound.

Pat's stop-watch indicated the moment when for the first time he would be heard speaking from his Marseille headquarters. He now gave all his attention to the messages he would be sending, as Ferière, a ghastly pale colour, sweated profusely in the last few seconds, awaiting Pat's order, 'Start now!'

London could be heard distinctly, urgently pleading with him to 'Speak'. . . Pat was himself obviously quite inaudible to them, and nothing that he was saying was getting through, though their 'Speak' call was proof that they were expecting to hear from him. The time was running out fast. Then suddenly, London stopped calling, and it was too late to try again.

It was at this critical moment of disappointment and frustration that the wretched Ferière chose to give himself away when he said, as though thinking out loud :

'You know, it's extremely dangerous doing transmitting like this, if it's to be heard in London. If they can hear us, then so can the Gestapo with their detecting devices.'

And Pat, incredulous, shocked, knew at last that this man was simply terrified of being caught and had never had any real intention of using his transmitter in such a fashion that the Germans as well as London might hear him.

It was a moment of complete shambles. Pat was disgusted, so much was at stake.

After trying to get some sort of sense out of the machine and failing to do so, he threw down the head-set.

'You bastard !' he remembers calling over his shoulder as he stormed out of the room. At six o'clock he tried again. But his hard-won transmitter, manhandled so dangerously all those perilous miles on streets, trams, and railway was useless without an operator.

Later that evening Séraphine admitted a distraught Ferière, who had failed to return to the flat to try again at the six o'clock transmitting time. Dishevelled, out of breath and totally confused, he had even managed to miss the train he was taking from the Gare St Charles.

There was no way that this man was ever going to be any good in any capacity, Pat decided. Such an incompetent, inefficient and weak character, who could not be relied upon in an emergency, was the sort of luxury the line could ill afford.

A man who knew too many precious addresses in the town, must go at the earliest possible moment. Such a vulnerable man was a constant threat to them all, and he and his wife must be removed to a place of safety at once.

Pat called on Ferière's Belgian wife Mimi who was completely taken aback to hear that her husband had undertaken such a dangerous job, and one that was completely out of character.

'He would only have done it because he loves me, and could think of no other way of rejoining me,' she said.

Pat was quick to see them both safely escorted along the line, and back to England.

Still minus a wireless operator, Pat approached Gaston Nègre, the man whose vast fourteen-roomed flat was almost continuously full of hidden parcels, and whose wholesale grocery business in Nîmes was a wonderland of black market food and drink. Characteristically he produced an unemployed radio operator who had once worked at the airport at Nîmes : a Frenchman called Roger.

Over glasses of *pastis* Pat confided in Roger, describing his needs, and the job was agreed.

Meanwhile Jimmy Langley sent Pat a substitute for the failed Ferière, and instantly and improbably there arrived their one-eyed friend Jean Nitelet.

'He was generally known as Jean le Nerveu, or Restless Johnny,' wrote Louis Nouveau, and continued :

> Having failed, owing to the loss of the eye, to find an active job in the RAF, and burning with eagerness to do something, he had volunteered to be parachuted back into France to serve with some underground organisation.
>
> He had taken a successful course in wireless, which his duties as an airman had made it easy for him to pick up.

Returning at night in an RAF Lysander, Nitelet had narrowly escaped arrest. The aircraft had come down near Châteauroux but the pilot had been unable to take off again. When all efforts to get the wheels out of the soft ground had failed, the plane had had to be abandoned.

Nitelet had struggled with his bulky radio set, and made his way to the Nouveaus' door.

In April 1942 everything seemed to happen. Paul Cole crossed the demarcation line and was arrested at the Hôtel d'Angleterre in Lyons by pro-Allied Vichy French Police. Later he was to be released by the Germans, when the latter occupied the Southern Zone in November of that year.

In April 1942 Léoni Savinos was arrested after carrying out numerous dangerous missions for Pat. And as if these dramatic events following so swiftly upon one another within that month were not enough – Pat's new wireless operator Roger was arrested too. He was in the very act of receiving a message from London, when with a gun pressed into his back he was dragged off to gaol.

Pat didn't hear of this arrest until a couple of days later, and had not been able to understand the total silence from London.

Meanwhile Nitelet was up in Brittany upon other work connected with trying to establish an escape route by sea through Brittany, as instructed to do before leaving London. His absence further aggravated Pat's loss of contact with London at this anxious time.

And by the end of that fateful month Donald Caskie was arrested at his Mission building, and imprisoned in the Fort Saint-Nicolas. There he was put on probation for two years, with the alternative of being offered a flight back to Britain. When he refused this safe conduct, he was told to remove himself from Marseille to Grenoble, well away from his old haunts and contacts and supposedly therefore out of harm's way. By this time, however, sensing that he had been blown, he had hastily begun to scatter his flock and was able finally to close his empty building as ordered.

It was surely a measure of his standing in the town that he managed during the short spell of grace granted to him, to disperse and hide more than sixty soldiers, sailors and airmen at a multitude of clandestine addresses in and around Marseille.

Before releasing them to their various Safe Houses, he was careful to see that each man was well prepared and equipped for the final stage of the journey home.

All were well clothed with stout boots for mountain walking, and for good measure he added a knuckle-duster apiece.

'I used to buy them in the seedier parts of the town,' he told me. 'One at a time, in all sorts of little shops. I felt that the lads ought to be able to defend themselves. They weren't armed of course. And many of them weren't really in peak condition after being kept in cramped situations and unable to take proper exercise.'

He was indeed the good shepherd to the end.

A network of French and other Christians had come to his rescue with offers of safe-housing in his crisis. These were friends, and friends of friends who bitterly regretted the betrayal of this good man by one of their nationals within the Milice.

Many had made it their business to spread careful word of Donald's needs.

The Sûreté, the Criminal Investigation Department, he felt sure, had turned a blind eye upon his desperate efforts against the clock to clear and close his building. No doubt they reckoned that he wouldn't be around to trouble them much longer, keeping them on their reluctant toes.

Donald, in his book *The Tartan Pimpernel** has written : 'Amongst such people I had friends in the police – though others did their duty to Vichy, and were ashamed of it.'

The arrest of Léoni Savinos was a personal tragedy. But it was also one for the line since being a fluent speaker of German, he was an invaluable member of the network for dealing with the Gestapo.

Having arranged to meet various contacts who would supply him with information about five British airmen hidden near to Tours, Savinos was arrested by plain clothes Gestapo, along with another member of the line 'Petit Pierrot' of Nîmes.

They were both sent under escort to Frèsnes, a gaol situated to the west of the present Paris/Orly airport.

This was a disaster for Savinos whose wife was German. She had left Germany some time between 1931 and 1933, and had like Léoni himself been a well-known anti-Nazi. Mercifully the Gestapo were unaware of this when they caught him.

Of late he had become invaluable to the Germans, acting as a thoroughly acceptable go-between, between themselves and General Plastiras the Greek statesman living on the Riviera.

From 1941 the German High Command had had it in mind to install this eminent Greek as head of the Greek government. Gruppenführer Nosek, a high-ranking SS officer, suspected by the organisation of being a member of the Gestapo, had been sent by the Germans to negotiate and win the Greek general over to their side.

For the good offices of Savinos, his invaluable fluency in French, Greek, and German, and the sophisticated manner in which he handled the blandishments so subtly employed by the Germans, they supplied him with an official Gestapo pass. This was a prize beyond compare, which enabled him to travel freely between Marseille and Paris.

On the day he was arrested he had arranged to meet an agent from another organisation at a kiosk at the Gare Montparnasse. For various reasons, and the intense heat which had caused tracks to buckle and faults to occur on the line, as well as the delays that affected nearly all wartime trains in those days, there was a muddle over the meeting.

Léoni and Pierrot had foregathered : but there was no sign of the other man. The plan was that Pierrot should accompany Léoni, and be responsible for escorting back to Marseille with him any airmen that

* Published by Oldbourne Book Co. Ltd in 1957.

Léoni might have been able to pick up, amongst whom would be the five men in hiding near Tours.

Now as they waited tensely in this public place for their unknown agent, they repaired to the station buffet, preferring to pass the time of anxious anticipation somewhere where they could at least be seen to be occupied with a cup of ersatz coffee, and not just hanging about suspiciously for no good reason.

They all now knew the chilling fear of arrest and interrogation. But in the meantime there was always the added frustration of not knowing whether the other person would actually turn up. Would the information so dangerously obtained and passed on, in fact reach the right person? And if it did, would it be recognised for the vital material that it was? Might it lose some of its impetus and import becoming, as it passed through more than one courier, of less significance, and over-processed?

And now, suddenly, against all recommended behaviour, the wretched man approached them directly, telling them that he would be in the waiting-room with his wife.

This was the moment the Gestapo were waiting for, and at pistol-point they cornered Léoni and Pierrot, demanding to know the identity and business of the man they had just been speaking to. How right Pat had been to keep his own network intact and separate from other organisations. With perfect truth they were able to deny all knowledge of this man. Nothing would have made them divulge the content of their proposed conversation with him.

As Léoni was to say to Airey Neave in London later that year*:

'I told the truth. I didn't know that man. I had never seen him before. They took me off to Frèsnes. I was in a spot I can tell you. I had on me the key to Mario's flat, the plan of a factory that was making parts for German fighters, and £1,500 in Francs.!†

'But I also had my pass from Nosek.'

Savinos must have had extraordinary presence of mind. He explained away the key, but the factory plans were 'more awkward'.

Puzzled, the Gestapo had sent for Nosek.

'Nosek questioned me at length, and did not believe my story, that

---

* *Saturday at MI9.*

† Some of this money was his own, and some belonged to the line, and was to have been handed over to Jean de la Olla. Couriers often had to travel with considerable sums of money on them. An added responsibility, and a compromising liability if they were arrested and had to explain their full purses.

I was engaged in trading between occupied and unoccupied France. He knew me well over the Plastiras affair, so I was able to explain away the key of the flat and the French money.

'He knew that I spoke French and German and began to hint that I might like to work for the Gestapo. I was to go back to Marseille as a spy for them, and report back to Paris.'

There were many cases of such propositions being put to prisoners arrested by the Gestapo. The offer was invariably that the prisoner would be released so long as he got on with the business of betraying his friends.

Savinos's only chance was to agree with this proposal, then disappear. The Gestapo knew little at this time about O'Leary. They may have learned his description from Cole at the end of 1941, but seemed unwilling to carry out wholesale arrests in unoccupied France. They were biding their time until they had complete control, and they needed a stoolpigeon.

At Frèsnes Pierrot Lanvers was cruelly beaten up, as would Léoni have been had the prison authorities not happened upon his official pass signed by Nosek.

Had he known at that time that arrrests* were being made at his home, amongst whom was an Australian airman in hiding there, Léoni would surely have reckoned his last hour had come.

Their cell was damp and evil-smelling, and they lived there for many weeks on near-starvation diet. Time and again Pierrot was removed for further questioning, and because he wouldn't talk, for savage attacks on his person. In the meantime the authorities had awaited the arrival of Nosek to interrogate Savinos himself.

How, Nosek was asking himself, could he allow Savinos his freedom, without some sort of security against his absconding if released? A hostage would be the simplest arrangement. Léoni's wife would be just

---

* Louis Nouveau records that: 'It was dangerous to trifle with the Germans. Until the end of 1942, they shot many they arrested. It was only early in 1943 that Laval, I believe, obtained the concession that German authorities would shoot only people who actually participated in armed attacks, or were carrying arms. This explains why the Abbé Carpentier, Bruce Dowding, Dideret, and others who were already awaiting trial before the agreement was concluded, were executed, though none of those belonging to our organisation arrested after 1943 were shot . . . during the last months of the occupation, the Germans again became perfectly ruthless . . . they acted quite unpredictably, without adhering to any general rules . . .'

such a valued pledge. Savinos was horrified. His wife's anti-Nazi record would surely turn up.

'How on earth could I operate without arousing suspicion in the south, if you free me, and arrest my wife?' he asked.

'Surely you don't imagine that she would not be missed straight away? How could I possibly continue convincingly as your agent if my wife is known to have been arrested by you? Any fool would soon work *that* situation out!'

'Alright,' said Nosek. 'We will hold Pierrot Lanvers instead.'

This was a much more difficult problem for Savinos. They might do anything they liked with Pierrot, and this was unthinkable.

They might move him to another gaol, torture him even more, or remove him to a concentration camp. And since Léoni fully intended not to give satisfaction as a stoolpigeon, then poor stoical Pierrot would surely pay the price for his, Léoni's, shortcomings.

With infinite subtlety Léonie succeeded in convincing Nosek that if he himself returned to Marseille to continue to work as a spy for him, then it was important that his old friend Pierrot was seen to be with him. Any change of this kind would immediately discredit Léoni and Pierrot too. Nothing would be more likely to cause suspicion within the network, and make it difficult for him to do Nosek's bidding. In fact he really could not even undertake to work efficiently for the Gestapo, unless the status quo was maintained.

The astonished Pierrot was soon released, and both men were free to leave Frèsnes : a rare achievement.

Savinos returned quietly to Marseille, where he went immediately to report to Pat at the Rodocanachis. He still had his priceless official pass. But the money taken from him at Frèsnes was never recovered.

Pierrot Lanvers travelling, as always, separately from his colleague was less fortunate. Still in pain from his repeated beatings-up, bruised and swollen with broken teeth, he had at first just not been able to believe he was free.

In his desperation to get away before the authorities changed their minds, he fled without collecting his papers. Without these, he was re-arrested and returned to Frèsnes as an escaped prisoner.

Eventually confirmation of his story came through from Paris, his papers were restored to him, and he was released to stagger home, a haggard and pitiful shadow of his former self.

Pat began immediately to make arrangements to get Léoni, his wife and Lanvers out of France. All three were now in the greatest danger.*

To add to Pat's anxiety, two suspicious-looking men had been seen hanging about outside the Savinoses' flat in the Rue Estelle. It was feared at first that these were Gestapo spies already keeping watch on Léoni, but they turned out to be members of the French Non-Collaborationist police force in plain clothes.

Having heard of the arrest of Savinos and his subsequent release, they were now naturally enough seeing him as a German spy and were keeping him under observation.

Since Whitney Straight travelled with the precious party on board the British-owned and crewed armed trawler *Tarana*, it was with considerable relief that on 24th July 1942 a message from Donald Darling was received by Airey Neave and Jimmy Langley in London, which ended :

SENDING BY AIR AND SHOULD ARRIVE HENDON TOMORROW 25 JULY STOP PLEASE REMIND SATURDAY MADAME SAVINOS IS GERMAN REPEAT GERMAN.

Back in England Léoni and Emy Savinos still had one more hurdle to clear. Being non-British arrivals in wartime, they had to face confinement at the Royal Victoria Patriotic School at Clapham, a forbidding interrogation centre across the road from Wandsworth Gaol, where they were detained until their story was confirmed. This dreary place built in the time of Queen Victoria as an Asylum for the Orphan Daughters of Soldiers and Sailors killed in the Crimean War, had been evacuated in 1939 when it was taken over by interrogation teams.

Here the entire system was calculated by a soulless procedure, punctuated by alternating periods of suspense and boredom, to wear down, and show up, the professional double, or German agent. Detention there for however short a time, must have been a bitter anticlimax and let-down for those who had for so long looked forward to their safe arrival in Britain.

But the Savinoses were soon released, and as has been related, were to meet Airey Neave and bring him up to date with the situation in the south of France, over dinner in the West End.

* The above account of Savinos' ordeal is drawn from *The Way Back* by Vincent Brome, op cit.

CHAPTER EIGHT

The O'Leary Line under Threat

1942-1943

In August 1942 escapers and evaders in ever-increasing numbers moved towards their distant goal the Mediterranean. A blue crescent, flanked by rust-coloured Esterel Mountains, it was for many the place where they had enjoyed holidays in peace-time. Now it was a dangerous area in which a false step could lead to arrest and imprisonment. Trained as they were in hiding and evading, even the scent of crushed rosemary, lavender or thyme carried on the wind might betray them as they crouched and crept their way to the coast.

By now the Americans had arrived on the scene and escalated the numbers of men seeking an escape route to England. It was not unusual for country people harvesting their crops to come upon men who spoke little if any French, hiding amongst their vines and fig trees on the aromatic terraced vineyards above the town.

Some of these exhausted strangers travelled the last few miles into the city, hidden, cushioned and cradled in fragrance. And many an Allied serviceman was given a discreet welcome and refreshment in an old Provençal farmhouse. Tall dark cypresses planted in pairs stood sentinel at the entrance to many of these properties : one for *la paix*, peace, and the other for *la prospérité*.

Americans were now establishing their own air force in England based on their former Eagle Squadrons which flew with the RAF, and their first bombing raid over France was to attack submarine pens at l'Orient in September 1942. This was at the height of the U-boat menace to Allied shipping in the Atlantic and elsewhere.

Lightnings and Thunderbolts now gave fighter protection to American bomber formations, and the French became adept at identifying them, and noting the giant Flying Fortresses, the B17's.

Over the chocolate corduroy fields of France came, too, Hudsons and Lysanders with containered supplies, their pilots seeking charted dropping zones.

(Right) Marseille, January 1943. Prisoners being herded into rail cars.

(Below) St Pierre Prison, Marseille, where Georges Rodocanachi was first imprisoned after he was arrested at 21 Rue Roux de Brignoles. From this gaol he was brought (handcuffed to 2 gaolers) to see Fanny for the last time, as it turned out.

(Left) Water-colour se[lf] portrait of Louis Nouve[au] painted in cell 508 at Fresnes prison in Paris From Fresnes Louis Nouveau was transfer[red] to Buchenwald where [he] briefly met Doctor Rodocanachi a few da[ys] before the doctor's he[art] attack.

(Below) Conditions in Buchenwald Concentration Camp when Doctor Rodocanachi died . . just such a bunk as on[e of] these.

In the south the hot scented air wafted the perfume of orange blossom, jasmine, and violet from the hillsides ridged with meticulous cultivation, and the acres of pin-cushioned lavender. Hedge-hopping, and familiar now with secret, intimate and private places, pilots combed secluded fields in search of reception committees. These, in peril of their lives, waited to pounce upon bags and containers, and to help any Joes* being dropped or picked up.

Selected fields with wood and scrubland close by, and torches shielded from view except from the air, were by now well-known to aircrews. Things didn't always go as planned, and soon Marseille became bogged down with alarming numbers overwhelming secret hide-outs, and blocking existing escape routes. This situation was a nightmare to Pat and his team, the more so since it was becoming daily more hazardous to risk involving others within the town in Safe Housing.

Only by getting men away in much larger numbers by sea could they avoid catastrophic overcrowding in Marseille.

On 14th July (Bastille Day) 1942, in response to a broadcast from London, the people of Marseille turned out in their thousands to demonstrate their pro-Allied and anti-Nazi feelings. Assembled on the Canebière at the BBC's suggestion they paraded up and down, a vast and purposeful crowd showing dissent.

Nothing seemingly could have been more innocent. And nothing as it turned out, could have been more encouraging and supportive of those who had felt themselves isolated and in the minority in their attitude to the Vichy government. For everyone who had kept this simple appointment engineered from London, had surely been listening illegally to the BBC, and had felt an irresistible urge to stand up and be counted.

Since no rules had been broken, no charges could be made, and the crowds were free to disperse afterwards to the fury and frustration of the baffled German and Vichy authorities.

Even school children were by now beginning to join in. The Germans didn't know that the French for a safety-pin was *une épingle anglaise*, with the result that safety-pins in varying sizes became the latest craze, worn conspicuously by all age groups. Unpunishable badges of support for the Allies.

More expensive and prestigious 'safety-pins' in the form of jewelled

* An agent being dropped or picked up.

brooches were also being sported by the wealthier Marseillais. But these, being made to order, could only be commissioned from a jeweller known to be a supporter of the cause. Only when the Germans realised the meaning of the French words for safety-pin, and recognised the badges for what they signified, were they banned in all schools. But by then it was too late. The pins (along with knitted caps, ladies' compacts and ear-rings, and children's yoyos with their red, white and blue RAF roundels), and the 'Great Walk' had served their purpose.

By the autumn of 1942 the Rodocanachis like the Nouveaus were experiencing new and unexpected problems with their American visitors. Unlike the British, the Yanks didn't alarmingly attract the attention of observant policemen by looking the wrong way when being escorted across roads. But their table manners and dress were conspicuously different from those of the French or British. Shirts hanging loose outside 'pants' and not tucked within the waist-band of trousers, could be dynamite and needed checking before sallying forth into the street.

Table manners didn't matter within the safe house. But couriers convoying men from house to station, from a bus-stop to a (pro-Allied) hairdresser or photographer, or sitting opposite them as they used their eating utensils differently in cafés or restaurants, were kept constantly on edge.

Americans seem also to have been more impatient and intolerant of house-rules than were other nationals in similar circumstances. Fanny Rodocanachi has recorded their first encounter with an American visitor.

The US Consulate, until its closure and departure, and the certainty of the entry of the US into the war, had brought us very precious help, by sending to the flat all pilots who were seeking refuge.

The first American pilot who came to Dr Rodocanachi very nearly got us into very serious trouble. We advised the Consulate of his arrival, and in their delight, they begged that he should be allowed to dine with them before being sent away by convoy.

We had made it an unbreakable rule that no refugee should ever leave the house except accompanied, either to be photographed, or to go to the station ... As a favour and an exception this first American was granted permission to dine with one of the Vice-

Consuls. After his long trials – flight, hunger, privations – the shock was too great for him.

He was brought back late at night in a state of great exhilaration, and it was not an easy job to bring from the front-door of the house two storeys up to the flat, a happy but too merry pilot who would persist in singing patriotic songs.

On 6th August 1942, at eight forty-five p.m. the massive carefully planned escape had begun at the Fort de la Revère above Monte Carlo. Squadron Leader Higginson, two other officers Barnett and Hawkins, and two sergeants Derrick Nabarro and a New Zealander Pat Hickton, together with some sixty airmen and soldiers staged a monumental exit. Of these sixty or so men, thirty-four reached hideouts of the O'Leary organisation.

Dr Rodocanachi, using his curfew permit, and Pat by day, escorted small groups to individual safe houses. Later they moved the men from this temporary accommodation to a villa along the beach, hired for this specific purpose. Here, herded together behind drawn blinds and closed shutters they remained quiet. The darkened room was filled with recumbent figures smoking, chewing gum, and tense until required to move on.

Meals were brought by the Misses Trenchard, two grey-haired Scottish sisters who delighted in being involved in helping with such exciting 'underground' work, and knew where their loyalty and their duty lay. For years they had kept a small Scottish teashop in Monte Carlo, a rendezvous now for men on the run, wherein Pat, to the sisters' entire satisfaction played God, took them into his confidence, and gave his instructions.

To the Rodocanachis* came Derrick Nabarro, and Pat Hickton (known as 'Hicky'), Hawkins and Barnett.

The Nouveaus, bulging at the seams, took six including Higginson and covered their drawing-room koor with sleeping figures. They could have done with Donald's accommodation too at this time.

Five ended up at Nîmes, seven were lodged at Madame Mongelard's

---

* Fanny Rodocanachi records that between June 1941 and February 1943, they sheltered 'British soldiers, sailors and airmen, and men from Scotland, Wales, Canada, Australia, New Zealand, South Africa, Poland, Belgium, Norway, and the USA. In all some 180–200 stayed with them at various times, of whom there were 3 Commandos from the St Nazaire raid, and 2 from the Dieppe raid.'

hotel in Toulouse, some went to the Martin family near Endoume, and the rest to the Duriez family at Antibes.

All in the event were to need this secret accommodation for three more weeks, as did the stragglers from the Dieppe Raid of 19th August, of whom two turned up and were hidden at the Rodocanachis.

Derrick Nabarro in his book *Wait for the Dawn** said of this episode:

> We made for the Vieux Port district. A doctor, a Greek, and his wife hid both Barnett, who had travelled from Monte Carlo the day before, and myself. Barnett taught me the rudiments of chess, a game which passed away many an hour and proved an antidote to the boredom of waiting in our bed-sitting-room. Pat called every three days, brought food, cigarettes and the latest news concerning our escape. The day after our break-out the remaining officers in the fort had been moved to Italy. Within a week of their departure the aircrew sergeants had organised a mass escape.

Derrick Nabarro told me that the library at the Rodocanachis had been a godsend to him, and their home a haven, though confinement to one room had worried the others.

He had spent long periods alone in Stalag IIIC in Germany, and in France, and slept a lot, having been on the run for about sixteen months.

'The doctor and his wife were calm in the face of the enormous risks they were running – not for one another – but for something far more important.

'For my part I wanted to know as little as possible about the operation, the house, or the people. We could so easily have been recaptured.'

His job, he said, was to keep out of sight. And he managed to remain ignorant of the name of his hosts until after the war.

'The flat was so clean and civilised – it was a sanctuary ... I never left it during those three weeks. But there remains with me to this day, the indelible memory of the same atmosphere prevailing in that place as at bomber stations during off-duty periods. A quietness, a calmness, and something else, unspoken.'

Another account of this period of incarceration at the Rodocanachis is given by Hicky, at that time aged twenty.

* Published by Cassell & Co. 1952.

Returning from a bombing raid on Turin in a Wellington in September 1941, they had crashed just north of Mont Blanc, when their starboard propeller fell off. After hiding in Paris for four weeks, the crew crossed the demarcation line at Vierzon, and made for Marseille. But they ended up in Fort de la Revère, where Hicky met Derrick Nabarro.

'At the Old Port,' Pat Hickton said, 'a Resistance contact took over, and Pat, for it was he, who had only just heard over the BBC that he had been awarded the DSO, took us with him to celebrate in sweet and dry Vermouth. At the new place I met the doctor and Madame Rodocanachi.'

In his diary, a French one given to him when he was still in prison by Donald Caskie, Hicky wrote :

Doctor's wife a bind, but otherwise good. Dr Rodocanachi a nice old gentleman. Stopped in room set aside for us on top floor* and looked out over the main street. Drapes or type of blinds drawn : they were not to be touched, and to be kept drawn all the time.

Sentries opposite the flat were the bane of Fanny Rodocanachi's existence, for their presence required her to set out on shopping expeditions for her enlarged household only when the sentry had been changed, and had not already watched her bring a load of shopping back with her.

Hicky's diary continued :

The doctor's wife used to say that she was brought up in England, and being a doctor's wife it intrigued her to read murder mysteries, and how the doctor's wife got poison, and poisoned her husband . . .

We used to think our tucker might be laced . . . but after a few days we forgot it, as she just liked to ready mystery books, and meals were adequate with plenty of bread, tomatoes, and meat. What meat we didn't ask !

Anyhow, we weren't really interested in what we got to eat. Only that we would soon be out of it : except that there was a lot of police movement, and the enemy now and again.

* They must have been unaware, never having left the flat since their hurried arrival there with Pat, that there was a floor above them.

His diary, with so little to say, gives a touching count-down after all these years :

Saturday, 5th. No news.

Sunday, 6th. Same place. Browned off.

Monday, 7th: Heard that 58 men and NCO's escaped from Fort de la Revère.

Tuesday, 8th. 36 of the 58 back in clink. 3 RAF safe. All's well.

Wednesday, 9th. 2 of 58 arrive at Doctor's place in Marseille by themselves.

So, from Thursday 10th. September, to Wednesday 16th. – 16 army chaps safe. Pat downhearted because there were only 3 RAF, and what they really wanted at present was as many airmen as possible, as they were the backbone. Army chaps only help to flood the 'Line' when quick and safe movement is essential.

Thursday, 17th. All is set. Leave on Sat. morning 7.0.

Friday, 18th. Bragging all day. But good fun, and fills in time.

Saturday, 19th. Left for Perpignan. All ranks arrived and journeys without incident.

Monday, 21st September. At 1.0 this morning boarded boat (schooner) feeling very happy.

Tuesday, 22nd. Sick all day : did not care about anything. Bully all meals.

Wednesday, 23rd. Same

Thursday, 24th. Met Destroyer. Schooner had about 200 Polish refugees on it for England. Then to Gibraltar.

Saturday, 26th September. Arrived Gib. Air raid first night. Left for England in HMS *Malaya* at 9.0 p.m.

Monday, 5th October 1942 arrived Greenock 7.0 p.m.

On 19th August the BBC reported the Dieppe raid. The two evaders hidden at the Rodocanachis after avoiding capture following this raid reached home safely.

Life at the Nouveaus' followed the same day by day strict routine. One escaper, Philip Newman, recalls his host vividly :

His appearance was quite unforgettable. Thin, of medium height, wearing a light grey, well tailored suit with a spotted bow tie, his attitude at once suggested activity and competence. He had a small moustache and more horn-rimmed glasses and his greying hair was slightly deranged. His expression of sincerity broke very quickly into one of humour and gaiety.

'I like to eat breakfast among my books, it gives me food for thought for a busy day.'. . . .

While he was talking and I was guzzling fish, he got up and reached for a large book, the first of a series of volumes on one of the shelves. He brought it down to the table. It was Volume I, *Oeuvres Completes de Voltaire*. . . .

'You are the sixty-fifth person through this file,' he said, with obvious pride and I noted that it corresponded to the number of the page.'*

Yet these extra mouths to feed were presenting an increasing problem. Food, Louis says, was in very short supply from the end of 1941 onwards, so that even his totally honest wife Renée was driven to helping herself to odd pieces of bread, or purloining 'bread tickets' at the station canteen at the Gare St Charles. The bread tickets were exchanged by soldiers, who left them in lieu of the sandwiches they bought. My aunt Netta tells me that she did in fact receive complaints from other Red Cross ladies working voluntarily at the station canteen. 'That Madame Nouveau, she's helping herself to bread,' they told her, full of righteous and justifiable indignation. But my loyal and disbelieving aunt would have none of it, and managed somehow to calm everybody down. Today Renée (much to my aunt Netta's amusement) says that she did indeed stuff hunks of bread into the bib of her Red Cross apron, or hide it under her cape as she hurried home to her hungry young visitors. The end, as she saw it, justified the means, and when she able to do so, she unburdened herself of her guilty secret to her good friend Madame Zarifi.

*

Clearing up after a drop at 2.0 a.m. Jean Nitelet and Gaston Nègre were arrested in the very act of manhandling the precious containers, and hauling them from the moonlit field where they had landed. With them had been Mario, also defying the curfew and hiding in a wood close to the dropping zone, waiting to hear the sound of engines before risking the prearranged signal for dropping. It was not unknown for

* *Safer than a Known Way*, William Kimber 1983.

containers to be picked up by a Gestapo reception committee and purloined by the enemy.

These drops were always fraught with possible hazards. The reception committees began their work as soon as they heard the 13.00 hours transmissions. They had in any case to reach the dropping zone before the time of the curfew, which in winter was a problem since curfew for four months of the year, was before the 18.00 hours confirmatory broadcast.

Group Captain Griffiths who carried out such operations over France, describes the situation in his book *Winged Hours**:

> If they lived some way away, they usually had to cycle to get to the DZ† area before sundown. Then there were the spades to be found to bury the load, or maybe a horse and cart to be procured to take the load away for hiding, so that the DZ would be clear by dawn.
>
> And all this had to be done in the greatest secrecy, for security was paramount. The fewer people involved the less could be revealed.
>
> Even when they arrived at the DZ their problems were not yet over. In wintertime, having arrived before curfew, one of their number living locally would listen for the confirmatory message at 18.00 hours.
>
> If there was no message the drop was not on, but they couldn't go home until the curfew was lifted next morning. This meant sleeping the night in the odd haystack, or if they were lucky on the floor in a friend's house.

RAF crews who regularly dropped supplies to reception committees were well aware that should *they* fall into enemy hands they would be treated as POW's. Their admiration was great for those on the ground who risked torture and death should they be caught if a drop went wrong.

This one had gone badly wrong as guards had come running from the very woods in which the Resisters were hiding. Bursting out into the moonlight, they had arrested Jean Nitelet and Gaston Nègre, and only Mario, distraught and dishevelled had managed to escape and carry the news to Pat at the railway station rendezvous.

* Published by William Kimber in 1981.
† Dropping Zone.

All should have gone well, and Pat, mentioning the arrests of two very precious members of their escape line to Derrick Nabarro at the Rodocanachis', said : 'We'll get over it.' But he was careful to hide his anxiety. Nevertheless, the money and supplies sent out in that most important drop, by Jimmy Langley, were recovered. However Pat was left to the torment of wondering what incriminating documents or information Jean or Gaston might have been carrying on their persons. And yet again he was without a wireless operator.

At this critical time and until London was able to send him a replacement, he was driven to send messages by the forbidden method of contacting agents in other networks, when he needed to be in touch with London.

The large party destined to foregather for return by sea to the UK converged via Perpignan on the accommodation arranged by Pat, close to Canet-Plage.

'For three weeks we hid in the doctor's house,' Derrick Nabarro said. 'Then late one evening we walked to the station and caught a train.'

Simple as this sounds, the Rodocanachis and Nouveaus must have gone in fear of all their lives through the deserted, curfewed streets of Marseille.

Louis has recorded that it was safer to travel *à deux* than alone. The police were more likely to interrogate a solitary person than two travelling in each other's company.

It was considered dangerous to escort more than two men at a time, unable to speak French, and looking 'a bit odd' in a railway carriage. You could never leave them alone, since you had always to be ready to jump in and speak up for them, or smooth over any difficulties.

Two other men travelled from Marseille to Perpignan at about this time. Georges Zarifi accompanied a very frail and limping André Postel-Vinay. Hobbling along, supported by a walking-stick lent by Georges this tall bespectacled man with the sad sensitive face was also destined to travel to England and safety. He had worked with Garrow and Pat over many anxious months, but had suddenly been arrested without any warning by two Gestapo agents as he was waiting at a rendezvous at the Café aux Deux Magots in Paris.

His first contact with the line had been made through Georges Zarifi himself, and the interview had been with Dr Rodocanachi at his flat in

Marseille on the afternoon of Cole's confrontation in Garrow's room there. Postel-Vinay had let it be known that he was in a position to collect military and other information concerning the Germans, but didn't know how he might pass this on to de Gaulle in London.

The rendezvous had been made after Pat had been approached, and had agreed to pass messages to London along with his own. A double-bottomed box of victuals destined for Georges Zarifi would reach the flat in the Rue Roux de Brignoles, and receive prompt attention. The whole business was quite separate from the escape network, and Georges Zarifi was desperately anxious not further to compromise his uncle. But the Rodocanachis' flat would surely serve as the ideal place for Pat to receive and transmit the material from Paris.

Because of his activities Postel-Vinay was arrested by two Gestapo agents at pistol point, and flung into gaol at Frèsnes where he was cruelly tortured. In despair, and fearing that under duress he might lose control and betray certain people, he made a courageous attempt at killing himself whilst he was being taken from his cell for yet another interrogation.

In solitary confinement awaiting torture he became acutely distressed to realise that amongst his possessions the Gestapo had removed a small notebook in which were the code names of a number of agents. Without any addresses to match them these people were safe. But he began then to doubt his ability to withstand continued torture. He determined to throw himself from the balcony, a drop of some thirty feet to the courtyard below. Freeing himself frantically from his guards, and crashing to the stone floor he fractured his spine, pelvis, and one leg. But he came to in mental anguish, to realise that he was still alive and able to be forced to talk.

Unconscious to begin with, and in hospital at last, he had in the meantime been manhandled back to his cell until it was realised that he could only be of use to his inquisitors if treated.

For six months he lingered on in hospital in a critical condition, until miraculously he saw and took his chance. With the implicit but unspoken connivance of the doctor, who had left him alone and unattended whilst he himself remained discreetly absent for long enough, the patient dragged himself from the room and mingled with a group of workmen leaving the building.

Struggling to the Metro, Postel-Vinay appealed to a group of small boys, telling them his pitiful situation, and begging the money for his train fare home.

They, delightedly entering into the adventure, pressed a few francs into his trembling hand. He had help too from the Stationmaster who phoned his sister, and kept him warm and under supervision until she arrived to fetch him.

Six weeks later Postel-Vinay turned up at the Zarifis' seeking a way to escape to England, before the Gestapo should catch up with him. He remained hidden at the Zarifis' under medical care from Georges Rodocanachi until he was strong enough to travel down the Line.

It was at this point that young Georges Zarifi helped himself to one of his father's fine walking-sticks : for how otherwise was the limping man to reach England on his weak and shaking legs, and his newly-healed fractures?

'I accompanied him by train as far as Perpignan,' Georges said. 'But I didn't witness the embarkation by boat or submarine.'

Now the cold weather had come round again. There was no heating at all and food was scarcer than ever. The Germans, frustrated by the known successes of the various Allied escape routes out of Europe, tightened things up.

In October they began infiltrating the unoccupied zone – thus breaking the terms of the armistice.

On 11th November Hitler hit back as a rejoinder for the American landings in North Africa, Operation Torch, and Montgomery's successes in the desert battle against Rommel, and German troops crossed the demarcation line. On 12th November 1942 they entered Marseille.

Intent upon taking over the powerful French Mediterranean Fleet at Toulon, German troops advanced in that direction. With only hours to spare before their arrival the French succeeded in sinking their fleet of 73 ships as they rode at anchor in Toulon harbour, and the myth of Vichy sovereignty was also at an end. The swastika was now to float over the whole of France.

Everywhere, the French were confronted by the Gestapo, and the German military presence was an obscenity to many.

For the O'Leary Line it was a disaster. Pat became anxious about Garrow's situation at Meauzac. For Ian, through one of the guards, had got wind of new plans and had managed to smuggle a message out to Pat, telling of his proposed deportation to Germany.

Pat immediately contacted London. Once in Germany, Ian would be destined to spend the rest of his ten-year sentence, according to the guard, in the hell-hole that was Dachau.

'Shall I take risks involved to save Garrow?' he asked London. Receiving a non-committal answer, he started to make his own plans, and sent Francis Blanchain to reconnoitre in the Meauzac area. The situation had to be sized-up, estimates of difficulties to be overcome, made, and local contacts established.

In October 1942, Pat had received a new wireless operator from England. A twenty-one-year-old Australian called Tom Groome* who, thanks to his French-born mother, spoke excellent French. He was landed from a Polish ship at Canet-Plage, and due to his competence and timely arrival, Pat was able to keep in touch with MI9 throughout the whole of the Meauzac affair.

One of the first messages with which Groome had to concern himself was the one which announced the departure from Marseille of the Nouveaus. As the German troops advanced towards the Mediterranean they launched major attacks on civilians running escape networks. Three hundred or more Gestapo and Abwehr agents had been deployed in advance of the occupation of the southern zone, and had entered the area, already in possession of police papers supplied by Vichy.

Intense police activity, and an alarming sudden increase in the numbers of hidden German agents operating and mingling with civilians in the town, greatly added to the daily hazards of the networks. Paul Cole, released by the new masters in the south, had just reappeared on the scene, welcomed and made much fuss of as their long-lost collaborator.

Pat was out to get him so that he should not escape retribution, now that for the first time since his confrontation with him at the Rodocanachis' he actually knew where Paul was. But much more urgent than nailing Cole was the need to get Renée and Louis out of Marseille.

Pat was in Toulouse when towards the end of June 1942 word had reached him via two agents, that the Gestapo were on to the Nouveaus' flat. It was only a matter of time now. They must be told to close their

* Tom Groome was awarded an OBE.

delightful home at once, every trace of their activities removed, and all members of the network informed accordingly.

No more visitors must head for that flat, wasting dangerous time knocking at a door that was sure to be watched, and walking straight into a trap. Louis was to take the train to Paris, prepared to take charge up there, and Renée went to live with Françoise Dissart in Toulouse, of whom more will be said later. It was the end of an era, and for the Nouveaus, of their home-life together. As Louis saw his wife off at the Gare St Charles, the clouds of steam that engulfed her face seemed symbolic of the unseen and unimaginable events that lay ahead of them. One thing they both knew, and accepted, was that they must not risk meeting again until victory was won.

Pat travelled with Louis as far as Montauban, where Tom Groome met him on the platform. One door had closed : but another was about to open. Ian Garrow was in desperate danger. Once at Dachau, there would be no way that the line could help him. This was Pat's opportunity for repaying the debt he owed Garrow for getting him out of St Hippolyte du Fort.

*

Francis Blanchain had played his part, and Pat had laid his plans accordingly. A Jewish tailor called Paul Ullmann was to make a guard's uniform, working with his wife against the clock to have it ready to be smuggled into the prison by one of the guards, prepared to see it into Ian's cell. The money demanded for this service was considerable : the bulk to be paid to the man's wife, and the rest in cash to him, once Garrow was safely free. Nancy Fiocca and Pat, with others, made elaborate plans, and Nancy contributed generously to help fund the enterprise.

Meauzac was reckoned to be a particularly difficult gaol from which to escape, and was habitually reserved for those sentenced to life imprisonment or death.

Unforeseen difficulties arose, however. The uniform so faithfully and hurriedly copied became useless once the new régime led to a sudden change in the routine of the prison. Under the Germans instantly in occupation, different guards in different uniforms took over.

Once again the Jewish tailor and his wife set to work and made a replacement for the uniform, and the new one was completed during a night of frantic cutting and stitching.

Next day, in the company of two Frenchmen armed with revolvers, Pat similarly ready to give battle if need be, remained hidden with them about fifty yards from the exit from the gaol. In an agony of suspense he watched the tall figure with its distinctive walk stroll nonchalantly through the gates amongst the night shift coming off-duty at dawn on 6th December 1942.

The familiar face was gaunt in the glare of the prison lights, the cheeks and eyes sunken. Three weeks of lying low were to precede Ian's departure along his own line. Pat travelled with him to the border where, in a shepherd's hut with restrained emotion, they parted.

Crossing the Pyrenees, within a few days Ian Garrow reached London, travelling by air from Lisbon. At Airey Neave's flat he told him about Pat's now desperate situation, and the poignant last words he had said to Ian as they shook hands :

'Can this go on much longer?'

With his habitual concern for the safety of the other members of his team, Pat had arranged that a submarine soon to be taking a large party to England would also include any of the network who wished to leave.

Since the Rodocanachis' flat was suspected of being under surveillance, he offered the doctor a passage to safety whilst there was still time to anticipate his arrest. But Georges Rodocanachi who well knew the gravity of his wife's condition, refused to leave her. She was, until her dying day, to feel responsible for his remaining behind, and blamed herself for his arrest.

Thanking Pat for his courtesy and concern, Georges Rodocanachi explained the need for him to remain, and continued his work.

After the departure of the last big party from Canet-Plage, with the small boat full to the gunwales making its fourth trip from the beach to the ship lying out in deep water, Pat and his team dispersed by torchlight.

Gaston Nègre, in gaol at Castres since his arrest at the drop, was Pat's next concern. With the occupation of the south, however, it was proving ever more difficult to find people willing to become involved in such a dangerous rescue-operation. Few wanted to have anything to do with such contaminating people as members of an escape network. Too many Marseillais had already been deported to Germany on the flimsiest of excuses, and ghastly rumours and stories were circulating about the treatment being meted out to anyone who could be said, however remotely, to be connected with a foreign power.

Everyone feared his neighbour. People looked warily round in the streets before they carried on a conversation. Military uniforms were to be seen everywhere. A sort of grey-green plague had engulfed the town. The atmosphere can even be sensed from the photographs in this book.

Alone, or in groups the Germans were conspicuous for the vacuum that seemed naturally to occur around them. Remaining aloof, they yearned for acceptance and approbation as the locals passed by, preferring to keep an irreproachable distance from the new authority.

Some neighbours, patients, and even friends of the Rodocanachis began now to shun them, crossing the road hurriedly if they saw them coming, preferring not to risk being seen talking to them. This deterioration in their hitherto happy relationships made them feel isolated and threatened. The net was surely closing.

Eventually after the doctor had been arrested and the news spread local tradespeople became aware of Fanny's difficult situation. It was then that countless 'little people' rallied around, pressing upon her small gifts of every kind according to their limited means and personal possibilities. Many were grateful patients of the doctor's who now lavished upon the convalescent Madame Rodocanachi, all the accumulated goodwill and gratitude of a lifetime's selfless doctoring in the town.

Visualising Fanny's newly straitened circumstances, her husband's earning abilities suspended, they pleaded with her to accept these gifts with no strings attached, and pressed her to use the food to hasten her own recovery, and to help improve her husband's miserable lot in St Pierre Gaol.

Even the little local *'garagiste'* went to enormous lengths to try to safeguard the four tyres on the doctor's car, against the day when he should return and need to use it again.

As a doctor, his car was exempted from such abuse: but the tyres were taken for all his efforts. But that was in the future. Now nobody knew what were to be the rules of the new game of 'occupation', and there was a fair amount of panic in the air.

The dreaded tabs with SS on the collars of the Gestapo, and Germans everywhere in all sorts of different uniforms not yet identified, caused people to keep their mouths shut and hurry on their way.

German officials now controlled all the railways of France. But the *Cheminots* who kept the service running, bravely continued to help the Allies as slow, overcrowded trains struggled across France despite sabotaged tracks, points, bridges and signal-boxes.

Secret listeners to London had learnt by tragic experience never to leave their sets switched to the BBC. Yet the radio was their most prized possession, and many crouched over their sets in the privacy of bedroom or bathroom, some listening through the deadening sound of running water.

Up and down the line, new German passes were stolen and copied, precautions redoubled, and passwords revised. Fanny Rodocanachi constantly busy decoding messages from London, was increasingly alert to comings and goings at her home. Heightened tension meant that a ring at the door, the sound of a lift being summoned to descend, and the vibrations as it clanked its metallic way up again, could cause the elderly household to tremble.

The clash of the lift gates, or an unfamiliar car seen cruising unduly slowly along the street below, its engines idling as it paused at intervals, its lights dimmed – or a telephone call that didn't quite fit into the usual routine of the family or medical pattern of the flat, could bring its inmates out in a clammy sweat.

From Pat's agent Bernard Gohon, once a French Air Force pilot and a new member of the line, came discouraging reports of the possibilities of rescuing Gaston Nègre from Castres.

Then Françoise Dissart came up with a friend whose brother was a gaoler at Castres. A man who was clearly discontented, and who was persuaded to cooperate in the rescue of Nègre in exchange for a guaranteed trip along the line to England, whether the mission was successful or not.

Conditions were far different now from before occupation. Since trains were now being much more heavily searched and passengers checked, it was better to avoid them, and road transport in the early hours of the morning when prison routine was at its weakest was being planned. Gaston Nègre must be spirited away from a town where no contacts or safe-housing existed, and using roads which at night were habitually full of lorries heading for Toulouse.

Supplied with a powerful sleeping draught by Georges Rodocanachi,

Photograph taken in 1946 just after Pat O'Leary was given the George Cross by the King –
left to right Sylvia Cooper-Smith (whom he married in 1947), Pat, Fabien de Cortes, Albert
Leycuras.

At the House of Commons in 1969 to launch Airey Neave's book *Saturday at MI9*. Front row, left to right, Mrs Langley, Ian Garrow, Jimmy Langley, Airey Neave, Donald Darling and Mrs Neave.

(Below) The street name-plate to commemorate Doctor Rodocanachi in Marseille today.

Robert* the slim blond jailer succeeded in doctoring a bottle of wine to be shared by the night shift to celebrate a fictitious birthday.

He managed unobserved to retain a glass for himself without the drug, and when the other guards were all asleep, in stockinged feet Gaston – together with two American and one British airman, a French sailor, and two of his friends, followed the man who had the great keys to the prison, into the deserted street, and a furniture van outside. By four o'clock that morning Gaston Nègre and his fellow escapers were being welcomed by Pat at Françoise Dissart's dress-shop in Toulouse.

A thin, pale Gaston with the inevitable cigarette in the corner of his mouth, and a glass of *pastis* in his hand was advised by Pat that his work with the line was finished, and he must leave for Paris at once. Disguised as a convalescent he travelled north to build a new life, and managed to hide himself away, riding out tthe rest of the war until victory was won.

Another whose days with the O'Leary Line were numbered, was the redoubtable Nancy Fiocca. Under pressure from the German authorities the French government decided that Nancy Fiocca who had married a Frenchman after 1938, was no longer entitled to hold French nationality. Unless she left the country, she would be subject to very different regulations.

She set off for England in April 1943 with the same convoy as Renée Nouveau, a Belgian padre who had been in the Resistance, and eight British airmen. After three night marches they succeeded in crossing the frontier, but were promptly arrested by the Guarda Civil at a farm where they were resting. Thanks to lengthy negotiations between the British Consul General at Barcelona, and the Spanish authorities, they were released three or four days later.

Louis in Paris was by this time making good use of the talents of a twenty-five-year-old Greek, a friend of Léoni's, whose name was Costa Dimpoglou.

He was doing advanced mathematical work, specialising in statistical technique, for which reason I nicknamed him 'Pythagoras' [writes Louis Nouveau].

* He was eventually to die at the hands of the Gestapo.

He began by helping me to change pounds and dollars belonging to our airmen, and the fact that he had a relation employed at the Stock Exchange facilitated matters.

We succeeded in getting 960 francs for £1 treasury notes (on the black market, of course), and about 400 francs for one dollar. These operations served to augment my cash reserve by about 50,000 francs.

It was understood of course that the amounts would be refunded to the owners on their arrival in London.

When Nancy Fiocca reached England, she trained with SOE, was parachuted back into France, and had a distinguished career as one of Maurice Buckmaster's stars in the 'Independent French' section of SOE.

She, who became known as the Terror of the Germans in the Auvergne, was awarded the George Medal for her bravery, and the important contribution she had made towards victory in Europe.

CHAPTER NINE

The Collapse of the Line

1943

In 1943 disaster and tragedy beset the O'Leary Line, thanks to Paul Cole. For by this time the network was completely penetrated by the Germans.

Pat had sent his best guide, Francis Blanchain, down his own line to England early in the year, after the young man had made a spectacular escape from the police at Limoges. He had been on a reconaissance job for Pat, and had been caught and detained. After that episode he was hopelessly compromised, and useless to the line. Crossing the frontier into Spain he disappeared from the Marseille scene, where he had so memorably rescued Whitney Straight.

At Airey Neave's flat in Elizabeth Street, Garrow warned of the terrible things that might happen, now that Cole had reappeared in Paris.

Early in January 1943, Pat who was staying with Françoise Dissart in Toulouse began to be anxious because he had not received his routine report from Tom Groome.

In hiding in a house at Montauban, 35 miles from Toulouse, provided by the Cheramy family* Tom was slipping furtively from flat to flat to make and receive his coded messages. Every fifth message from London saw him move elsewhere, and he was using a young French girl, Edith Reddé, as a runner. Pat, waiting in room 202 at Madame Mongelard's Hôtel de Paris would get Tom's decoded messages from the girl, and send her back with his replies for London. It worked well, and there were fewer detector vans than by this stage of the war, operated in Marseille.

But unbeknown to Pat, Tom Groome had been located and caught at his set by a direction-finding team, and both he and the girl, and

---

* The Cheramys were both sent to a concentration camp. Patricia Cheramy who was English, suffered great hardship and ill-treatment at Ravensbrück, but survived to be released.

the Cheramys had been arrested. Jumping on to a table, and diving through an open window, he fell thirty feet to the ground, but was given away by a bystander as he rushed through the street.

In the chaos of his attempts at escape, Edith Reddé had had the presence of mind to slip away and get news of Tom's arrest to Pat. What she didn't know, was that in extremis, with a gun in his back, Tom Groome had managed to signal to London by leaving out a security check, that he was in enemy hands. This omission was spotted at once at MI9, and all messages thereafter were coloured by London's awareness of Groome's altered circumstances.

With the vultures closing in for the kill, the line's next tragedy was the arrest of Louis Nouveau, also in January 1943. He was betrayed by Roger Le Neveu, also known as Roger Le Légionnaire. Together he and Louis were escorting five American airmen, survivors from a Flying Fortress shot down in Brittany.

Pat had sent a letter to Louis in Paris through Raffarin* on the overnight express asking him to come to Toulouse to take over while he visited Gibraltar to discuss the dangerous situation now Tom Groome had been arrested.

Louis therefore arranged to leave Paris immediately, travelling with the American airmen as an escort with Roger. The five evaders had been passed by Louis to Jean de la Olla who had seen them safely to the flat in the Avenue d'Orleans. There they had all shaved and got cleaned up, and had been issued with their new identity cards. As Louis has recorded : 'It all seemed routine enough.'

So was the plan to rendezvous at the Gare d'Austerlitz at 10.00 for the 11 o'clock train. Since there were five men with no French, Roger and Norbert Fillerin were to travel with them to the station. By now Paris was alive with German troops, and suddenly Louis realised that they now needed special passes to gain access to the main station. Waiting about in the cold January air from 10.00 until 11.00 had made him angry and fearful. It was always dangerous not to keep to agreed schedules. And now they would all need the extra passes which would delay them still further.

Beside him a kiosk was bright with the earliest mimosa from

---

* Raffarin was arrested eight months after Louis' arrest, and they met again at Buchenwald Concentration Camp. But after being transferred to another camp, he was never seen or heard of again.

Provence : a nostalgic reminder of happier times down there. Astonishingly, flowers were still cheap, and he was amused that the old woman had decorated her bunches with strips of silver metallic ribbon, dropped by the RAF to confuse enemy radar detectors.

'*Cela vient des aviateurs anglais,*' she smiled at him. 'They come from the English airmen !'

'*Ça porte bonheur, Monsieur! Tenez . . .*' 'They bring good luck, Sir . . . here, have some . . .'

It was as though those silver threads were a token of goodwill : a pledge of better things to come when victory would see an end to all their troubles. Country people collected the silver strands reverently, harvesting them as a new and valued crop, finding them dropped mysteriously during the night, knowing that young men had risked their lives to dispense this largesse.

Those who seemingly innocently chose to add them to the flower arrangements in their homes, Louis recognised, were implicit supporters of the Allied cause.

At last, at 10.45 to Louis' relief, the party showed up. The airmen looked ill-at-ease in their new clothes and were walking in the centre of the group. But since they like Louis had no passes, they were promptly refused entry to the station. Louis, with little time in hand, foresaw that the journey might have to be abandoned, and the five escorted back into hiding again.

Suddenly, as they were debating what they should do, Roger announced : 'Leave it to me. I'll go and get some passes !' And so saying he plunged into the crowds milling around the station approaches unable, as they would normally have done, to spread themselves amongst the spacious platforms. With only five minutes to go, miraculously Roger returned carrying cards for them all. The relief was so intense that nobody thought to question how this had been done.

With hindsight, Louis was to record that he should have remembered Cole, and his uncanny and unnatural successes at the demarcation line. But Roger had in the past escorted several groups quite satisfactorily, though it must be said that not everybody had been entirely happy to trust him in the early days.

'It just never occurred to me,' Louis said later, 'to ask him how he had managed it.'

'There was a great crush at the barrier,' he continues. 'We went along the train looking for places. There were only five minutes to go.'

They separated to look for seats. Two of the airmen were with him in one compartment. Two others were standing in the corridor with a courier. The fifth was in a different compartment, also accompanied by a courier. Louis could see Norbert Fillerin's face as he wished them a good journey. Jean de la Olla's kindly smile. Roger waving, also smiled pleasantly . . . oh so pleasantly!

Louis was very tired and slept much of the way, except that he talked for twenty minutes or so with the senior officer amongst the airmen. The rest of the time he spent dozing on his feet. They were to cross the line at a place that was new to him, and not as he usually did at Montpont. That evening they would sleep at Loches. Next day they would all be in Toulouse. A wintry scene with bare fields flashed by.

At St Pierre-des-Corps they changed trains and all went well as they climbed into the last compartment of a little local train. It was an old-fashioned carriage which didn't communicate with the other carriages. They were all together. Louis mentally checked them all in, as he waited as patiently as he could for the train to start. He remembers feeling nervous and uneasy, and would have preferred to have been sitting on the side away from the platform.

Suddenly the door was flung open. He had noticed that there were still one or two vacant seats in their carriage, so turning his back on the door he didn't even trouble to look round. Those little local trains were much less systematically searched than were the expresses, which was why the Line used them whenever possible.

Immediately, he felt something hard sticking into his ribs. It was the barrel of a gun. Then he heard a voice with a German accent say:

'Hands up, you're for it!'

He was shattered. There was a great commotion. German plain-clothes police revolvers at the ready invaded the carriage. He could feel the gun pressing hard into him. In his own words: 'It was the end of the show.'

Within twenty-four hours news of Louis' arrest reached Pat. It was unthinkable. He decided to go at once to break the news to poor Renée. This was when he decided to send her down the line to safety in England.

With a heavy heart he set off for Toulouse where he knew that he would find her, and where Françoise would be around to comfort her in her distress.

*

Paul Cole, free again, was reaping a rich harvest in Marseille. The shadow of what he might do to the few members of the O'Leary Line still at large, hung over them all.

It was to be Georges Rodocanachi's turn next. But he had in any case been living each day as it came, waiting for the ring at his door which didn't announce a patient, nor yet an escaper or evader. Just the Gestapo come to arrest him and take him away.

'Things had slowed down until February 1943,' Fanny Rodocanachi records.

But activities became more and more difficult. On every side our organisation was being betrayed. And the location by special cars, of radio-transmitting, made the sending of messages more dangerous.

Dr Rodocanachi however was not interfered with, and became more wary. But on 26th February at 6 a.m. the Gestapo in the shape of two officers and six men invaded the flat and arrested him.

They didn't make a very thorough examination of the flat, nor any particular charge. During the battle for the liberation of Marseille for instance, four revolvers and ammunition, together with some petrol were given to the FFI.* All had been carefully hidden behind the skirting-board beside the mantelpiece in the drawing-room by Dr Rodocanachi before his arrest.

For two months we feared that all the work of sheltering men would be discovered.

But in spite of all the workers of our Organisation being arrested, one after another by successive betrayals of Fari† and Roger the Legionary, the doctor was never suspected of his real activities and work.

Three times he was subjected to cross-examination, but he was

---

* Forces Françaises de l'Intérieur: the French paramilitary resistance organisation.

† A member of the French Police introduced to the line by Gaston Nègre. He had thought it might be advantageous to have this link with the police: for which payment was made. But the man turned out to be working as a double-agent.

never questioned on what he had really done : but each time on silly, vague accusations of different kinds.

The last cross-examination concerned a gambling-hell at Cannes which he was supposed to be running, and to which town he had never been.

There was one saving miracle however – the day after his arrest, the 27th February, six pilots came to the house at 7.00 a.m. If the Germans had come a day later, or the pilots a day earlier, all would have been discovered and arrested.

On the morning of her uncle's arrest, Helen Vlasto became aware that something must be wrong upstairs when the Rodocanachis' telephone continued to ring unanswered. This in the doctor's house was unheard of. Later she learnt from her aunt that the Gestapo refused to allow anyone to touch it.

Once Georges Rodocanachi had been taken handcuffed from the flat, it was Séraphine who had gone shakily downstairs and said :

'*Madame voudrait vous parler, Madame.*'

'At least I was able to help poor Auntie Fanny get rid of all those compromising pairs of bedroom slippers,' Helen told me. 'The Red Cross soon found good homes for them.'

*

Four days after Georges Rodocanachi's arrest, on 2nd March 1943, Pat O'Leary was arrested – betrayed as Louis Nouveau had been, at Roger le Neveu's instigation, and arrested by the Gestapo. And on the night of 5th/6th March RAF Bomber Command opened its heavy night bombing offensive with an attack by nearly 450 aircraft on Essen. Thus began the Battle of the Ruhr.

They had rendezvoused at a café in Toulouse. The meeting had been arranged by Roger, using the tailor Paul Ullmann as an intermediary. Unwittingly Ullmann was being conned into acting as an innocent third party to draw Pat into Roger's net. He had no reason to mistrust another member of the line, the big blond Frenchman in his middle twenties, who regularly brought men south, and was proposing to give Pat details and information about Louis' recent arrest at St Pierre-des-Corps.

Traitors who could infiltrate a network were in a position to eat their way the length of a line, like a canker. As movements expanded, close-knit organisations like the O'Leary Line became more remote and difficult to supervise and control.

At that time Pat had not in fact ever set eyes on Roger Le Neveu, the man who had spent three years in the Foreign Legion, though he was of course known to him as a recent recruit brought into the *réseau* by Louis. Jean de la Olla approved of him, but Norbert and Jean Fillerin weren't so sure, and were reluctantly persuaded that he was trust-worthy. Nor would Pat in the normal course of events have made time in his busy day, to meet and talk with the courier Roger. But any source of information about possible weak points in their organisation's defences, or details of how Louis had been betrayed and arrested, would be invaluable.

Arrived outside Paul's tailor's shop, Pat paused just long enough for Paul to fall naturally into step alongside him as he led the way the length of the avenue of pollarded trees to the bar. Now Paul was talking. He told Pat that he had seen Roger go into the café. But he was worried about two men who for no obvious reason had been hanging about outside for some time. The Gestapo were becoming more difficult to spot, having by this time shed their identifiable sort of uniform, which had become almost a music-hall joke. But Pat, well armed beneath his nondescript anonymous clothes, was undismayed as they walked in, and over to the bar. Most customers were drinking the noxious black liquid made from grilled barley that passed for coffee by this stage of the war.

Roger sat with his back to the door. Pat, after the introductions were over, chose as was his invariable habit, a seat facing the door. Paul settled himself between them. As always Pat got straight down to business, asking Roger about his most recent journey south with parcels to collect and deliver.

He asked to see the card Roger had used at the now more strictly guarded demarcation line. A new and different stamp was now required on identity cards. He wanted to see for himself how difficult this might be to reproduce.

Returning after a few minutes from the lavatory downstairs, he noticed as he drew level with the ground floor that the two men they had seen hanging about outside the bar, were now inside.

This was not so very surprising, and Pat returned to his seat. Naturally enough, and thinking nothing of it, he turned to Roger and asked him what he knew about Louis's arrest.

'Tell me,' he said quickly, his look penetrating; 'who is it who is giving us away in Paris? Do you happen to know?'

Roger's reply to this question was quite definite.

'Yes,' he said, 'I know him extremely well!'

Instantly, just as Louis had felt it, Pat was aware of the cold pressure of a gun in the small of his back.

Simultaneously Paul Ullmann* too was being covered, and they realised as they stared about them in disbelief, that nearly everybody in the bar was part of the business of their arrest.

Customers all around them were on their feet, and six revolvers were trained on them from various angles. Pat who had already experienced the frustration and degradation of prison, anticipated what was to come. In German hands, incredibly for him the war really did appear now to be over: and who was left who could take his place?

At the time of his arrest, Pat didn't know that Georges Rodocanachi too was in gaol. It was the German interrogator Dunker Delage† who broke the news to him that his elderly host had been taken from his wife and home only four days before his own arrest.

At the St Pierre gaol in Toulouse, as Pat lay on straw he heard one day to his horror, the heart-broken wailing voice of his old friend Françoise Dissart calling his name over and over again. By some miracle she was not arrested, and was no doubt seen as some old eccentric with a deranged mind, and of no account.

From Toulouse he was sent under guard by train to Marseille and not as he had expected to Frèsnes. In Marseille the Gestapo held other prisoners arrested in the area: Dr Rodocanachi, Fabien de Cortes, and Monsieur Dijon, proprietor of the Petit Poucet. It had just occurred to the Germans that Pat might have some connection with these.

Already they had an *Acropolis File*, as he had discovered when he tried to read it upside down during his former interrogation by Dunker Delage on the sixth floor of the Gestapo Headquarters. It seemed that the authorities were at least aware that there were a number of anti-

---

* The arrests of Louis Nouveau, Pat O'Leary, Jean de la Olla and others were conducted by the *Paris* Gestapo, with the connivance of the French traitor, Roger-le-Neveu.

† Arrested after the war by the French, sentenced to death, and executed.

German Greeks active in the town. The wonder of it was that they didn't carry out their usual procedure, which was to interrogate such prisoners separately, and then face them with each other. Discrepancies in the accounts given soon showed up disastrously under these circumstances.

Pat's arrest meant the end of the O'Leary line. Though other evasion lines continued to the end, it was a bitter blow for MI9. Donald Darling in Gibraltar recalled in *Secret Sunday* what had happened :

[It] was obviously the work of Roger, who, when Nouveau could not initially obtain tickets at the Paris station, had 'arranged' to get them and thus was able to hand over the whole party, neatly, in a train compartment. Roger . . . was a German agent and within another few days had engineered a meeting with O'Leary himself at a Toulouse café, where Pat was also detained by the Gestapo. Roger then attempted to trap Françoise in the same way, but the wily old lady let it be known that she was 'not interested' in meeting him. The Gestapo, who could not identify her, though they knew of her existence, was frustrated on that count at least.

This appalling news reached London and then me, thanks to a desperately courageous leap from a moving train by one of Pat's most trusted lieutenants, young Fabien de Cortes. Arrested along with Pat, they were being taken to Paris in an ordinary railway compartment, but under armed guard. When the train slowed down on the outskirts of the city, Fabien spied an approaching tunnel, and opening the door he leaped out just before the tunnel mouth, so that the guards could not see which way he had gone. Fabien after a long journey reached Switzerland illegally and contacted the British Embassy to have them inform P15 of O'Leary's arrest. He also named the traitor and asked that he should be liquidated at all costs.

Fanny Rodocanachi told me of the bug and louse infested conditions at the Marseille prison. They fell from the clothes she collected there, and which Séraphine washed and ironed with her usual meticulous care. They were returned by Fanny's own hand, spotless and sweet-smelling, together with small gifts of a nourishing kind, which it later transpired never reached her husband. Pat called it the dirtiest, most infested, stinking gaol imaginable.

For trying to improve the lot of others confined with him, Georges Rodocanachi fell foul of a sadistic warder* who kept him for a long time in solitary confinement. Yet in other gaolers his stoicism and courage in adversity aroused admiration, and Fanny has recorded that he was allowed to keep his hands in his pockets in winter, which was normally strictly forbidden.

After Fanny's operation at the caring hands of one of her husband's colleagues, a Dr de Vernejoul, she was not expected to live. It was Netta Zarifi, as head of the Red Cross in Marseille, who managed to obtain permission for Georges Rodocanachi under guard, to visit his wife at the Clinique Bouchard. Handcuffed to two gaolers he spent a few minutes at her bedside, remaining as close to his two warders as possible, so that Fanny should not see the handcuffs that so odiously linked them.

They were never to meet again.

From St Pierre in Marseille on 17th December 1943, Dr Rodo-canachi was moved to another prison at Compiègne where he remained for a month. It was considered dangerous to leave local prisoners too long in their own area, for fear that attempts might be made to rescue them.

Fanny, making a slow recovery after her operation, was grateful that at least her husband was still in France. On 17th January 1944, how-ever, he was transferred to Buchenwald concentration camp in Ger-many, travelling as Fanny has recorded, 'in one of those atrocious convoys of which we have all heard.'

'We made that appalling journey, 120 to a truck, deprived of all garments, in Siberian weather,' Jean Blanc was to write to Fanny in a letter dated 12th May 1944, in answer to hers asking him for anything he could tell her about her husband's imprisonment. These two men had shared all three prisons, and Jean Blanc dwelt much on the angina that had so plagued his companion. His letter continued :

We were obliged to walk with lowered heads, our eyes on the ground, and to doff our caps when we met up with an SS.

* *'L'odieuse Madame,'* Fanny calls her. G.R. spent ten months in St Pierre gaol in Marseille.

Rodocanachi would never bend to these orders. On the contrary, he walked proud and erect, his head held high, and refused to salute the SS. With the result that at every meeting he received a violent blow from the riding-crop full in his face, so that the little striped* cap fell off.

We had *appels*, roll-calls, in the snow which lasted for about three hours at 30° below zero, wearing only the lightweight convict outfit, a little pullover without sleeves or a collar, and a striped shirt to match.

We slept in a large wooden hut with a passage down the middle and on either side, racks one upon another, three or four tiers high. Each of these racks was about 1 metre 60 wide, 2 metres deep, and 55 centimetres high.

We lived sometimes 7 in those infamous, vermin-infested boxes, without a palliasse, with only one blanket.

It was February 1944, I can't remember the exact day, and very cold, minus 30°, and snowing. After a disinfection session, Rodo began to feel ill.

Realising that he was determined not to be taken to the infirmary, and that he wanted to die in his block, amongst his comrades, he asked me to gather around him as many French prisoners as I could. And he asked us to sing the *Marseillaise* for him.

I admit to you, *madame*, that our national song came very painfully from our tightened throats. Nevertheless, we managed somehow to sing for him the hymn that is so dear to all French patriots, and Doctor Rodocanachi passed away in this fashion, whispering with his last breath :

'*Vive la France. A bas les Boches.*'

Madame, you should be proud of your husband. His son and all his family may, and should proclaim a hero, victim of odious Nazism, and here one must say it, the unspeakable activities of certain individuals who proved themselves to be French in name only . . . I hope that I have succeeded in reconstructing for you with all the sincerity within my power, dear Madame, what I know of the life of Dr Rodocanachi during the time he spent in Nazi prison and convict camps.

* The dark blue and white striped clothes of cotton sacking were designed to be humiliating, and easily seen if any prisoner tried to escape and survive outside the concentration camp.

I was proud to have been considered by him as a friend.

Another old friend who saw him at Buchenwald for a few painful moments was a Monsieur Robert Delmas, who spoke to him through the barbed wire which separated their compounds.

'I only knew him by his voice,' he said in Paris years later. But he was aware that it was being said of Dr Rodocanachi : *'il va crever,'* – he is finished : it's all up with him.

The only communication Fanny received from her husband from Buchenwald was a stereotyped postcard dated 24th January 1944. But since this was not posted until 12th February 1944, two days after Georges's death, on 10th February 1944, it was a bogus request for items which he could never have received. A very free translation of the postcard runs like this :

My dear wife. I am glad to be able to give you the latest news. I am in fine spirits [morale] and this [spirit, morale] continues. I have permission to write to you once a month in German, and ask you only to answer in German. I've got permission to accept 600 Francs per month. The number and weight of parcels are unlimited. Please send me a bag [this is the sort of bag used for carrying bread in], and some cigarettes, tobacco, and paper for rolling cigarettes. You may send me whatever food you are able to. But please do not send anything perishable, because parcels sometimes are on the way for up to four weeks. I also have permission to accept one parcel per month from the Red Cross. If possible 'clear' (declare) these parcels before you send them off. My thoughts are always with you. Be embraced in love by your Georges Rodocanachi.

The writing, needless to say was not his.

*

Louis Nouveau also ended up at Buchenwald, but survived his monstrous incarceration there. He was probably the first to bring Fanny direct news of her husband's last days. He recorded :

He arrived at Buchenwald in January 1944, and a week later I heard that he was in one of the blocks, like myself in quarantine, and that he had only arrived a short time before me. Although communication between the two sections of the small quarantine camp was strictly forbidden, I managed to slip in and spend three quarters of an hour with him . . . poor dear, generous, Dr Rodocanachi . . . he had been arrested, not on account of his own or his wife's activities as a member of the organisation, but because he had been denounced by some unknown person as a Gaullist, and also because of his activities on the Medical Board.

To think that he could have obtained his release if he had only consented to sign an undertaking never to do anything against the Germans : but he absolutely refused to do so.

After Georges Rodocanachi had died, Louis tried hard to establish what had happened, and to hear details of his death. It transpired that as he was lying in his bunk, only a few hours before his death, he heard the *Schreiber** call out his number. With the sort of sardonic humour that was so characteristic of him, he called out :

'*Présent. Et bon pour le crématoire!*'†

*

So, via the one or two scarecrow figures who stumbled out of Buchenwald, and the letters she in time received, Fanny was comforted by accounts of her husband's great humanity, and of the magnificent example he gave to those around him.

With no medical equipment or drugs of any kind, he was frustrated in his instinctive endeavours to treat and alleviate the deprivation, suffering and disease which surrounded him. But by his strong character, his own personal courage and stoicism under extreme adversity, and his unswerving loyalty to the cause he had always espoused, he was able nevertheless to encourage, support and comfort others.

'He died of a heart attack,' Fanny was to record later, 'some say in January, others in February or March, after a cold shower in Arctic weather. He was entirely conscious of his condition.'

---

* A prisoner acting as a clerk.
† 'Present. And ready for the crematorium !'

It was not until 19th February 1947 that an official letter informed Fanny Rodocanachi that her husband had indeed perished at Weimar-Buchenwald. How strange and bureaucratically punctilious that after a delay of three long years, they had felt it appropriate to be so precise as to the actual hour of his death.

He died at 14.00 hours on 10th February 1944.

Postscript

Before my marriage to Dr Aidan Long, my maiden name, like my aunt Fanny's, was Vlasto. In 1946 whilst on demobilisation leave as a naval VAD, I spent a few weeks living with her, and with Séraphine in the flat in the Rue Roux de Brignoles.

My aunt put me 'in your uncle's room, darling', and I began then to learn a little of what had happened in that flat but a short time before.

Séraphine had as always set out on my bedside table the small silver salver with its decanter of brandy, the cut-glass bowl containing cubes of sugar, and the familiar boudoir biscuits in their canister with the silver lid. Rationing, like the war, was apparently over.

Yet, as I leaned out of the window to look down into the street – as Hicky had done, through the slats of his closed shutters – there were still loose ends of aerial dangling from the sill in the hot Mediterranean sun.

And my bathroom, from whose window Cole had once leapt to freedom, now boasted a new pane of frosted glass on to the courtyard.

It all seemed part of a dream. Too strange and improbable really to be believed. Yet there were all those piles of tattered pre-war magazines and paperbacks in English stacked against the walls of my bedroom, and the pitted marks on the parquet beneath the nail where the darts-board had hung.

As I lay in my bed I was sure I could hear, distantly, scarcely audibly, the sound of men's voices talking quietly in the room across from mine. The soft shuffling of slippers in the corridor outside, and the ethereal strains of a Chopin étude being played with tenderness and pathos on the piano in the drawing-room.

Since that visit, I have been in touch with many people connected with my aunt and uncle during those dramatic days. With my husband I have visited Marseille on a number of occasions, and sought out the locations that form the background to this story.

My fluency in French has enabled me to talk freely with many who shared the clandestine life that was lived in and around the flat between 1940 and 1944, in a way that many journalists could not easily have done.

My uncle's first interrogation took place at the Gestapo Headquarters in Marseille, 425 Rue Paradis, which stood at the junction with the road already called Boulevard Rodocanachi. The property, and part of the town on which the road had been built had once belonged to the Rodocanachi family.

Upon the tall white-painted building there is now a plaque which reads :

Remember
behind the walls of this building the Gestapo
between 1942 and 1944
tortured hundreds of Resistants
those who did not die under torturing
were deported to Nazi extermination camps
they did not all return from these (places)
we never forget them, for they gave their lives
to preserve the honour of France.

After the war the street was renamed Boulevard du Docteur Rodocanachi.

Every Liberation Day, a ceremonial laying of a wreath takes place. The plaque does not specifically record the number of attempted or successful suicides that occurred in the building, and I feel mention should perhaps have been made of these brave acts, carried out to eliminate the danger of putting the lives of others at risk under torture.

At the Hôtel Dieu Hospital behind the Hôtel de Ville on the Vieux Port a ward has been named after Dr Georges Rodocanachi who served the town so well in peace and war.

The fact that my aunt was not arrested, and that the flat was only superficially searched, indicated that no member of the line, who would have known of the Rodocanachis' real activities, had given them away.

This *must* include Cole, and through him Roger le Neveu as well. To the end of her life my aunt firmly maintained that they were not denounced, as Pat and Donald Caskie believed that they were, by Paul Cole. My aunt told me after the war that she had formed her own opinion, but being the kind of person she was she remained silent until her death. Nevertheless she left documents written in Marseille after her husband's arrest. The concierges, she stated, had gossiped and noised abroad the Rodocanachis' anti-German attitude.

But her chief recorded bitterness was directed against the medical fraternity who had at no time offered Dr Rodocanachi or herself any support in their hour of need; what was much more significant was that certain of them, some of whom she mentions by name, for personal reasons and possible jealousy had without doubt chosen in bad faith to witness against them.

Today the 'listed building' of which the flat forms part, is occupied by the national tax authority. When I visited it in 1981, they knew nothing about the dramatic events that had taken place there during the war years. Their enthusiasm and demands to know more, finally made me realise that this was not just a family story, but one in which others also were interested.

I recall that Hicky had written when he was barely twenty – 'Doctor's wife a bind' . . . Perhaps she had been. But she had surely had good reason to discipline her young visitors. She had managed to keep her safe house safe. And that was no mean achievement. For, as Airey Neave had said :

'Safe houses were very dangerous places.'

Appendices

I

After the War

Fanny Rodocanachi: Moved to live near her brother Michael Vlasto and his family, and her many friends in London after the war. She lived quietly with her memories, and died of the cancer which had required surgery in Marseille, at St Mary's Hospital in April 1959.

Kostia Rodocanachi: Their only child, was most helpful over this story of his parents' wartime activities. It is through him that I have had access to Fanny Rodocanachi's typed account of their clandestine life. He died in Geneva in September 1981.

Netta Zarifi: Holder of the Légion d'Honneur for her many years of devoted service to the Red Cross; still lives in Marseille.

Lt-Col James – 'Jimmy' – Langley, MBE, MC: The young lieutenant with the Coldstream Guards who lost an arm at Dunkirk, and was passed as 'unfit for further military service' by Dr Rodocanachi, was awarded the MBE and MC. He was demobilised as lieutenant-colonel in 1946, spent many years with Fisons, and became a bookseller in Suffolk from 1967–1976. He also took to writing himself. *Fight Another Day* was published in 1974. *MI9 Escape and Evasion 1939–1945* written in co-operation with M. R. D. Foot was published in 1979. Jimmy Langley died on 10th April 1983.

Georges Zarifi: Travelling down his own line, left Marseille on 22nd April 1943. The organisation had by this time collapsed like a pack of cards. Only Françoise Dissart was left who knew the network and the strings linking the guides. She organised his departure, travelling with several others, and they reached the frontier at 4.0 a.m. on 28th April. Their guide promptly deserted them instead of seeing them as far as Barcelona as he had been paid to do.

They had no money, spoke no Spanish, and it was raining! At a village called Aguellana they were picked up by the Guarda Civil and imprisoned in the gaol at Figueras the following day. After a series of removals from one unsavoury prison to another they were finally released from Miranda de Ebro on 16th August. Donald Darling had seen to their reasonable

196

comfort for their four weeks spent in Madrid. But in England they too were faced with the misery and anti-climax of four days at the 'Patriotic School', and exhaustive interrogation. In London Georges joined de Gaulle as had so many French nationals who had made their way along the O'Leary escape route out of Marseille, and his help and encouragement in the writing of this story of our mutual aunt and uncle, have been invaluable. He is in business in Marseille today, and enjoys the company of his three small granddaughters and one little grandson.

Pat O'Leary, GC, KBE, DSO: Pat had survived Mauthausen (Austria), Natzweiler, and Dachau concentration camps, being freed from Dachau on 29th April 1945, when USA forces liberated the camp. But he chose to stay on there to fight an epidemic of typhus raging at Dachau. Thereafter he ceased to be Patrick O'Leary Lieutenant-Commander RN – though it was in this guise that in 1946 he was awrded the George Cross by King George VI.

Recently released from Dachau, Pat was called to identify the body of Paul Cole, shot by the French Police in a flat in Paris. After World War II he rejoined the Belgian 1st Lancers as a medical officer, and in 1951 was appointed Chief of the Medical Service to the Belgian Volunteer Battalion in Korea.

In retirement he lived with his English-born wife Sylvia at Waterloo near to Brussels, a close neighbour of his doctor son and his young family. Sylvia Cooper-Smith was working for Donald Darling at the Paris Awards Bureau when she met Pat, and they married on 18th December 1947. Though plagued by eye-trouble, as have been so many who suffered torture and near starvation in Germany's concentration camps, Pat remains the charming, indomitable personality whose qualities of leadership and friendship proved irresistible to everyone who came within his orbit and under his command. He is one of the highest decorated men of World War II with medals and decorations lavished upon him from all sides for his personal bravery and genius for conducting clandestine work of the most hazardous kind. He is also President of the Society of Ex-Inmates of Dachau Concentration Camp. Sylvia Guérisse died on 9.1.85.

Elizabeth Haden-Guest: She left Marseille with little Anthony, and arrived in Lisbon, reported to Donald Darling who already knew of her clandestine work in Germany, and her connections with her brother-in-law David Haden-Guest who was killed fighting in the Spanish Civil War.

She stayed about 2 months in Lisbon reporting on the situation in France, and being checked out before being returned to UK by air via Limerick to London. Being the first woman and child out of France, she was given front-page coverage in all the London papers, and was interviewed over the air by Ed Murrow for CBS.

But her desire to return to continue her clandestine work in Marseille, or elsewhere on the continent (she speaks fluent German as well as French), was blocked, and she was told she was 'brûlée', burnt out, blown. She was admired even by the Vichy officers who admitted to her ... '*Vous avez grande mérite pour la France et l'Angleterre Madame*'.

Now, as Elizabeth Furse, the mother of five children, she is a journalist in London. Through Margot Fonteyn she met Patrick Furse, when she herself was working as a continuity girl in films, and together they ran an art gallery. Later she opened the first Bistro in Great Britain, and was taught how to toss an omelette and grill a steak by Clement Freud.

Her Bistro became a refuge for many who 'had survived the war, and needed the "one for all, and all for one" spirit.'

But nothing has ever been more to her instinctive liking than was the clandestine work of arranging escapes, saving lives, and looking after 'her boys' that she undertook before, and during the war years.

Anthony Haden-Guest: Now a writer and journalist and living in the USA.

Pat Hickton, 'Hicky': Lives back in his native New Zealand. He is referred to in Derrick Nabarro's book *Wait For The Dawn*. He has been most helpful with his memories of Safe House life as a 'visitor' at the Rodocanachis. He is a member of the RAF Escaping Society.

Séraphine: Lived in retirement in an old people's home at Aubagne, near to Marseille, after Fanny Rodocanachi moved to London. The citation given to her by an appreciative British Government, and which Fanny had framed for her, was for the rest of her life, her proudest possession.

Nancy Fiocca (Nancy Wake, GM): (Née Nancy Wake) is now Nancy Forward and lives in Australia. She married an RAF officer at the end of the war. Her exciting and dramatic war story has been told in a book called *Nancy Wake*, by Russell Braddon. Like so many characters in my story, she is an honorary member of the RAF Escaping Society, and a member of the Special Forces Club. She was awarded the George Medal.

Airey Neave, DSO, OBE, MC, MP: was assassinated in March 1979 by a bomb planted by the IRA. For a man who had escaped from Colditz, and had hated being shut into confined spaces, this was a tragic and monstrous end to his life. Lady Airey, Baroness Neave, has been most helpful with memories of Airey's time in the Safe House care of the Nouveaus. She is still in touch with Renée Nouveau at Aix-en-Provence. Lady Airey is a trustee of the RAF Escaping Society.

Ian Garrow, DSO (1943), Croix de Guerre: Joined Langley and Neave at MI9 after his return from France along his own escape line. He was promoted major, and was to have been operations officer for Crockatt in the Overlord landings and thereafter. But he suffered a badly broken heel following a fall at the training headquarters of the unit to which he had been appointed. By the time his heel was usable, a delay of several months, he was left with a permanant limp. He was then sent to an interpreters' unit which in due course was posted to Berlin at the end of the war, at which time he was promoted lieutenant-colonel. He remained in Berlin from 1945 to 1947, when he returned to the UK and was demobilised.

He died in his native Scotland on 28th March 1976.

Mario Prassinos: Warned by a Special Branch French policeman that Mario's activities had become known, Pat strongly advised him to disappear, and sent him down the line to Gibraltar.

In England he trained with SOE and returned to France, dropped by parachute. But he was later caught in a German trap as he was enjoying a drink at a friend's house. He was deported to Germany where all trace of him was lost, just before the final surrender. Some say he died of typhus in the concentration camp, others that he was massacred during the transfer from one camp to another, for it was not uncommon for the SS to finish off any prisoner who was too exhausted to keep on walking. Mario was posthumously awarded the OBE which was presented to his widow on the same day as Louis Nouveau was decorated with the George Medal.

Françoise Dissart: Awarded the George Medal and equivalent decorations from the French and American governments. When the O'Leary Line was all but dead, with Pat, Louis, Dr Rodocanachi, and Tom Groome all in gaol, Françoise, whose flat was opposite the Gestapo HQ in Toulouse, continued to send escapers into Spain right up to the liberation. When it became too dangerous to operate any longer from Marseille, she accompanied the men herself as far as the frontier.

Having been Pat's chief organiser in Toulouse, she became his successor after his arrest in March 1943. Georges Zarifi travelled down the line with the last party out of Marseille, organised by Françoise, which left on 22nd April 1943.

Postel-Vinay, André, Commandant de la Légion d'honneur, Compagnon de la Libération, Grand Officier de l'Ordre National de Mérite: Became a director of a French bank after the war. The walking-stick which my cousin Georges Zarifi lent him for the journey to England was never seen again. It became an on-going family joke with the Zarifis, for Georges's father Theodore Zarifi who had known nothing of his son's activities missed his fine stick in due course, and was mystified and irritated that it had been mislaid. Nor of course had he known of his brother-in-law's medical visits to care for a convalescent André Postel-Vinay, hidden, unbeknown to him, in his own house, until his departure for England.

Air Marshal Sir Denis Crowley-Milling, KCB, CBE, DSO, DFC: Pilot Officer Denis Crowley-Milling flew with Douglas Bader. In the film version of Bader's story, *Reach for the Sky*, Kenneth More, creating a row because there are no tools or spares on the station, asks if nobody has a tool to offer. Someone pipes up : 'Yes, sir, Crowley-Milling's got a penknife!'

Air Marshal Sir Denis Crowley-Milling is a Vice President of the RAF Escaping Society.

Wing Commander 'Taffy' F. W. Higginson, OBE, DFC, DFM, RAF: Shot down near St Omer. Evaded capture and stayed with a local doctor who had two daughters. Was introduced by the doctor to Paul Cole in Lille, and left Madame Deram's home with him on his way to cross the demarcation line. Chocolate suitcase incident at check-point.

In Marseille spent two nights at the Rodocanachis, where Ian Garrow and Pat O'Leary were both resident, and heard the announcement with them ... *Adolphe doit rester.* August 1941.

He was passed to a Spanish guide in Marseille, who took him to Banyuls. Getting off the train his habitual chivalry made him allow all the women to go ahead of him as they left the train, and he was stopped by the police who weren't happy with his papers, since he was so far from the north. These had been made for him by the Abbé Carpentier at Abbeville. He was put into solitary confinement at Banyuls, and then sentenced to 6 months in Perpignan Civil Gaol. He served about 2–3 months there, before being transferred, handcuffed by an armed guard to St Hippolyte du Fort. A month later, the crowd he was with were all transferred to Fort de la Revère. From there he escaped with Hicky and Nabarro, etc., they went to the Rodocanachis, and he stayed at the Nouveaus until they all left in the *Tarana.* His escape from Fort de la Revère was the first big one. There was to be a second and much bigger exodus shortly after the first one.

Now back in his beloved Wales, he combines farming with consultancy to an international company, which brings him up to London. It was on one of these business trips that he was good enough to recall for me some of his memories of crossing the line with Paul Cole, to whom he will always be indebted he says, for the saving of his life.

He also treasures to this day his memories of two nights spent at the Rodocanachis, and of my aunt Fanny Rodocanachi giving him her arm, and asking him to take her in to dinner at the flat in Marseille. The polished mahogany table was decorated with flowers, but the meal was frugal due to food shortages, and only one platter was to be shared between them all. It was while he was staying at the Rodocanachis that he too heard the message from London ... 'Adolphe doît rester.'

'Taffy' Higginson is a member of the RAF Escaping Society.

Donald Caskie, OBE: After long months of imprisonment in seven different prisons, and being sentenced to death, he was released when the

Germans left Paris. He opened a canteen for the RAF at Le Bourget : the first British canteen in newly liberated France. He was called upon from time to time by the Intelligence Service, and his manse in the Rue Piccini became a rendezvous for old friends and visitors, as had been his Mission building in Marseille.

As visiting Chaplain to various camps, and to military offenders in prison, he was confronted with Paul Cole – disguised as an American colonel. For three months he, Cole, had been attached to a special unit engaged in tracing and recovering art treasures sent to Germany. This had given him the opportunity to do some pilfering on his own account. But the Americans had at last rumbled him, and Donald was able to identify the man they were only too delighted to find was not after all an American. Cole, face-to-face with Donald, denied ever having seen him before.

In 1957 HM the Queen laid the foundation stone for a new Scottish church in the Rue Bayard, a momentous day for the Reverend Donald Caskie, who was appointed an OBE.

He retired to live at the Royal Scots Club in Edinburgh, and died in December 1983, aged 81.

Louis Nouveau, GM: Miraculously Louis survived the monstrous conditions at Buchenwald, despite having been badly gassed in 1917. After the war he was soon to be seen around Marseille, driving his Bentley again, immaculately dressed and London-tailored as always.

His business threads picked up, he continued to prosper, and extend his entrepreneurial activities.

He received the George Medal on the same day as Mario Prassinos's widow accepted the posthumous OBE awarded to her husband.

Renée Nouveau, MBE: Renée now lives at Aix-en-Provence. She too was decorated by the British government, and takes pride in the MBE that recalls for her the wartime activities in which she played such a courageous and active a part.

I visited her with my husband recently, and she was delighted to show us the volumes of Louis's set of *Voltaire*. Recorded in delicate and precise handwriting the length of the seams of the books, are the names, units, and details of the dates of arrival and departure of their many wartime 'visitors' at the flat overlooking the Vieux Port.

Jean-Pierre Nouveau, Croix de la Libération in 1944, Légion d'Honneur in 1945, Croix de Guerre neuf Citations, created Grand Commandeur de la Légion d'Honneur in 1966, created Grand Officier de l'Ordre de Mérite in 1974: Having crossed into Spain in January 1941, he was arrested at the frontier with Portugal. After spending time in eleven Spanish prisons, he ended up at Miranda de Ebro, from where he was released in August 1941. Joined the Forces Françaises Libres and saw action with a tank regiment in Africa. Fought in Normandy, Paris, the Vosges, Royan, and Germany before going out to Indochina as a lieutenant, and left the army in 1947.

In 1947 he joined his father's business and ran the Paris office until he took over from Louis Nouveau on his retirement.

Jean-Pierre retired in 1976, and the business is now in the hands of his son Nicholas, the child of his first marriage. By his second marriage he has two daughters, who have given him three grandsons.

Paul (Harold) Cole: Following the Allied invasion of France in June 1944, the Gestapo, realising they had lost the war, rounded up and killed or deported to concentration camps in Germany, hundreds of Resistants. Cole actively assisted them in this, betraying countless more French people known to him to have been hiding airmen along escape routes. Most of these people were tortured or executed.

On 17th August 1944 Cole, dressed as a German officer, and regarded by them as a trusted agent, left Paris. He only reappeared on the scene in the spring of 1945, when he turned up at an American Cavalry Regiment posing as a British agent called Captain Mason.

Unsuspectingly, the Americans gave him an American uniform, and a job in connection with interrogation. In this capacity he began denouncing his former Gestapo associates to the Allies.

In the end he outraged the American authorities by stealing from under their noses, art treasures pinched by the Nazis, and which were about to be returned to their rightful owners. So at this point he was being sought by the British, Americans *and* the French because of his monstrous betrayals of their nationals. In the end he was shot by the French Police in a flat in Paris in 1945.

Pat O'Leary newly out of Dachau, and at the time on holiday with Ian Garrow in Skye, was called to identify Cole's body. Roland Lepers was also asked to come, and he too travelled from Britain, where he was serving with the Free French forces.

Roger le Neveu (Roger le Legionnaire): Was one of a small number of Frenchmen who were blackmailed or bribed to work for the Germans against their own countrymen.

After betraying Louis Nouveau and Pat O'Leary he continued to work for the Gestapo. He was transferred to Rennes to penetrate escape lines in Brittany, and later escape routes into Spain, right up until June 1944.

History relates that at the liberation of France, he was dealt with in an appropriate manner by the Maquis.

Derrick Nabarro, DCM: Fanny Rodocanachi, who unlike Louis Nouveau did not keep any records of their wartime visitors, nevertheless remembered just a few by name. Of Derrick, she wrote : 'A young Nabarro, airman and poet . . .' He has in fact continued successfully to write, and still remembers with admiration and gratitude the hosts in Marseille whose name he did not at that time come to know.

Flight Lieutenant Nabarro, then a sergeant pilot was shot down in June 1941 in the sea near the coast of Germany. In November that year he escaped, but was recaptured in the December and interned in a fort in the south of France. But in October 1942 he escaped again and reached England. For these escapes he received the first DCM to be awarded to the RAF.

Donald Darling: June 1940 he escaped from France and returned to London. In July 1940 he was asked to go to Spain and Portugal to establish communications with France, and to organise evasion routes for British servicemen. Spain having proved useless for his purposes he set up shop under the official guise of Repatriation Officer in Lisbon.

In January 1942 he was sent to Gibraltar to continue evasion operations, and remained there until March 1944. April to September 1944 found him working in, and eventually heading the 'Evasion Office' in London. September 1944, and he was in Paris setting up the combined War Office and Foreign Office Awards Bureau, and with the rank of Major, keeping in touch with 'Special Services'.

He died on 15th December 1977.

The Cheramys, their baby, Tom Groome and Edith Redde were taken handcuffed to the Gestapo Headquarters at Toulouse, opposite Françoise Dissart's flat. There the parents were told that unless they 'talked' their baby would be killed.

Madame Cheramy bravely told them to go ahead and kill him, and after that to kill her. But by some miracle the baby was looked after by the Red Cross, and after her return from prison in Germany, Madame Cheramy, after much searching for him, was reunited with her child.

She herself was monstrously ill-treated at the concentration camp, but survived to live in England with a useless hand, and unable to turn her head as a result of physical abuse under interrogation. She now lives in Hove, and her portrait hangs in a place of honour in the officers' mess at RAF Odiham.

Tom Kenny: Tom, who met Sue Martinez of the Hotel Martinez at Cannes, through Nancy Fiocca, married her in July 1941 when she was 17, and he was 31. Tom was arrested three days after their marriage, but later released. Arrived in England, he joined the RAF, and spent the last part of the war in Holland and Belgium.

After the war he, Sue and their three sons settled in Paris, where he went into the film business, selling French films abroad as part of his work. He suffered badly from ulcers just after the war, and came to London for an operation in 1950.

He died of cancer in Paris in February 1971, aged 60.

II

LIST OF NAMES OF ALLIED TROOPS, MAINLY AIRMEN, AND MEMBERS OF THE ORGANISATION, WHO STAYED SECRETLY WITH LOUIS and RENEE NOUVEAU. *From the manuscript by Louis Nouveau released to me by Dr G. M. Bayliss, Keeper of the Department of Printed Books at the Imperial War Museum, at the request of Madame Renée Nouveau, MBE.*

The documents in my possession, which have served as a basis in compiling these memoirs and are reproduced below, are exceedingly scanty. They consist :

Of the list of airmen who spent a few days, varying from one or two to fifteen, in our flat in Marseille between May 1941 and November 1942. I wrote down their names in the inner margins of separate pages of Volume 44 of a Complete Edition of Voltaire's works, in 70 volumes, published by E. A. Lequien, Paris, in 1823. Unfortunately, I only began to do this after a certain number of them, perhaps 25 or 30, had stayed with us, having at first omitted to do so; so that the names of our earliest secret guests are missing, except the very first one of all whose name I remember perfectly, as he stayed in the flat a fairly long while. The names written down on the different pages include not only airmen and soldiers who had been shot down or had escaped, but also members of our own organisation who slept in the flat; but there were not more than a dozen or so of the latter. The entries I made on each page are faithfully reproduced. In some cases, very little information is given; and what is available is often extremely succinct; it would, therefore, be very difficult for me to furnish any details except those which actually appear in the 'Voltaire'. It may be estimated however, that approximately 156 visitors in all, of whom 145 were not French, were secretly harboured in our flat at 28A, Quai Rive Neuve, Marseille.

On the inner margins of volume 1 of the 'Voltaire', I also noted the various journeys I undertook in 1941, and up to November 1942, on instructions, first from Captain Ian Garrow, and subsequently from Lt. Cmdr. P. A. O'Leary; but I have probably forgotten some of these. In any event, this list of 42 journeys undertaken during a period of from 18 to 20 months will serve to give some idea of our activities.

To have noted the names of our secret visitors and the journeys under-taken on the pages of two volumes of a complete set, comprising seventy in all, forming part of a library of some 2,000 volumes, was really not so risky as may at first sight appear : for it must not be forgotten that at the time I made these entries, Marseille was still in the unoccupied zone, and consequently only the Vichy police were to be feared.

Page   1 – Sergeant Philip HERBERT – 15 days.

„   5 – No names given, roughly about thirty.

„   24 – Peter SCOTT JANES.

„   25 – LOCKART ? Sergeant Pilot.

„   26 – Pilot Officer GONZOR (Polish).

„   27 – Mario PRAXINOS.

„   28 – Capt. GARROW (Ian) Chief.

„   29 – 101 Sq. Robert SAXTON – 3 Alexander Road, Burton on Trent, Staffordshire.

„   30 – Franck ALLEN – Mill House, Ramsbury, Wiltshire, 101 Sq.

„   31 – Ed. DIMES B.O. Battery 1st Reg.

„   32 – Archie NEILL – Gordon High.

„   33 – Robert REID – Royal Eng.

„   34 – Andrew POW – Gordon High.

„   35 – Serg. Patrick BELL – 602 Sq.

„   36 – Serg. William CRAMPTON – 9 Sq.

„   37 – Flight Lieut. George BARCLAY – 611 Sq.

„   38 – Pilot Officer NITELET – 609 Sq. mobilised Oct. 1940.

„   39 – Serg. Kenneth READ – 9 Sq.

„   40 – Sq. Leader Harry BURTON – 9 Sq.

„   41 – Gunner John CLAPHAM B.O. – 1st Reg. R.H.A.

„   42 – Pilot Officer Oscar COEN – 71 Sq. (probably the first American).

„   43 – Pr. Joseph ROSS Gordon High.

„   44 – Juan CASTELLIO – Guide.

„   45 – Salvador AGUADO – Guide.

„   46 – Jean HULZENHAUTS – (Member of a gang of terrorists).

„   47 – Joseph HANTSON – (Member of a gang of terrorists). Dec. 1941.

„   48 – Oliver JAMES 745340 83 Sq. Shot down Morlaix 22/3/41.

„   49 – William McGRATH 587464 82 Sq. Dec. 41 S. High AALBURG 13 A 1940.

„   50 – Jan. 42 – Capt. Richard CF ASTON 151 PROVOST C° CMP Calais region 18 months.

„   51 – Sq. Leader P. A. O'LEARY[1] – Chief from Oct. Dec. 1940 – Jan 42 (who slept and took his meals with us during those months).

[1] We took him for an Airman, though he was in fact a sailor and, above all a doctor.

,,   52 – Victor REINER S. Lieut. 5° Regiment Jan. 42 Carpathian Rifles (Polish).

,,   53 – Jan. 42 – Januez WAHL 9° Division D.C.A. (Sub. Lieut).

,,   54 – George REEVES – Captain RNVR, called up by British Admiralty. Feb. 1942.

,,   55 – Major Robert CHALLONER 97586 (?) Royal Eng. Beaumont Div. Second in Command of Royal Eng. Bat. Feb. 42 Escaped from Herlag near Rouen – Prisoner 1st of June Nolleval north of Rouen.

,,   56 – Flying Off. Mieczyslaw TARAS – Sq. 300 bomb. shot down over Ostend after bombing Munich.

,,   57 – X Monsieur BENOIT (Secret Agent).

,,   58 – Lt. Colonel (or Colonel) KAMIONKO, G.S.O. had been at Norwick, in France, since the Armistice, and had made several abortive attempts to join the Free Polish Forces.

,,   59 – Patrick HENRY (Mechanic).

,,   60 – James Terence HENRY (Mechanic).

,,   61 – X Virginia HALL.

,,   62 – CUISENIER.

,,   63 – Van den MERRET.

,,   64 – Ladislas RADWANSKI – Flying Officer – Sq. 300 – M P 1006 – from Geneva.

,,   65 – Major Ph. NEWMAN R.A.M.C. (taken prisoner at Dunkirk) escaped from Rouen, c/o Jh. NEWMAN, Mansfield, Ingatestone, Essex.

,,   66 – 16 April, Lieut. A. M. S. NEAVE, R.A. 1° Light anti-aircraft – Escaped from Oflag 4/C near Leipzig Straflag 10th Jan. 42 – from Geneva.

,,   67 – 16 April – Capt. H. A. WOOLATT – 2° Bat. Lancashire Fusiliers – Escaped Oflag 5/B near Biberach 15 Sept. 41 – from Geneva.

,,   68 – MARIE – 17 March.[1]

,,   69 – M. G. DUNCAN – Oxf. and Bucks Light Inf. – Escaped 13 Sept. Ofl 5/B near Biberach near Ulm. September from Geneva.

,,   70 – Aug. Rowan HAMILTON – Black Watch – Escaped 12 Sept. Oflag 5/B Biberach Ulm Left – from Geneva.

,,   71 – A. M. HECHT – 5 Reg. Inf. Escaped from Holland 25 November – from Geneva – from Amsterdam.

,,   72 – 28 April – Lieut. Marian KOZUBSKI – Motorised Cavalry 2° DV GRDI – in Switzerland since 28 June – from Geneva.

,,   73 – Cap. Barry O'SULLIVAN – 3rd Bat. R. Tank Reg. captured in Calais – Escaped 5/B.

[1] Virginia HALL.

„ 74 – Driver William BACK R.A.S.C. (Captured St. Valery) escaped Stalag 3/D Berlin.

„ 75 – 2nd Lieut Rudy BLATT – 5° Art. Motor antitank – Escaped from Holland – Amsterdam.

„ 76 – Serg. W. MILLS – 19 Sq. shot down near Abbeville 24 March – via Lyons – 9 May.

„ 77 – Flying Officer Ian WAGINSKI RAF – Sq. 304 – Shot down near Charleville – 27th April – 10 May – (Navigator).

„ 78 – Pilot Officer Ian FUSINSKI – 300 Sq. shot down near Mézières Charleville – 27 April – 10 May.

„ 79 – Flying Officer Julien MORAWSKI 304 – Jumped near Avallon 27 April – 15 May. Wellington.

„ 80 – 1st Lieut. Victor VAN LEATEM – 9th Inf. Reg. Machine Gun Officer – Escaped Ofl. 2/A near Preuzlau 17 Oct. (Tel. N° 415 16 Dec. 41).

„ 81 – 2° Lieut. J. OAK – 1° Bat. Montreal Reg. – Escaped Oflag 5/B Tel 28 April – N° 427 ??

„ 82 – Naval Lieut. Montchilo STANENKOVITCH – 3° Reg. Hydravion – shot down near Corfu – 17 April.

„ 83 – Sq. Leader Royce Clifford WILKINSON (44125) shot down near Abbeville – 3 May (Hurricane Hurribomber).

„ 84 – Serg. Wireless Operator MALECKI – 300 Sq. shot down near Namur – N° 783809 – 27/28 April.

„ 85 – Serg. Edward POLESINSKI – 304 Sq. Shot down near Charleville – Mézières – N° 792693 – 27/28 April.

„ 86 – Fl. Officer Stanislas KRAWCZYK – Sq. 305 bom. Cross-bombing 20m. north Mettet (Namur Charleroi) 6th of May on way back.

„ 87 – Cdt. Aviat. Wladislas TUCHOLKO – 2° Bat. General Staff 3° Army Air Force – entered Switzerland 18 June 1940 – from Geneva.

„ 88 – Lieut. Henry EDW. STEWART – Australian division Staff Off. Intell. Corps attached to the 8th and 9th Australian divisions captured at Derna escaped from Italy 1st October 1941 – Camp Sulmone Abbruzi – from Geneva – 7 April 1941.

„ 89 – Simon HERGENBERG – entered Switzerland end April 1941 – from Geneva.

„ 90 – Serg. Boleslaw WOZNIAK – Sq. 304 (792865) shot down near Mézières 27th April – Wellington.

„ 91 – Serg. Albert Leslie WRIGHT – Sq. 61 548615 – Shot down (bomber) 31 Jan. near Brest mid upper gunner on a Manchester *(He actually arrived wearing a dinner jacket)!*

* It struck me at the time as remarkably touching that the people in the little town or village who harboured him, probably having nothing suitable to give him to wear instead of his uniform tunic, had managed to find a 'smoking', a relic no doubt of some village wedding. It was so funny and very touching. (Louis Nouveau)

  „ 92 – Major (Engineers) Ilitch LYOUBOMIR – captured 21 April Sarajevo – interned at Nuremberg as officer captured in Italian occupied territory. Passed as an Italian prisoner of war. Although born at Belgrade, passed as a Montenegran. Interned Fiume-Avessa – Escaped 15 April with nine others from Geneva.

  „ 93 – Serg. Pilot Frederick BARKER – 102 Sq. (1377581) shot down near Dunkirk 28 April 1942 – Walked to Chateau-Thierry – train to Vesoul – walked to Swiss frontier. Halifax aircraft.

  „ 94 – Serg. Mechanic apprentice pilot Miloutine GARDACHE-VITCH Sq. 702 (Belgrade) captured Sarajevo 18 April 1941 – Escaped Tilingen 5/B 28 March 1942.

  „ 95 – Serg. John PRENDERGAST 1° Batt. The Welsh Regt. – Captured in Crete June 1941 – Escaped from XX/A near Thorn.

  „ 96 – (sic) X left with Drouet "Fullager" Gordon Highlanders.

  „ 97 – Y left with Drouet. Prady – idem –

  „ 98 – Drouet.

  „ 99 – 23 June – Barnabé.

  „ 100 – Sq. Leader WHITNEY STRAIGHT M.C.D.F.C. 242 Sq. Shot down 31 July 1941 near Fecamp – 27 June 1942.

  „ 101 – Serg. MIMAKOWSKY (Stephen) 300 Sq. Shot down 27 April near Givet Cap. Crew Fushinsky – 27 June 1942.

  „ 102 – Pr. Charles KNIGHT – 2nd Batt. Worcester Regt. prisoner 27th May 1940 near Béthune wounded 27 June.

  „ 103 – André SIMON – Flt. Lieut. RAF Intelligence – Prisoner 26th May 1942 – Châteauroux – arrived here 7/7/42.

  „ 104 – John BEECROFT Serg. RAF 101 Sq. Shot down near Mézières 20th May 1942 – 9/7/42.

  „ 105 – Henry HANWELL Serg. RAF 101 Sq. Shot down near Mézières 20th May 1942 – 9/7/42.[1]

  „ 106 – Anthony Deane DRUMMOND Lt. 2 Commando – prisoner Italy 13th Feb. 41 – 9/7/42.

  „ 107 – René DEBRETS (known as Antoone Olivier) betrayed.[2]

  „ 108 – Pilot Officer Darrick PERDUE Sq. 12 – Shot down near Le Havre – landed near St. Oppertune 1st April brought back by me.

  „ 109 – S Lieut. Kristo KOUSTOUDITCH – Airman Group 34.

[1] Additional note page 105 "Brought Andrew EVANS", rear gunner RAF, and VAN LAERT (Belgian betrayed) from Paris. Others at Gaston's (end July).
[2] As the next one arrived on 11 August, some names must be missing, for I was absent for several weeks and it is unlikely that four weeks could have elapsed without any new arrivals unless the batch of 9/7/42 made an exceptionally long stay.

Captured 22 April 1941 at Sarajevo – Escaped from camp at Bordeaux (Stalag 5/C–5/B previously) as a worker 26 June. Arrived from Geneva 11 August.

„ 110 – Abbé Josef MIRDA.

„ 111 – Jacques WATTEBLET – Slept at home several times, especially 17 and 18 August (was one of our men at Toulouse). Francis ACHILLE (BLANCHAIN) left 15 August. Had escaped after being betrayed and arrested about 1 August.

„ 112 – 23rd Aug. Serg. Ronald CHAPMAN 174 Sq. shot down near Ruuningham 30th of July – Hurry bomber (brought by Fillerin).

„ 113 – 26th August F/O Brian HAWKINS – 245 Sq. shot down near Cherbourg 25/10/41 Hurricane (La Turbie).

„ 114 – 2nd Sept. F/L Frederick HIGGINSON (Bennet) 56 Sq. shot down St. Omer 17/6/41 Hurricane (Turbie).

„ 115 – 2nd Sept. Serg. Hickton HAURY – Accident near Dijon 11/9/41 Wellington (Turbie).

„ 116 – 3rd Sept. Corporal James WILKIE R.A.M.C. Concealed in a convent for 15 months. Captured Arras 22/6/40.

„ 117 – 6th Sept. S/L Harold AUTRAM – Sq. 138 Shot down 24th August 1942 Whitley at St. Loup near Vierzon.

„ 118 – 6th Sept. F/Lt HOLLIDAY Henry – Sq. 138 – shot down near Vierzon at St. Loup – Whiteley – 24th August 1942.

„ 119 – 6th Sept. P.O. Wilson LESLIE – Sq. 138 shot down 24th August 1942 near Vierzon at St. Loup – Whitley.

„ 120 – 6th Sept. P.O. WOOD. Sq. 138 – Shot down 24th August 1942 near Vierzon at St. Loup – Whitley.

„ 121 – 6th Sept. Serg. FOSTER Gilbert – Sq. 138 – Shot down 24th August 1942 near Vierzon at St. Loup – Whitley.

„ 122 – 10th Sept. Serg. Conrad LAFLEUR – Mount Royal Fusiliers D 62077 – 19th August 1942 at Dieppe.

„ 123 – 10th Sept. Guy JOLY – Mount Royal Fusiliers – D 61265 19th August 1942 at Dieppe.

„ 124 – 10th Sept. Robert VANIER – Mount Royal Fusiliers – D 61748 – 19th August 1942 at Dieppe.

„ 125 – 11th Sept. Gordon FISHER – Sq. 408 – Shot down 28th August 1942 near Charleroi Hampden.

„ 126 – Serg. L/Lt Douglas BAKER – Sq. 149 – Shot down 25th August 1942 North East Tournai (here 22nd Sept. Stirling brought back by me from Lille).

„ 127 – Serg. Jeffries ROBINSON – Sq. 149 – iden – (brought back by me from Paris) Stirling.

„ 128 – Pr. Robert MCDougall CAMERON 2932302 4th Batt. Cameron Highlanders; prisoner at St. Valery en Caux 12th of June 1940 – Escaped early July. Escaped from La Turbie 5th Sept. 1942.

„ 129 – Forgotten in Sept. 42 François KULUA 2° Serg. Pilot Sq. 3 or 5. Shot down near Brussels.

„ 130 – Serg. Alan MILLS 926726 – Sq. 103 – shot down 7th Nov. 1941 near Lons le Saulnier – Escaped from La Turbie 5th Sept. 1942.

„ 131 – Serg. Douglas WALSH 754104 – Sq. 15 – Crashed in the Mediterranean – same crew as Herbert N° 1 – Escaped La Turbie 5th September 1942.

„ 132 – 30th Sept. P.O. Denys BOOTHBY – Sq. 161 – Whiteley – Baled out near Reims 25/9/42.

„ 133 – 30th Sept. Pte. Richard WATSON – 1° Batt. Royal Regt. – Escaped from Fort Duchere, Lyons 28/9/42.

„ 134 – 2nd Oct. Serg. Thomas John JENKINS 1.379.417 Shot down near Tournai (same crew Baker Robinson). Brought back by Jean de la Olla.

„ 135 – Sergeant Frederick BERTHELSEN – Sq. 149 – N° 41530 – iden –

„ 136 – Sapper (one word unreadable) LINS (?) 2053171 (1940) Escaped La Turbie 5th September 2nd October.

„ 137 – Pr. John PARKER 129574 – From Switzerland (1940) Escaped La Turbie 5th September 2nd October.

„ 138 – Gunner John MORAN 3609361 Switzerland (1940). Escaped La Turbie 5th September 2nd October.

„ 139 – Serg. Leslie PEARMAN – Sq. 101 – shot down near Düsseldorf came to France tried in March to pass to Spain – Arrested sent to La Turbie. Escaped from La Turbie 5th Sept. 2nd October.

„ 140 – Corp. Arnold HOWARTH 3448514 N° 2 Commando – escaped from St. Nazaire caught by Gendarmes at Bazas. Escaped from La Turbie 5th Sept. 2nd Oct.

„ 141 – Pr. Duncan LIVINGSTON 2817510 Seaforth Highlanders. 2° Batt. Captured at St. Valery – escaped in Belgium end of June 1940 – caught in Marseilles Feb. 1941; escaped from La Turbie 5th Sept. 2nd October.

„ 142 – R.A.S.C. Driver Francis McFARLAND 112276 – Captured at St. Valery – Escaped at Bethune end of June – Escaped from La Turbie 5th September 3rd October

„ 143 – Michael DOMILLY 2883908 – Gordon Highl. 1° Batt. captured St. Valery – Escaped at St. Paul 26th June – Escaped from La Turbie 5th September 3rd October.

„ 144 – Pr. Thomas McKAY 2821959 Seaforth Highl. captured St. Valery – Escaped at Lille 28th June (8 months in Lille). Escaped 5th September La Turbie – 3rd October.

  ,, 145 – Abbé MIRDA.
  ,, 146 – Jean da la OLLA.
  ,, 147 – Pat.
  ,, 148 – Sq. Leader Donald Beausire BARNARD 40352 142 Sq. Wellington – shot down 16th–17th September near St. Omer, brought by Fillerin 23rd October.
  ,, 149 – Pilot Officer Raymond GLENSOR N° 403442 142 Sq. – idem –
  ,, 150 – Sergt. Ralph FORSTER 1653891 142 Sq. – idem –
  ,, 151 – Sergt. Ezwin D. WISSENBACK 1900/4589 Flying Fortress shot down North East Lille in Beligum at Nechin Heynaut 23rd October 367 Sq. Second air force, brought by de la Olla 9th October.
  ,, 152 – Lieut. William J. GISE 0660484 – idem –
  ,, 153 – Walter GOSLING – 10th November 2 3 B G cl (???).
  ,, 154 – Thomas George GOODWIN 260613, one of our men, 13/14 Nov. G 6778.[1]

III
Simulation of Disease

Relating to Dr Rodocanachi's simulation of disease in the case of Whitney Straight – and other candidates for return to UK with inaccurate diagnoses, specifically contrived :

Often it was enough that the doctor was able merely grossly to exaggerate the importance of a disability where some such might be found to exist – encouraging the man to ape the more serious manifestations of it. Occasionally however it became necessary to simulate a chronic conjunctivitis, to support the medical report which stated that a man was suffering from intractable inflamation of the eyes. Or to encourage a nasty discharge from he ear. As the doctor knew : there were ways that this might be done, and the end, as he so fervently saw it, justified the means at his command.

[1] I have forgotten Norbert FILLERIN who, I believe, slept at the flat several times, at all events two or three nights in August 1942. Also young d'ASTIER de la VIGERIE, whose alias I have forgotten. The minimum is therefore 156. Nos. 57 BENOIT, 62 CUISENIER, 99 BARNABE were secret agents whom Virginia HALL, known as Marie Jambe de Bois, had recommended to us.

212   *Safe Houses Are Dangerous*

IV
HMS Fidelity

She had been the SS *Rhin* of the French Paquet SS Co. A 1,500-ton heavily armed merchantman registered in Marseille, but of dubious origin and obscure purpose. Later she was renamed *Fidelity*, and was tragically torpedoed in the South Atlantic – lost with all hands on 30th December 1942.

After the war, Louis Nouveau and Pat O'Leary tried in vain to organise some form of tribute to the ship and her gallant crew, but the Chairman of the company, who had been a member of the National Council of Vichy during the war, seemed disinclined to take any action in the matter.

V
Citations

After the war Fanny Rodocanachi found herself reluctant to accept an award which she felt should have been given to her husband. The following correspondence shows that it took some time for the War Office and her son Kostia to persuade her that not only did she herself deserve this honour, but that it perhaps reflected an attempt by His Majesty the King to give higher recognition to Georges Rodocanachi's services than was otherwise possible.

The War Office,
c/o. Room 327,
Hotel Victoria,
Northumberland Ave.,
LONDON, W.C.2.

Ref : IS9/Awards/2/7184.

7th January, ,1946.

Dear Mme. Rodocanachi,
    I have been asked to find out from you the following particulars :
1.   Your full Christian names.
2.   The date and place of your birth.
3.   Any honours or decorations previously awarded you, with dates.
4.   Your permanent address.
    I shall be greatly obliged if you could furnish me with the information asked for at your earliest convenience. A stamped addressed envelope is enclosed for your reply.

Yours sincerely,
L. Winterbottom.

Ref : IS9/ Awards/2/7184

January 11th 1946

From : Mrs. G. Rodocanachi
16 Sussex Gardens,
W.2.

Dear Colonel Winterbottom,

I am extremely touched and infinitely honoured by your letter, but I am certain you will understand why I cannot send the particulars you ask for.

I honestly do not feel that the little I was able to do in helping my husband deserves any recognition. I could not have done less – neither he nor I could have remained indifferent. He gave his life knowing what he did – the mere fact of being allowed to assist in his good work is sufficient. Thousands of women have accomplished so much more.

I want to thank you very earnestly indeed for thinking of me, and please do believe that I appreciate your remembrance more deeply than I can express.

Yours sincerely,

From : Maj Gen C. D. PACKARD, DMI.

The War Office,
Whitehall, S.W.1

By Registered Post

4 August, 1948.

MI 9/19 BM/3158

Dear Madame Rodocanachi,

I am extremely glad that you have now consented to accept your appointment as an additional Member of the Order of the British Empire (Civil Division) to which His Majesty The King has graciously given approval. In accordance with the wish you expressed to Major Roberts on Friday last, I am therefore forwarding the Insignia of the decoration under cover of this letter.

At the same time I am taking tthe opportunity for forwarding a Certificate of Commendation for Brave Conduct, which was awarded to your late husband, Dr. Georges Rodocanachi, for his outstanding services to the Allies during the recent war. I would like to explain that this award is the highest which can be given posthumously to a foreign subject, who has carried out work of the kind undertaken by your late husband. . . .

*

By the KING'S Order the name of
Dr. Georges Rodocanachi,
was placed on record on
18 June, 1946,
as commended for brave conduct.
I am charged to express His Majesty's
high appreciation of the service rendered.

C. R. Attlee
Prime Minister and First Lord
of the Treasury

The President
OF THE UNITED STATES OF AMERICA
has directed me to express to
GEORGES RODOCANACHI
the gratitude and appreciation of the
American people for gallant service
in assisting the escape of Allied
soldiers from the enemy
DWIGHT D. EISENHOWER
General of the Army
Commanding General United States Forces European Theater

Bibliography

Wait for the Dawn by Derrick Nabarro. Published by Cassells in 1952.

Saturday at MI9 by Airey Neave. Published by Hodder & Stoughton in 1969.

They Have Their Exits by Airey Neave. Published by Hodder & Stoughton in 1953.

The Way Back by Vincent Brome. Published by Cassell & Co. in 1957.

The Tartan Pimpernel by Donald Caskie. Published by Oldbourne Book Co. in 1957.

Fight Another Day by J. M. Langley. Published by Collins Ltd. in 1974.

MI9 Escape and Evasion. M. R. D. Foot and J. M. Langley Bodley Head in 1979.

Secret Sunday by Donald Darling. Published by William Kimber in 1975.

SOE in France by M. R. D. Foot. H.M. Stationery Office, 1966.

Resistance by M. R. D. Foot. Published by Eyre Methuen Ltd. in 1976.

Des Capitaines par Milliers by Louis Nouveau. Limited edition published in France in 1958, by Calmann-Lévy.

Winged Hours by Frank Griffiths. Published by William Kimber in 1981.

Sunday at Large by Donald Darling. Published by William Kimber in 1977.

The French Resistance 1940–1944 by Frieda Knight. Published by Lawrence & Wishart in 1975.

The Week That France Fell by Noel Barber. Published by Macmillan in 1976.

Evader by T. D. G. Teare. Published by Hodder & Stoughton in 1954.

SOE Recollections & Reflections 1940–1945 by J. G. Beevor. Published by Bodley Head in 1981.

Escape to Live by Wing Commander Edward Howell, OBE, DFC. Published by Longmans in 1947.

The White Rabbit by Bruce Marshall. Published by Pan Books in 1970. (Yeo-Thomas.)

Safer than a Known Way by Philip Newman, published by William Kimber 1983.

Fighter Pilot: A Self Portrait by George Barclay. Edited by Humphrey Wynn. Published by William Kimber in 1976.

Index

Acropolis, 89, 187
Aguado, 61
Andorra, 61
Armistice Commission, German–Italian, 19, 36, 60
Arnaud, Mme, 103

Barcelona (British Consul), 47, 79, 177
Barclay, George, Flight Lt, 102–3, 116, 117
Barnabe, 105
Barnett, Flight Lt, 163–4
Bassin de la Grande Joliette, 53
Belgians, King Leopold, 69
Bennett, Capt, see Higginson
Bensi, 96
Berthet, Guy, 145
Besançon (the Citadel. Offlag 142), 31, 50
Bismarck, Battleship, 84
Blanc, Jean, 188
Blanchain, Francis, 88, 90, 141–2, 172–3, 179
Bontoux, Maître, 109
Buchenwald, 180, 188–192

Café aux Deux Magots, 169
Café de Paris, Paris, 62
Canebière, 19, 31, 51, 53, 87–8, 134, 161
Canet-Plage, 142, 147, 169, 172, 174
Carpentier, Abbé, 93–5, 117, 124, 157
Caskie, Rev Donald, 30 (meets Dr Rodocanachi) 35–7, 40–5 (sets up Seamen's Mission) 47–8 (describes Pat O'Leary), 72, 77, 86, 135, 154

(arrested) 155, 165, 195, Appendices
Catala, Madame, 61–2
Chamberlain, Neville, 25
Change Into Uniform, published by Terence Dalton, 1978
Cheramy family, 179, Appendices
Chope du Pont Neuf, bar, 101
Christmann, Richard, 117
City of London Safari published by Abson Books 1983
Clinique Bouchard, 188
Coates (M & P, Mr Gosling), 59, 89
Cole, (Sgt Harold, alias Paul, alias Delobel) 64, 85–94 (convoys men from the north) 96–99 (Pat O'Leary suspects him) 99–103 (Pat O'Leary investigates) 110–113 (confrontation) 115–125 (first arrest) 145, 153 (second arrest) 157, 170–2 (released) 179, 183, 193–5, Appendices
Compiègne, 17
Concentration Camps, (German) see under Buchenwald, Dachau, Natzweiler, Ravensbrück; (Austrian) Mauthausen
Cooper-Smith, Sylvia, Appendices
de Cortes, Fabien, 186, 187
Coventry raid, 56
Creswell, Michael, *Monday*, 63, 92
Crowley-Milling, Air Marshal Sir Denis, 91–2, Appendices

Dachau, 172–3
Dansey, Colonel, 124
Darling, Donald, *Sunday*, 63–4, 122, 124, 146–7, 159, Appendices
Dean & Dodds, Messrs, 41, 50–1

217